GERMAN PIONEERS IN TEXAS

A Brief History of Their
Hardships, Struggles
and Achievements.

Compiled for the

FREDERICKSBURGER WOCHENBLATT

And

FREDERICKSBURG STANDARD

By

Don H. Biggers.

Gillespie County Edition.

Press of the Fredericksburg Publishing Co.

1925

Library of Congress Card No. 8 3-812 31

Copyright © 1983
By Fredericksburg Publishing Co., Inc.

Printed in the United States of America
By Eakin Publications, Inc., P.O. Box 23000, Austin, Texas 78735

ISBN 0-89015-385-x

Second Reprinting 1986
Third Reprinting 1996

INDEX.

CHAPTER I.

General History of German Settlements.

CHAPTER II.

German Emigration Company Organized.

CHAPTER III.

Flash Lights of History.

CHAPTER IV.

Civil Wartime Outrages.

CHAPTER V.

Human Interest History.

CHAPTER VI.

Scraps of Unusual History.

CHAPTER VII.

From the Old County Records.

CHAPTER VIII.

Historic Old Mills.

CHAPTER IX.

Sketches of Less Ancient Days.

ILLUSTRATED SECTION.

FOREWORD.

One of the most conspicuous elements in the educational, social, industrial and commercial pre-eminence of Texas today is its German citizenship. This citizenship is not of recent origin. It is descended from the hardiest class of pioneers that ever blazed a path through adversity to great achievement. Fully 80 per cent of the German citizenship of Texas trace their ancestry to the colonists who came here from 1828 to 1850.

General histories and school histories utterly fail to do justice to these pioneer German colonists, and to the same degree such histories fail to perform the functions that history is presumed to perform. Why so? The history of the German people in Texas is important and interesting. It is history of which any state and all people should be proud. It belongs not only to the history of Texas, but to the history of the entire country.

Two valuable contributions to the history of the German people of Texas is a pamphlet published by W. von Rosenberg in 1894, and a far more elaborate history published by Robert Penniger in 1896. Both of these works were published in German, and, so far as this writer knows, neither has been translated into English. Von Rosenberg's pamphlet is devoted principally to a denial of the charges brought by Dr. Schubert, at one time connected with the Adelsverein or German Emigration Company, against the officials of the Adelsverein and to the refutation of charges that England had in any way at any time, financed the German colony projects. But in disproving these charges Mr. von Rosenberg presents a great deal of valuable history. Mr. Penniger's book, while specializing on the pioneers, hardships, progress and achievements of Gillespie county and of Fredericksburg, of which county he was for many years a distinguished citizen, gives a great deal of general history. It goes much farther than does the von Rosenberg history and constitutes a valuable contribution to the history of Germans in Texas. By far the most exhaustive contribution to the hisory of the German people in Texas, that has ever been published in English, is the work of Professor Moritz Tiling, now deceased, but formerly instructor of history in the Houston Academy. This work was published in 1913.

Another history of the Germans in Texas is the book of G. G. Benjamin, published in Philadelphia in 1910. None of these works have been given even a respectable degree of the circulation their merits deserve.

The essential facts presented by all of these able and impartial writers belong in the school histories as well as in the general histories of Texas, not merely because such history is the history of the German colonists and the German people of Texas, but because it is essentially a part of the history of the state. By the elimination of these facts the history of Texas is woefully incomplete.

The writings of all of the men mentioned has been of great assistance in the preparation of this work. Particularly have the essential elements of Professor Tiling's work been conserved.

The purpose of this work is to put into as brief but accurate form as possible the salient facts of German colonists and German achievements in Texas. The work has required a great deal of research, and the examination of much matter that has at different times appeared in newspapers and magazines, and personally interviewing many people familiar with the pioneer colonization history of Texas. The work is, in some material respects, a condensation, while in other respects it is an elaboration of what has been written by others. If it adds in even a small degree to the dissemination of meritorious truths it will have accomplished its mission in so far as the writer is concerned. If it does nothing more than assist in carrying the message of von Rosenberg, Penniger, Tiling and Benjamin to the public it will have served a good purpose.

CHAPTER I.

GENERAL HISTORY OF GERMAN SETTLEMENTS.

Dawn of Texas' Colonization History.

The colonization of Texas is unsurpassed both in romance and achievement. It abounds in adventure, hardships, loyalty and treachery.

Spain first claimed Texas by right of discovery, and the first attempt at colonizing was made by the Frenchman LaSalle in 1685. This was accidental. LaSalle was hunting for the mouth of the Mississippi river when fate decreed otherwise and he landed in Texas, not knowing where he was at the time. In 1685 LaSalle located a colony in the vicinity of Matagorda bay, and proclaimed all the territory within the scope of his imagination as a province of Spain. In 1687 with a small band of followers he left his colony and started in search of the Mississippi, but met death at the hands of one of his men. Several months later the Spanish government was informed, perhaps by Indians, regarding the French colony. The Spanish governor in Mexico immediately investigated, with a view to chasing LaSalle and his followers out of the country, but when the Spanish authorities reached the scene of the LaSalle colony they found the spot where the French had built a fort and a church deserted. Practically every soul LaSalle had left in the colony when he started in search of the Mississippi had perished, and thus the first attempt to colonize Texas had met a tragic end.

Then the Spaniards undertook to colonize Texas, this era known as the "mission period." The scheme of the Spaniards was to build forts and missions and make the Indians good and useful. The Spaniards had a good plan but it wouldn't work. They didn't understand the Indian, but even at that they made a better success of it than the French did. They left landmarks that grow more rich and mellow in romance as the years and centuries roll by. Neither the French nor Spaniards had any real program or intention of material development. The main idea in those old days was territorial expansion—beat the other fellow to it and then have a war about it.

In 1821 Mexico succeeded in establishing its independence of Spain. Prior to the revolution by which Mexico became independent of Spain, Spain had been very strict in the matter of granting colonization privileges to the subjects of other nations, but the new Mexican government adopted an entirely opposite policy, and for its own selfish good got too liberal. It was the pioneer in the land grant boom business. With wild liberality it made enormous concessions to any foreigner or native making application. All a promoter had to do to secure a vast grant of land was to agree to pay for surveying the land, recording the deeds, and to promise to locate a certain number of families on the land awarded him within a certain period of time. Naturally such a policy would lead to land grant and colonization schemes, if not to immediate and permanent results.

In 1823 there was a revolution in Mexico, and Emperor Iturbide was forced to abdicate. A new republic was established and the land granting and colonization policy of the government was changed to some extent. Under the new government not more than eleven sitios, or practically 50,000 acres, would be granted to any one person. The purpose of this law was to prevent land monopoly. Fifty thousand acres would be a gigantic land monopoly at present, but it was a mere pittance in those days.

Moses Austin was the first American to secure a Texas colonization grant from the Mexican government, his grant being secured some two years before the change in the colonization laws of Mexico. Moses Austin died soon after securing his land grant, and the colonization project was transferred to his son, Stephen F. Austin. This was followed by numerous colonization grants.

There was a great deal of humbuggery and promotion graft in connection with many of these colonization schemes. In several projects good intentions were all mixed up with lack of common sense and with impractical methods, and a few of them were failures because of unavoidable misfortunes. Stephen F. Austin stands out conspicuously as the greatest of all Texas colonizers. He was earnest, honest and practical. Even with the Austin colonists material development was more of a vague dream that a fixed purpose and planned policy. Courage was their chief asset, determination their outstanding characteristic, honesty their guide and love of liberty their creed. They were the fighting forerunners of a new republic. They were the instruments destiny would in due time use to expel the last vestige of Spanish authority from the domain north of the Rio Grande.

And in the meantime another element was introducing itself. This element was the force that had a plan and a fixed purpose for real development. It was an element that planned to build, create and utilize. This was the German element.

Hecke Gets Enthused and Writes a Book. Adventurers Get Arrested.

It is not a clearly established fact as to when the first Germans came to Texas. One of LaSalle's adventurers was presumably a German. Contemporaneous with Austin's colonization work the Mexican government granted concessions to two Germans, at that time residents and presumably citizens of the United States. One of these was Joseph Vehlein, the other Robert Leftwich. If Vehlein ever attempted to put a colony on his grant the records fail to disclose the fact. Concerning the Leftwich grant Prof. Tiling in his history says:

"Leftwich's grant dates from the year 1822, and his extensive lands were situated near the old San Antonio road, leading from New Orleans to Texas, between the Colorado and San Marcos rivers. He built a small fort and settled a few families on his land in 1826, but soon afterwards returned to Tennessee, where he had formerly lived and died there. After his death a company was formed at Nashville in 1830 to carry out the conditions of his contract, but the Mexican government did not recognize the transfer of Leftwich's claim to this company and gave the land to Austin and to S. M. Williams. Four years later the Mexican government reversed its decision and permitted the Nashville company to succeed as owners of the Leftwich grant. Thereupon Sterling C. Robertson brought 500 families from Tennessee and South Carolina as settlers on this fertile land.''

In the meantime Texas was getting a great deal of publicity, not only throughout the United States, but in Europe. Among the pioneers in this publicity business was J. V. Hecke, an educated gentleman, an ardent adventurer and a former officer in the Prussian army. As a part of his itinerary in the United States he arrived in Texas some time in 1818, then a part of Mexico, and there spent several months. He returned to Germany, and in 1821 published a book relating his travels in the United States. He gave an especially glowing description of Texas and its possibilities. He was the first man to see the possibilities of limited acreage and intensive cultivation. He maintained that fifty acres properly tilled would make the owner independent and enable him to repay to the government the cost of transportation and for necessary provisions and farming implements. As Prof. Tiling puts it: ''When we remember that the Monroe doctrine was at that time not yet promulgated, and that Iturbide who had just proclaimed himself emperor of Mexico, might have been quite willing to part with the province of Texas for a monetary consideration, Hecke's plan for a new Prussia on this side of the Atlantic does not look like an iridescent dream, and leaves a wide field for speculation as to what might have happened had his ideas been carried out.''

At any rate the publication of Hecke's book created a great deal of interest throughout Europe, and especially among the German people.

According to Mr. von Rosenberg's pamplet: ''A troup of 53 adventurers of different nationalities landed in New Orleans in the fall of 1821, and in October of the same year they reached the Texas coast and marched into the interior. In due time they reached Goliad and being heavily armed, were suspected by the Mexican authorities as hostile invaders and were arrested. An investigation disclosed the fact that their intentions were peaceful, and they were released, with permission to take up any occupation they desired to pursue. At least six of these men were Germans, their names as disclosed in the archives at Austin being Eduard Hansen, Joseph Dirksen, Ernest von Rosenberg, Wilhelm Miller, Carl Cuans and Gasper Porten." It is probable that some of the names as registered in the archives are not properly spelled. At different times many mistakes were made in spelling German names, and this instance was perhaps no exception.

According to Mr. Penniger's history all of these men were educated and had served in the German army. Mr. Penniger also says: "That they kept up a correspondence with fellow officers in Germany is evidenced by the fact that when the movement for independence from Spain started in Mexico much interest was manifested in various German garrisons."

Ernst von Rosenberg joined the Mexican army. He had been a lieutenant in the Prussian artillery, and was given a commission as colonel of an artillery regiment in the Mexican army. After the abdication of Iturbide Rosenberg was shot. Whether he was courtmartialed or killed in a political riot is not proven. Practically nothing is known as to what became of the other members of this expedition. A brother of von Rosenberg came to Texas in 1849, and he and his descendants are recognized as among the most prominent citizens of Texas, both in the past and at present.

This little band of 53 were more than adventurers. They were trail blazers, forerunners that exercised a future influence in German colonization in Texas. Their correspondence with friends in the Fatherland contributed in no small measure to the immigration that followed.

A great many German names appear with the list of Austin's colonists. Perhaps few of these were directly from Germany. Possibly all or most of them had come from

Germany to some portion of the United States, later joining the Austin colonists and coming to Texas, but very naturally these colonists kept up a correspondence with relatives and friends in Germany and in this way contributed to advertising the new found territory.

But during all of this time elements and agencies were at work preparing the way for the great German colonization movement that had its greatest momentum from 1830 to 1849.

First German Settlements in Texas.

Baron de Bastrop was one of the first Germans identified with the history of the colonization of Texas. He was a Prussian by birth and served under Frederick the Great. Later he was employed by the King of Spain and sent to Mexico on an important mission. He possessed great influence with the Spanish government, later with the Mexican government, and was the close personal friend of many of the most prominent men in the United States. He secured a grant of land thirty miles square from the Spanish government, this grant being situated between the Mississippi river and the Red river. Four hundred thousand acres of this land he transferred to Aaron Burr. What be did with the balance (about 175,000 acres) of this particular grant history fails to disclose. Soon after Spain ceded Louisiana to France Baron de Bastrop moved to San Antonio and was made an alcalde, a most important office at that time. When Moses Austin went to San Antonio and made application for a colonization grant it looked as though his mission would be a complete failure. By good fortune he met his friend Baron de Bastrop. The Baron immediately took up the cause of Austin with the Mexican authorities, and it was through his efforts that Austin secured his grant in 1821. Baron de Bastrop was the first man to plant a German colony in Texas. He secured a considerable grant on the Colorado river some thirty miles east of the present city of Austin, and by 1823 had induced quite a number of Germans to locate on this land.

In his "German Element in Texas," Tiling says: "Nearly all of these pioneer settlers came from the county of Elmenhorst, Grandduchy of Oldenburg. For sixteen years, until the founding of the City of Austin in 1839, this was the farthest northeastern settlement in Texas. Here the sturdy German pioneers, surrounded by ferocious and barbarous Indian tribes, in a wilderness a hundred miles from civilization, toiled faithfully and undaunted, plowing their fields with guns on their shoulders and performing all the hazardous work incident to pioneer life. When in 1836 Bastrop county was organized, this county comprised all of the present Travis county, and the five commissioners named by the Texas congress in 1839 to select a suitable site for the capital of the republic of Texas, bought 7735 acres in the township of Waterloo, on the banks of the Colorado river where the city of Austin now stands, for $20,000, the deed to this property being executed by the sheriff of Bastrop county. It may be of interest to note that when the state agents John Edwin Waller and surveyor W. Sandusky, appointed by President Lamar to survey and plot the grounds purchased for the future capital, arrived at their destination, they found two families, Becker and Harrel, the only inhabitants of Waterloo. Two miles south of Waterloo was another city with the proud name of Montpolis, the rival of Waterloo, also inhabited by two families. On August 1, 1839, Judge Waller sold the first town lots, substantial houses were quickly built, and on October 17 President Lamar with part of his cabinet arrived at the new capitol of the republic of Texas.

"The capital of the young republic of Texas grew rapidly, quite a number of Germans taking part in the building of the city. Many highly educated men, who had first adopted the strenuous life of the pioneer farmer when they came to Texas from the Fatherland, gradually left their farms for the more congenial life and employment in the city, and the Germans of Austin have forever been a prominent social, political and industrial factor of the capital of Texas."

What is conceded to be the first permanent German colony founded in Texas was at Industry, in Austin County, in 1831. It is today one of the most substantial and prosperous German settlements in Texas.

This colony was founded by Friedrich Ernst and Charles Fordtran. Both men had come as immigrants from Germany to New York. There they became acquainted, formed a partnership and decided to "go west and grow up with the country." Their destination was probably Missouri, but arriving in New Orleans they heard glowing accounts of Texas, and caught the Texas boom fever. They reached Harrisburg in April, 1831, and after a stay of several weeks there set out for the location selected near what was later the town of Industry.

Mrs. Ernst is by most writers conceded to have been the first German woman to come to Texas. She died at Industry at the age of 88 years, having lived there for nearly sixty years.

Many writers state that a number of German families located on the land grant of Baron de Bastrop in 1823, and remained there for a period of several years. It is probable, however, that a number of Germans and not a number of German families located at Bastrop. It is certain that a number of Germans located at Bastrop, but they were probably single men.

Letters written by Mr. Ernst to friends in Germany were published and added materially to the other influences then attracting the Germans to the Western continent.

According to the narrative of Mrs. Ernst a few families coming direct from Germany, reached Industry in 1833, while quite a number arrived in 1834. Until the coming of these families Mr. Ernst and his family had lived alone in the wilds of Austin county. To their privations must be added the misery of isolation and lonesomeness.

The first, and really the only failure, in attempting to establish a German colony in Texas, was made perhaps in 1832. Johann von Rackwitz, a German nobleman of limited means, obtained a land grant from the Mexican government, this land being on the Nueces river. A few German families were induced to locate on this land. The sporty Rackwitz went broke, having encumbered his grant for more than it was worth, and the colonists lost everything they had put into it. It is not known what finally became of these colonists. According to Tiling's history part of them were killed and others fled when Santa Anna's army invaded Texas in 1836.

Among the first and greatest of the early German immigrants to Texas was Robert Kleberg. No name shines more conspicuously in the material history of Texas than does that of Robert Kleberg. His name and great works form a chapter in Texas history that even prejudiced history writers cannot ignore.

He, with his young wife, and a number of highly educated persons, reached Cat Spring, in Austin County, in 1834. According to Tiling's history Industry and Cat Spring, in Austin county, and Biegel's settlement in Fayette county, were the first pure German settlements in Texas.

First German Emigration Society Organized.

The first Spanish, French and English visitors to the American continent were, with few exceptions, bold adventurers, soldiers of fortune, gold hunters, land grabbers and empire extenders. Their courage and capacity to suffer privations and endure the most brutal tortures was equalled only by their vivid imaginations. The glowing accounts they gave to a credulous people when returning from their tours of discovery did not perhaps exceed the wonderful possibilities and boundless resources of the countries they had visited, but they always took a romantic rather than a practical view of the matter. As a result most of the colonists came anticipating an easy acquisition of wealth. They didn't take into account the distances that would separate them from their native land, from their friends and kindred. They didn't take into account the conditions with which they would have to deal, and for that reason usually failed to make the necessary preparations.

During the early part of the nineteenth century many of the most talented Germans visited the United States and made extensive tours of the country. In the majority of cases their purpose was to find a place to which their impoverished countrymen could emigrate. In many instances their enthusiasm clouded their judgement. They saw only the glorious dazzle of a virgin country, and were blinded to the serious side of the situation.

According to Tiling the Germans who contributed most by their travels, writings and reports to create a desire among Germans to emigrate to the United States were Hecke, Bromme, Gerke, Ahrends and Duden. Hecke's book was published in 1821, the others at later dates. Tiling considers Duden's work published in 1829, the greatest of them all, creating the greatest interest and contributing most to direct results.

Perhaps the first emigration society organized in Germany was the Giessener Auswanderungs Gesellschaft (Emigration Society of Giessen.) There were a number of such societies organized about the same time, but this was the most prominent if not the first. The purpose of these societies, and of this one in particular, was to further wholesale emigration to the United States. This society was organized and its first pamphlet, setting forth its aims, was promiscuously distributed in 1833. This organization seems to have been entirely too utopian in its ideals. It started off with too much theory and landed on the rock of reality. Speaking of this society G. G. Benjamin says: "It was organized originally by a number of university men, among whom Carl Follen was the leading spirit. Its aims, as stated in a pamphlet issued in 1823, were: The founding of a German state, which would of course, have to be a member of the United States, but with maintenance of a form of government which will assure the continuance of German customs, German language and create a genuine free and popular life. The idea was to occupy an unsettled and unorganized territory in order that a German republic, a rejuvenated Germany, may arise in North America. The members were men of means. Some held high official and professional positions. They sailed in two vessels from Bremen to New Orleans in 1834. After their arrival in this country dissentions arose and the company was broken up. An account of this undertaking is given in Niles' Register and shows clearly what vague ideas existed at that time."

Professor Tiling adds: "While these utopian plans were never and could never be accomplished, still the western part of the United States gained much by this immigration, and so did Texas, then still a part of Mexico. It brought to this country a great number of highly educated and energetic men who not only assimilated themselves readily to existing conditions, but who became the basic element of these embryonic states. It was their hard and persevering labor that opened a vast territory to civilization and made millions of acres productive.

Texas-Mexico War Starts—Hardships and Heroism of German Settlers.

German immigration to Texas was just getting well underway when Texas revolted against Mexico and Santa Anna flooded the state with his army of barbarian invaders. During the war, and even while war was imminently pending, immigration from all sources ceased. In fact, it was not until some months after Texas had gained its independence that immigration again began flowing in. Owing to the proximity of most of these German colonists to the Rio Grande river they were the principal victims of Santa Anna's savage revenge. It is probable, and reasonable to presume, that Santa Anna had a more bitter feeling toward the German settlers than toward even the colonists from the United States. He had expected nothing but united rebellion on the part of the colonists from the United States, whereas he had very erroneously assumed that the German colonists would at least be friendly, if they did not actively support the Mexican tyrant. He very glaringly misjudged the German settlers. They had suffered their share of tyranny, and they were not the type of people to compromise with it. They were liberty lovers and tyrant haters. It was the German outpost colonies that presented the heroic and pathetic scenes when the armies of Santa Anna came. As the armies approached the German women and children were mounted on horses, and driving such livestock as they possessed trekked across the wilderness toward Louisiana, while the men and even mere boys who had not already joined the Texas army, shouldered their guns and marched to the front. When the war ended these German soldiers and their separated families reunited and returned, only to find their homes burned, their improvements destroyed and their crops devastated. But with characteristic determination they rebuilt and reendured the hardships which they thought to a great extent ended when the war started.

Among the Germans who played especially conspicuous and honorable parts in the Texas war for independence were: Robert Kleberg, Colonel Eduard Harcort and Adolph Stern. No man gave more unselfishly of his funds and his services than did Robert Kleberg. "Eduard Harcort was General Houston's chief of Staff. After the victory of San Jacinto he was ordered to construct a fort on Galveston Island for the detention of Mexican prisoners. There he contracted fever and died in the fall of the same year that had secured the independence of Texas."—Tiling's German Element in Texas.

Squire Storn, the German justice of the peace at Nacogdoches, was the Benjamin Franklin of the Texas revolution. Being commissioned by the provisional government of Texas he went in the fall of 1835 to New Orleans. There he not only raised thousands of dollars in cash for the needy army of independence, but organized three companies of famous volunteers, these being the Tampico Greys, the New Orleans Greys and the Mobile Greys, and among these companies of famous fighters were a number of Germans. The muster rolls of the army of independence gives the names of more than one hundred Germans who served under General Houston. The same public archives contains the names of 23 Germans who were with Fannin, and all of these with the exception of possibly three, met the fate of all of Fannin's men at the butchery of Goliad. Of the 365 men under Fannin only 27 escaped the massacre. Two Germans, William Langenheim and Joseph Spohn, had been detailed to hospital duty by the Mexicans. Hermann Ehrenberger made a remarkable escape. The German prisoners were offered the choice of joining the Mexican army or being shot with the other captured soldiers. Without exception they declined to join the Mexican army. They, with the other captives, were later lined up for execution. Just as the fatal volley was fired Ehrenberger made a dash for liberty, dived into the nearby San Antonio river, swam to the opposite side amid a hail of bullets, but miraculously escaped, and lived to write one of the most thrilling narratives ever published in regard to the Fannin massacre.

If there had been a spark of cowardice or treachery in the German makeup and blood it would have revealed itself by reason of and during the Texas war for independence. By siding with Santa Anna they would have not only not been molested, but could have had anything within the gift of the Mexican tyrant. Had the Germans, for any reason or consideration sided with Mexico the history of Texas' struggle for independence would most certainly have been different. It could not have succeeded without their assistance, for with these trained, intelligent fighters lined up with the Mexican army the little band of Texas patriots would have had a different proposition on hand at the battle of San Jacinto. Without his German soldiers Houston would have had less than seven hundred men to meet Santa Anna. With the Germans in Houston's army under his command Santa Anna would have had more than a hundred soldiers on his side equal in fighting worth to nearly all of his ragged Mexicans. When the Mexican general offered the German soldiers the choice of joining the Mexican army at the Goliad massacre his motive was not one of mercy. His scheme was to align the fighting

Germans with the Mexican cause. He needed them in his scheme of conquest. They preferred death to dishonor.

There had been no character of census of the population of Texas when it declared war on Mexico in 1836. The best estimate would be little more than a wild guess. The settlements were scattered, and the citizenship, with the exception of the Germans, was shifting and uncertain. A great many settlers coming from different states of the United States would soon get discouraged with the isolation, privations and hardships and return to their former homes. The Germans had neither this opportunity nor inclination. They had not the means to return to Germany had they so desired. It is probably conservative to estimate the total white population of Texas in 1836 at forty, possibly forty-five, thousand. Of this number perhaps less than ten per cent were Germans. Yet we find according to the muster rolls that more than ten per cent of Houston's army was Germans, and practically one man of every fifteen to meet death when Fannin's men were murdered was a German.

German Colony History Under Texas Republic.

The congress of Texas continued the liberal land grant policy of the Mexican government. It fact, the land policy of the Texas republic was more extravagent than liberal and more impractical than judicious. This was excusable for many reasons. The state was having a hard struggle in the matter of finances. Land was its only source of revenue, and necessity compelled the giving of much land for a few dollars. Again the prospect of war with Mexico was always imminent. Santa Anna had signed a treaty acknowledging the independence of Texas. This treaty the Mexican government refused to approve, and claimed Texas as a Mexican state. To be prepared for another Mexican invasion Texas needed more population and more men available for military service. But the too liberal land policy of the republic worked much mischief in the long run. Out of it grew a great deal of graft, although the republic itself was not a designing party to the evils that resulted. In its liberality and perplexity congress had failed to properly safeguard the interest of the state and the future immigrants

Two things contributed to a heavy influx of population to Texas from 1836 to 1845, the republic of Texas being admitted to the Union in 1845. The fact that Texas was independent of Mexico and dominated by the white race contributed in great degree to this and the liberal land policy was the second factor.

In 1837 the Texas congress passed a land grant act, under the terms of which each family settling in the state would be awarded 320 acres and each single man 160 acres. Had the state granted land in such quantities to actual settlers only it would have been much better for the material welfare of the state and for the protection of the public. But the same act carried with it a proviso making grants of enormous acreage to colonizing companies. It was this clause in the act that finally led to great mischief and fraud.

From the close of the Texas-Mexican war in 1836 to the annexation of Texas to the Union in 1845 there was a heavy immigration from all parts of the United States and from Germany. It has been estimated that more than 120,000 Germans reached the United States from 1832 to 1846, covering a period of thirteen years.

"During the six years from 1840 to 1846 there arrived at Galveston from Bremen alone 7161 German immigrants, among them many men of culture and refinement who had received a college or university education. They were all induced to seek these shores through love of liberty, and partly through the glowing accounts of travelers who had traversed Texas and in their reports did not hesitate to pronounce it the finest country on earth, suitable in every way for colonization by Europeans."—Tiling.

It has been openly charged that ship companies and immigration concerns had a big hand in this publicity work. They certainly profited by and very naturally encouraged such publicity, if they did not contribute to and direct it.

There was certainly a shameful amount of misrepresentation, whether intentional or by reason of blinded enthusiasm. These glowing accounts failed to mention the hardships confronting the settler. The truth about this matter coupled with the presentation of the great possibilities, would have educated the immigrants, and the German interest behind German emigration, to have made better preparations for the colonists, and would have safeguarded against the untold misery to which the colonists of 1845-1846 were subjected.

The bitter complaint has been often made that the Germans were not given a square deal in the matter of land grants by the Texas government. This complaint has been more often made by Americans than by Germans.

The richer lands in east Texas was reserved for the American colonists and colonizing companies. Not only were these east Texas lands richer, but they were more protected and being nearer the coast gave great advantage in the matter of marketing livestock and farm products and receiving supplies. The Germans were located in the western part of the state, given the poorer lands, subjected to the greater isolation and dangers, for they must serve as a bulwark against both Indians and Mexican marauders, and in the event of a Mexican invasion they would have to suffer the first onslaught of a destroying army. One may argue that the Texas republic was justified in giving preference to its kindred citizenship of the United States. Admit this and the fact remains that the Texas republic was not showing proper appreciation of, nor giving proper reward to, the Germans for their loyalty, heroism and sacrifices made during the war for independence. To say the least the Texas republic and later both the state and federal government, should have given the exposed German colonies better protection.

This was the first injustice done the Germans. And behind it there may well be a suspicion that such treatment was not without a certain degree of prejudice and ill feeling.

The Germans were not slave owners and were opposed to slavery. Under the Mexican government slavery was abolished by law, but permitted by indifference. As a republic Texas permitted slavery and was annexed to the Union as a slave holding state. Under the republic and during the heaviest colonization days a great many slaves were introduced into Texas. The American immigrants, and particularly the immigrants from the southern and slave holding states, considered slaves necessary to clear the land, cultivate and gather the crops, etc. The German believed in doing this work himself or with free labor. This democratic idea of the Germans subjected them to the ill will of the slave owning Americans.

However, the German element in Texas was too strong and too essential to be entirely ignored. In 1843 congress directed that the laws of Texas be published in German, and treated with favorable consideration the proposition to establish a German university, granting "a franchise in 1844 to the Hermann University, which was to be the 'alma mater' of philosophy, medicine, theology and jurisprudence. The professors of these four faculties must be competent to lecture in both the English and German languages, while the professors of theology should not belong to a special religious denomination nor teach doctrines of any sect."— Tiling's German Element.

Just how a teacher belonging to no church and teaching no sect would get along teaching theology was never demonstrated, for the reason that the German university in Texas was never established. The effort failed among the German people themselves. They either could not or would not subscribe the necessary funds to finance it, although the incorporators obtained a considerable land grant from the state and made at least two strenuous campaigns to raise the necessary money. Enough money was raised to erect a two-story stone building at Frelsburg in Colorado County, now used as a public school house. Tiling says "the plan of establishing a higher institution of learning in 1845 was premature and not feasible." In this he is certainly correct, for it was not until many years later that the state was able to make an unpretentious start in the matter of founding the present state university.

The principal German settlements in Texas between 1836 and 1840 were:

The settlement of the von Roeders at Shelby, in Austin County. This grew to be one of the largest and most prosperous German communties in that area. The von Roeders were immigrants with Robert Kleberg, but undertook this enterprise perhaps in 1836 of the early part of 1837.

In 1837 William Frels established Frelsburg in Colorado county.

In the same year the town of LaGrange was founded, and was a German town and settlement by accident. A number of German immigrants on their way to a location in Bexar county, reached the Colorado river at a point near the present town of LaGrange. For many weeks the river was on a highwater rampage and the immigrants were unable to cross. A man by the name of Moore had plotted the townsite. He made the waterbound Germans a proposition. If they would locate in his town he would give each man a town lot, and assist them in securing farm lands in the vicinity of the town. The town lots were of considerable dimensions, being 81x171 feet, or practically the third of an acre. The Germans accepted Moore's offer and thus was founded the greatest German town and community established prior to the admission of Texas to the Union, a town that has ever maintained its German character and elements.

These were the last German colonies to be established in the most favored part of the state. During the period from 1836 to 1840 a great many grants of land were issued in the names of individual Germans, but doubtless most of these Germans had first landed in some other state and later migrated to Texas.

In 1838 a German emigration society was organized in New York, the purpose being to establish a colony in Texas. This organization sent its first ship load of emigrants in December, 1839. This party consisted of more than 125 people. On reaching Galveston Christmas day they received the shocking news that the awful yellow fever epidemic was raging at Houston. Only a few of the most courageous of the colonists disembarked, the others, together with the leader returning to New York. According to Prof. Tiling, most of the colonists that remained in Texas went to Cat Spring and purchased land from Robert Kleberg, who, it may be mentioned, moved from Cat Springs to DeWitt county in 1847. Here he died October 23, 1888, at the age of 86. His wife died 19 years later, aged 90 years.

We come now to the area of the most stupendous, the most tragic and the most important of all German colonization projects, the coming of the Gillespie and Comal county colonists.

CHAPTER II.

GERMAN EMIGRATION COMPANY ORGANIZED.

Gets Victimitized by a Frenchman and an American.

Reference has been made to the character of literature by different German writers portraying the great opportunities and the blissful inducements in Texas. The productions referred to cover the period from 1821 to 1836. It was after Texas had secured its independence that the greatest flood of tracts, books and treaties on Texas was turned loose in Germany. In addition to dozens of tracts and newspaper articles, at least four books by men of considerable note were printed and distributed in Germany, none of which perhaps whetted the German desire to emigrate to the United States more than did a novel by Sealsfield, picturing the peacefulness and independence of the Texas pioneer. The political, social, industrial and economic conditions of Germany at that time especially prepared its people for the reception of such literature. It created a mania and produced its effects on people in all stations of life. The nobleman, the peasant, the tradesman, the mechanic, the professor and the physician alike heard and listened to this call of the wilds, to this message of imagination from beyond the seas.

It was a typical boom, effectively staged, whether by design or otherwise.

This led to a council of German princes and noblemen at Biebrich in April, 1842, "the result of which was the forming of an association for the purchase of lands in Texas." This was the beginning of the society for the protection of German emigrants to Texas, which was formed at a general meeting held at Mainz on March 24, 1844. As only princes and representatives of the higher nobility could become members of it, the society became generally known as the League of the Nobility, (Adelsverein)—Tiling.

It developed later that this organization couldn't protect itself.

Eighteen princes and nobles comprised the membership, with an incorporated capital of $80,000. The small amount of its capital reveals the utter lack of practical knowledge on the part of its incorporators, for as Professor Tiling remarks, one million dollars would have really been insufficient to carry out the plans of the company, and this would have required the best of executive control, whereas the company or association, had about the worst possible management.

Two representatives, Counts Victor von Leiningen and Boos-Waldeck, were sent as representatives to buy land from the Texas government. Count Leiningen seems to have been empowered with the gratest authority in this matter, though endowed with the least ability. He seems to have presented the matter to President Houston very awkwardly and improperly. He lacked both diplomacy and judgment. At any rate he failed in his mission, apparently because of his own mistakes. He requested too much and haughtily refused to accept anything less than full compliance with his demands. Count Boos-Waldeck was a man of entirely different temperament and judgment. He had visited with and listened to the advice of Mr. Ernst, the founder of Industry, a man of many years' experience as a pioneer. As a result of Mr. Ernst's advice Boos-Waldeck bought an improved tract of 4428 acres in Fayett county, together with all slaves on the place, this being the first, and perhaps the only instance of Germans owning slaves in Texas.

It is evident that there was utter lack of agreement between the two representatives of the Adelsverein or German Emigration Company as it was named. Notwithstanding the fact that he had failed to secure an acre of land for colonization purposes Count Leiningen returned to Germany and recommended a big colonization movement. Count Boos-Waldeck counseled against an undertaking on such an elaborate scale, particularly pointing out the difficulties to be encountered and the great cost that must be incurred. He favored the colonization proposition, but counseled conservativeness. Had his advice been heeded the history of German colonizing would not only have been a financial success, but the horros to which thousands of German colonists were to be later subjected would have been avoided.

Leiningen had been elected president and Count Castell secretary of the German Emigration Company (Adelsverein.) Both were evidently impractical theorists if not supreme egotists, but notwithstanding their lack of qualifications their influence was supreme with the organization, and Boos-Waldeck's wise suggestions were rejected.

And then a French sharper appeared on the scene. His real name was Bourgeois, but for this special occasion he had added many titles indicating nobility. He was just a common fraud working the land-shark game then being so promiscuously played by promoters of Texas colonization schemes. At that time a great many sharpers secured big grants with no other intention than to find a victim on whom they could unload for a good profit. He was one of the type having no intention of attempting to comply with the requirements under which the land grant had been secured. But he was eloquent and persuasive and easily trapped the gullible Castell. His grant had practically expired when he presented his proposition to Castell, but he claimed to be a close personal friend of President Houston and assured his prospective victim that he would have no trouble getting the grant extended.

Bourgeois' grant was dated July 3, 1842, and by the terms of this grant he was required to settle 400 families on the land within eighteen months. He had made no pretense at colonizing. As a consequence his grant expired December 3, 1843. His deal with the Adelverein was finally closed April 7, 1844, more than four months after his grant had really expired, both because of the time limit and of his total failure to comply with the requirements and conditions under which the grant had been awarded.

This deal was made over the advice and protests of Boos-Waldeck. The Bourgeois grant was in the territory to the west and northwest of San Antonio. The company now having, as it supposed, a great tract of land proceeded to advertise its proposition throughout Germany. It certainly seemed a fair proposition and was doubtless presented in good faith. To each emigrant it guaranteed a tract of good land in a wonderful fertile and healthy county, this being a present from the company and for which it would expect no compensation whatever. For the cost of transportation to the land and to provide a fund to sustain the colony each applicant, if a single man, was required to deposit $120, and each married man was required to deposit $240. The company would receive as its compensation a portion of the land granted by the republic of Texas to each settler, this being 640 acres to each married man and 320 acres to each single man. It developed when the real test came that it took more than three times the amount the Adelsverein had calculated to carry each colonist to the land and provide a sustaining and necessary improvement fund.

After the bogus land transaction with Bourgeois Prince Carl Solms-Braunfels was appointed commissioner general for the colony with Bourgeois as his assistant. They immediately came to Texas, and Bourgeois made an effort to get his grant extended, but his "close friend" President Houston, who had probably never met nor even heard of him before, emphatically refused to grant his request. Thus in addition to being out a considerable sum of money the Adelsverein was again without an acre of land for its colonization program, Prince Solms declaring the Waldeck purchase unfit for colonization purposes, and with a large number of colonists booked to sail soon for the promised land. Bourgeois was dropped as an officer, employee and stockholder in the company, and Prince Solms continued his search for suitable land.

And in the midst of the desperate situation another fakir appeared on the scene. To add shame to fraud, however, this fakir was an American, one Fisher by name, from Houston, Texas. Henry Fisher had arrived in Bremen as the consul for the Republic of Texas. Naturally his official position gave him creditable standing. He had formerly been in the real estate business in Houston, and had not overlooked the colonization land grant graft. He and one Burkart Miller had secured an immense land grant in West Texas. The conditions of this grant required among other things, the settlement of 600 families within eighteen months, and the settlement of 5400 more families within a reasonable time. Each settler would receive 640 acres if a married man, 320 acres if a single man, the agent or immigration contractor to receive not more than half the land awarded each settler. The Fisher grant was represented as containing nearly four million acres and lay between the Llano and San Saba rivers. And again, contrary to the advice of Count Boos-Waldeck the Adelsverein made a land deal. It contracted to pay Fisher & Miller $9000 and carry out all their contract with the state. Fisher, it later developed, had never seen the land, yet he represented that every acre of it was the very finest farming land while in fact but a small per cent of it was tillable. He also assured the Adelsverein that 6000 families could be easily located on the land and provided with necessary implements and supplies to run them several months for $80,000. In this Fisher deliberately misrepresented the matter. He had been in Texas for several years and knew better. Among the conditions of the grant it was stipulated that the contractor should survey the entire tract into sections each alternate section to be the property of the state. The cost of surveying alone, Professor Tiling estimates, would have been more than $80,000, the total incorporated capital of the Adelsverein. But in addition to the $9000 and the assumption of their obligations to the state Fisher & Miller were to share in all profits the company might make from the sale of lands or industrial establishments, they in turn generously obligating themselves to not sell their interest in the enterprise before 1848, a deceptive agreement of fair promise to which they could safely consent, for they really had nothing to sell at any time.

With the acquisition of the Fisher & Miller grant the Adelsverein proceeded with confidence to carry out its colonization project. The association "entered into an agreement with each emigrant in which the German Emigration Company in consideration of the payment of $120 by each single man or $240 by each married man, contracted not only to bring the emigrants to Texas, but also to furnish free transportation from the place of landing to the colony in wagons and tents of the society, and furnish a rude dwelling to be built on each emigrant's land in the colony. The other half was credited to the emigrants, who could draw on it for farming implements or extra rations from the company's store until they had made the first crop. The officials of the German Emigration Company had calculated that the cost of transportation from Galveston to Port Lavaca and from there to point of destination, about 300 miles, would be $4.00 per head and that a log house could be furnished for $24.00, whereas the cost of transporting each emigrant was more than $20 and the cost of each log house more than $100. "Neither Castell nor any other official of the association had the slightest idea of the conditions, price or cost of living in Texas, and neither Bourgeois nor Fisher found it to their interest to enlighten the German officials on these important points. Burgeois d'Orvanne and Henry F. Fisher were the evil spirits of the Adelsverein, and it was primarily their scheming and misrepresentations that caused the early collapse of the enterprise. But this can in no wise excuse the stupendous incompetency and childish credulity of Count Castell and other officials of the German Emigration Company, whose actions were an unbroken chain of blunders."

After the deal with Fisher the Adelsverein published the following notice:

"The grant of Burgeois d'Orvanne has been declared forfeited by the congress of Texas, but the company has made another contract with H. F. Fisher by which the more northerly situated, extra ordinarily fertile and healthy lands on the right bank of the Colorado river have been acquired and come into possession of the Adelsverein." This was signed by the directorate.

In this the directorate had been badly deceived or was seeking to deceive others. By its deal with Fisher it had acquired nothing but an obligation and right to colonize. The grant it had acquired had not then been surveyed, as the terms of the grant required, and the association had not secured title to a single acre of land.

As the result of the chicanery of an unscrupulous American and an unprincipled Frenchmen and the monumental blundering of German nobility thousands of German immigrants men, women and children, were doomed to suffer the tortures of death and to meet the bitterest of disappointments.

First Immigrants Arrive—Disasters Befall Them.

In November 1844 more than 700 of the German immigrants landed in Galveston. What to do with them was a question that sorely perplexed Prince Solms. The Fisher grant had not been surveyed, and it would not do to take the colonists 300 miles in the dead of winter into a wild country where they as yet had no rights, and from which the republic of Texas could eject them any time if it so elected. All that could be done was to take care of the new arrivals in the best way possible. They were transported to Indianola about 100 miles from Galveston. There the miserable colonists spent their first miserable Christmas in the new world of golden promise and sore disappointment. There in tents and in the meanest of quarters the colonists remained for more than two months. Assisted by Dr. Ferdinand Lindheimer, a distinguished botanist who had spent several years in Texas, Prince Solms was able to purchase a 1300 acre tract of land near the intersection of the Comal and Guadalupe rivers for which he paid $800.

The first colonists exhausted from an overland journey of more than 150 miles reached New Braunfels March 1, 1845.

Each colonist was given a town lot and a ten acre tract near the townsite. This gift in no way invalidated their rights to land to be allotted when the Fisher grant had been surveyed.

The immigrants quickly built a number of log houses, while Prince Solms had a more pretentious building erected for himself and his fellow officers, giving to this log hut the high sounding title of "Sophienburg."

The town itself was named in honor of the Castle of Prince Solms on the Lahn river in Germany.

In less than a month after the arrival of the first of the colonists Prince Solms returned to Germany, departing even before his successor, John O. Meusebach, could arrive. Prince Solms had a most excellent military record, but his army training and battle field experiences did not equip him to combat the arduous and complex problems that would confront him and with which he would have to do battle in handling the colonization situation. He was a first cousin of Queen Victoria of England, also of Emperor William 1, of Germany. He was a stepson of King George I of Hannover.

Meusebach quickly discovered that the finances of the company were in bad shape, its credit at a low ebb and its contracts unfulfilled, with another large consignment of immigrants on the way or due to soon start for America.

Every calamity and emergency produces its heroes and its men of the hour. The history of the German Emigration Company is no exception. In fact it is a shining verification of this adage.

Boos-Waldeck had advised wisely but his advice and suggestions had been ignored. Time and results vindicated him in every contention he had made and in every suggestion he had offered.

John O. Meusebach the successor of Prince Solms, was one of the wisest and most determined men that ever headed a colonization project or salvaged a forlorn hope. He has been described as a man of iron will, calm judgement, an unyielding sense of justice, tireless energy and dogged determination.

The first thing he discovered on his arrival at New Braunfels was that there had been no pretense at system in the management of affairs. He requested the treasurer to furnish him a financial statement. All kinds of petty officers had issued orders promiscuously and no proper account had been kept. The treasurer informed Meusebach that it would be impossible to prepare such statement owning to condition of the books. Meusebach went to Galveston, hoping to overtake Prince Solms and get things straightened out. He found the Prince and he incidentally found a lot more sad revelations. One of the many creditors of the German Emigration Company had served the Prince with an attachment. Meusebach paid the amount out of his limited funds, with the understanding that the Prince would hasten to Europe and see to it that more funds were forthcoming at once. Meusebach returned to New Braunfels, and being unable to get any satisfaction from the treasurer went to work on the books himself and in due time had them in respectable order. With order in the books and financial affairs of the company and by judicious business methods he soon restored the confidence of creditors. The books when balanced showed that the company was then in debt to the amount of nearly $20,000, an amount that in spite of the most rigid economy and the best of business attention, had increased to $24,000 by the first of November, 1845.

Despite this financial embarrassment and handicap several thousand immigrants were due to arrive in November of 1845. Meusebach knew that preparations must be made for these newcomers. They could not be quartered and cared for at New Braunfels, so he started in search of a new location. This he found on the Pedernales river, about 80 miles northwest of New Braunfels. He is said to have been the first whiteman to visit that particular section of the Llano and Pedernales rivers country. At a considerable distance from the Fisher & Miller grant he selected a 10,000 acre tract. It was good land, well watered and with ample timber to supply the needs of the colonists. This land was surveyed into ten acre tracts for distribution among the immigrants, due to arrive, on the same plan as had been followed at New Braunfels. And thus was prepared the settlement of Gillespie county and the founding of Fredericksburg.

Returning to New Braunfels Meusebach found awaiting him official notice that 4000 colonists were on their way to Galveston, and that credit to the amount of $24,000 had been provided for him at a New Orleans bank. What a miserable pittance. Six dollars per head to transport 4000 people a distance of nearly 300 miles, sustain them through the winter, build even the crudest log houses for them and provide for their needs until the first crop could be harvested, and this in view of the further embarrassing fact that the company was already in debt to the amount of approximately $24,000. To pay its debts and care for the colonists as the German Emigration Company had contracted to do, $240,000 would have been none to much.

From October, 1845, to April, 1846, 36 ships bringing

5247 German immigrants reached Galveston. This was 1200 in excess of the number Meusebach had been advised would arrive, and reduced the amount of money placed to Meusebach's credit to less than $5.00 per capita. Meusebach had his hands full and his treasury empty, for the amount placed to his credit wouldn't pay the debts of the company.

Many of the immigrants had brought along much luggage they didn't need, while nearly all of them had failed to provide the very things they would need. This horde of immigrants with their piles of luggage must be transferred from the ships to light schooners and then transported to Indianola 100 miles from Galveston, and thence overland to the land selected on the Pedernales, and this was the biggest task of all. After several weeks' strenuous effort Meusebach succeeded in contracting with a Houston teaming concern to haul the immigrants to New Braunfels, trusting by other means to get them from New Braunfels to their location. Just as the job was well underway, and after 100 wagons of immigrants had left Indianola, war was declared between the United States and Mexico. The government needed every available means of transportation for which it paid a much higher price than the contract between Meusebach and the teamsters. The result was that the teamsters repudiated their contract to transport the immigrants, and Meusebach was left without help or hope, with perhaps 4000 immigrants still in the miserable tents and shacks at Indianola, for not more than 1000 could have been taken in the first and only trip the teamsters made.

Even the elements were against the luckless immigrants. There had been an unusual amount of rain and dismal weather. As a natural consequence of the miserable, unsanitary conditions there was an epidemic of fever and many deaths among the colonists while at Indianola. The people were wretched and despondent, and when advised of the plight they were in after the teaming contractors had refused to carry out their agreement, despair was added to the situation. Some five hundred of the young men joined the United States army and went to Mexico, and a few weeks later the other immigrants, men, women and children, set out on a miserable march across an uninhabited and an unknown country, drifting toward New Braunfels. It was the march of death to the goal of disappointment.

"This proved disastrous to many, hundreds perishing on the way from exposure, hunger and exhaustion; while those who arrived at New Braunfels and later at Fredericksburg, carried with them the germs of disease that soon developed into a frightful epidemic, in which more than 1000 died."— Tiling.

It is impossible to describe the condition of these colonists, not only while on their long march but after they had reached their destination The Emmigration Company had failed to provision the immigrants, just as it had failed in many other vital matters. Particularly had it failed to provide the proper medical service and medical supplies. With ample justification the colonists were sorely angered at the Adelsverein, but in their insane rage they even threatened with death their best, most loyal and co-suffering friend, Meusebach. To have harmed this man would have been nothing less than the crucifixion of the only man that could save them. In the discharge of his duties Meusebach braved dangers, inspired the respect and confidence and finally won the adoration of the colonists. Tiling says that "while the scurvy epidemic was at its height men and women became bereft of reason, family ties were broken and the wretched people tried to forget their misery by dancing, carousing and drinking. Dr. Koester, the only physician at New Braunfels, was powerless against the attacks of the disease, which only spent its force after one-third of the inhabitants had fallen victims to its death grip."

Authorities differ as to the number of deaths, nor is there any reliable data available as to the number of deaths at Indianola, along the line of march, and later at New Braunfels and Fredericksburg. Meusebach reported the total number of deaths as not exceeding 850, while Dr. Knapp estimated the death list at two-thirds of the immigrants. All told 7380 immigrants had arrived, and two-thirds of this number would have been 4920. This is probably excessive, while Meusebach's report was possibly too conservative. One authority estimates the total deaths at 3800, which figures may be accepted as a fair compromise.

In his history Robert Penniger says: "In the middle of December, 1845, Commissioner Meusebach sent out from New Braunfels an expedition of 36 men under the command of Lieutenant and Surveyor Bene, with instructions to establish a wagon road from New Braunfels to the north bank of the Pedernales, where he had bought land for a new settlement. This expedition was well equipped with wagons, provisions, weapons, instruments and tools, and besides Lieutenant Bene, two engineers, Gross and Merchison, accompanied it. They arrived at their destination after a march of three weeks and at once began the construction of a block-house, which was only partly finished when they had to return to New Braunfels for lack of supplies.

"On April 24, 1846, the first body of colonists started for the new settlement in 29 heavy ox-carts and some Mexican two-wheeled vehicles, amid the cheers of their. countrymen who remained at New Braunfels. When they approached the Pedernales they were met by a number of Indians from the tribe of the Delawares, who, fortunately, were friendly disposed and the colonists passed the Indian camp unmolested.

"Friday, May 8, the weary immigrants reached the place where the surveying party had begun the erection of the first house in the new colony in an opening of the virgin forest of gigantic trees and dense coppice. The new settlement, named Fredericksburg, in honor of Prince Frederick of Prussia, a member of the Adelsverein, was platted by surveyor Wilke, the fearless pioneers began the construction of their new homes, their number being constantly increased by the arrival of new immigrants, and soon Fredericksburg had 1000 busy and industrious inhabitants."

These were undoubtedly the immigrants who left Indianola early in March when the caravan of 100 wagons departed for New Braunfels. It is the reasonable conclusion that not more than 1000 people left with this wagon train and that 4000 remained at Indianola or arrived on ships after the train left Indianola.

At different times surprise has been expressed as to why the state (for Texas had then become a member of the Union) and federal government did not come to the relief of these dying people during the awful epidemic. New Braunfels was little more than fifty and Fredericksburg little more than eighty miles from the state capital. Surely the state and federal authorities must have known of this epidemic of death.

It must be remembered that the whole population of Texas at that time was in little better condition than were the German immigrants. It was a state of scattered, impoverished pioneers. It took weeks to carry a message that can now be telegraphed or telephoned or sent by wireless in a few seconds. To add to this condition the country was at war, and the state and federal government was mustering every resource, both of men, money, medicine, food, clothes, and teams and rushing them into Mexico. It is doubtful if the report of the deplorable condition of these immigrants reached the capital of Texas until the epidemic was over. Had it reached there sooner, the state with its treasury empty and its citizens in the army could have done nothing.

New Braunfels is commonly considered and generally referred to as the parent German community of Fredericksburg. This is erroneous. New Braunfels was the first and Fredericksburg the second and really the last German settlement under the colonization project of the Adeluverein. The colonists at Fredericksburg came direct from Germany the same as did the New Braunfels colonists. They merely passed through and remained in New Braunfels for several weeks while on their way to Fredericksburg. All of these colonists were intended for the Fisher & Miller grant.

The Adelsverein Fails.—Fisher & Miller Show Up Again.

The disasters that befell the immigrants of 1845-46 sealed the doom and marked the end of the Adelsverein. It is hardly fair to assign any selfish or improper motives to the originators of this organization. It has been charged that it was a money making scheme, and that the nobles and royalists were planning a foreign possession in the United States over which the aristocracy would have supreme control, a feudal realm that would pay tribute to the offspring of nobility. This is possible and at that time would not have been improper but it was impractical, in fact impossible, and if true was nothing more than a wild dream. It was at one time openly charged, and the charge was made by a German, that England financed the movement as a means of settling Texas with foreigners and preventing the annexation of Texas to the Union. This charge was fanciful and unfounded. In the first place, the organization was never financed. Had it been financed it would not have failed, both as to its own interest and in the matter of carrying out its contracts with the immigrants.

That it was shamefully imposed on by a couple of land sharpers and that its management was impractical are conceded facts. Beyond this there is little cause for criticism.

When Meusebach received the first consignment of colonists the company was deeply in debt and placed only a pittance at Meusebach's command. He appealed to the Adelsverein in vain. He scoured the country and bought all he could from the planters on credit; he tried to borrow money, but bankers had but limited funds in those days and they had less confidence in the success of an organization that had been so wholly mismanaged. Finally through a published appeal to the people of Germany, this appeal inspired by Meusebach but signed by the Adelsverein's agent in Galveston, Mr. Klaener, the Adelsverein was compelled to send another but more respectable sum, $60,000. It was this remittance that enabled Meusebach to save the immigrants from dissolution if not from total destruction.

Although the Adelsverein continued to do some advertising, to maintain an existance and to make contracts after 1847, it was to all intents and purposes totally bankrupt. A number of the immigrants signed up by this organization on reaching Galveston and learning of the calamities that had befallen the New Braunfels and Fredericksburg immigrants, went elsewhere and located.

The German Emigration Company sent a total of 7380 colonists to Texas, all of them destined for the New Braunfels and Fredericksburg settlements. Of this number, as stated elsewhere, perhaps five hundred joined the United States army and went to Mexico, approximately 3800 died during the spring, summer and fall of 1846 and perhaps two hundred on reaching Galveston late in the spring of 1846, and learning of the misfortunes of their countrymen who had preceded them, went elsewhere. Of the 7380 colonists to arrive in 1845 and 1846, not more than 2800 of them were alive and living in the New Braunfels and Fredericksburg colonies January 1, 1847.

New Braunfels and Fredericksburg were selected only for temporary sojourning places, all of the colonists being intended for the Fisher & Miller grant. Instead of temporary affairs the two towns have become about the most permanent propositions in the United States. Only two German colonies were ever located on what had been the Fisher & Miller grant. These were Bettina and Castell in Llano county. Bettina was the dream of several German scholars and professional men. They soon found that there was considerable difference between a beautiful, utopian dream and a cold reality, so Bettina was abandoned. Castell was settled by a number of farmers and mechanics and is today a flourishing community, practically all of the citizens of the community descendants of the original colonists. It seems that neither of these communities was in any way identified with the German Emigration Company. Leiningen and Meerholz were located near the Fisher & Miller grant, but not actually on it. The German Emigration Company had nothing to do with these colonies, as has often been erroneously stated. They, too, were big dream propositions, and were soon abandoned by the original colonists.

Practically all the New Braunfels and Fredericksburg colonists got out of the Adelsverein were a number of town lots, ten acre tracts near the towns, disappointment, disillusionment and an awful lot of misery and temporary poverty and privations, conditions from which they eventually recovered by reason of their own heroic struggles and iron determination.

In 1848 the Texas legislature renewed the Fisher grant for the apparent purpose of taking care of the Adelsverein colonists, and certificates covering several thousand acres, mostly in Llano, McCullough and Concho counties, were issued to the colonists. The land was in the heart of the Indian country at that time, the colonists felt that they had all the hardships they could endure in their humble homes at Fredericksburg and New Braunfels, and they did not care to move farther into the Indian country and farther away from the semblance of civilization. As a result most of them sold their certificates for mere trifles, some certificates, covering a section of land being sold for less than ten dollars each. Just a few held their certificates, located their land and became wealthy as a result.

In July, 1847, just before he started on his famous and successful visit to the Indians, Meusebach seems to have irrevocably tendered his resignation as commissioner of the Adelsverein, although this resignation did not reach head-quarters in Germany for many weeks, becoming effective in July, 1847. He was succeeded by Herman Spiess. The New Braunfels and Fredericksburg colonists still believed that they would in due time be awarded the land to which they were entitled, in addition to the town lots and ten acre tracts. In 1847 Commissioner Spiess frankly told them that the Adelsverein was hopelessly bankrupt. "And," says Professor Tiling, "the colonists were left to their own resources. Not one of these unfortunate people would have remained at New Braunfels or Fredericksburg if he had possessed the means of returning to the Fatherland that he left only a short time ago with fine hopes and under such glittering promises. But it proved well for them that they were forced to remain at these primitive settlements. After the first outburst of despair and agony was over they all set determinedly to work, and by hard and persistent labor in cultivating their ten acres and living on the barest necessities for several years they not only succeeded in establishing a firm existence for themselves and their families, but in course of time made Fredericksburg and New Braunfels the garden spots of Texas."

Commissioner Spiess was succeeded in 1852 by Surveyor

L. Bene, the last official representative of the Adelsverein in Texas. In September, 1853, the company made an assignment of all of its properties and colonization rights to its Texas creditors. The deed to the 10,000 acres purchased by Meusebach at Fredericksburg was made to J. O. Meusebach. Bene as commissioner for the Adelsverein signed all deeds to settlers as the agent of the German Emigration Company. This caused no little trouble and resulted in several suits to perfect title. Meusebach had the land deeded to him as a means of safeguarding the interest of the settlers. He could have taken advantage of the fact that the original deed was made to him and have caused a great deal of trouble to the colonists and have greatly benefitted himself. But he was not that kind of a man. Many years ago Judge Moursund, as attorney for Meusebach and the colonists, filed an affidavit in the office of the Gillespie county clerk setting up the fact that the land belonged to the Adelsverein, that it was purchased with money of the association. By this means the missing link in the title between Meusebach and the German Emigration Company was perfected.

In 1851 Fisher & Miller came again booming into port with their sails of brazen fraud spread wide to the winds of chance. They appeared before the land commissioner and stated under oath "that the German Emigration Company (the Adelsverein) had introduced and settled in Texas 1600 families and 1000 single men and that therefore said Fisher & Miller were entitled to 160 sections of 640 acres each, and to 100 half sections of 320 acres each, making a total of 134,400 acres as the stipulated premium for settling European immigrants. By the terms of their deal with the Adelsverein Fisher and Miller were represented by three votes in the "colonialrat" of the Adelsverein, but in 1851 this committee had been out of existence for many years. Despite this fact Fisher & Miller had produced a judgment against the German Emigration Company which ordered that the certificates and titles to these 134,400 acres should be made out in their names. Commissioner Sherwood did so, but the commissioner of the general land office refused to issue the patents to the lands."—Tiling.

Then Fisher & Miller carried their fight to the house of representatives. Hon. Sam Maverick, of San Antonio, then a member of the legislature, lead the fight against Fisher & Miller, declaring that their judgment was a snap judgment and a fraud. The proposition was overwhelmingly defeated and the commissioner of the general land office sustained in his refusal to issue patents to Fisher & Miller. But that resourceful pair did not despair. Through court rulings and legislative enactments they finally got practically all they claimed.

And so the Adelsverein, "organized to protect German emigrants to the United States," came to an inglorious end. It had doubtless meant well, had promised much, but erred disastrously. Had the association listened only to Boos-Waldeck and Meusebach how different would have been its fate.

The Adelsverein Meant Well.—Why It Failed.

These colonists had left Germany with the assurance that they would receive a great tract of land, that each married immigrant would receive 320 and each single immigrant 160 acres of land, this being half the land awarded each immigrant by the state, the other half going to the Emigration Company. The immigrants before depositing the required amount of money—$240 for every married man and $120 for every single man—were assured that they would get prompt transportation from the port of arrival to the colony lands, ample provisions, clothing, farming implements, houses, etc., to care for them until the first crop had been made and harvested. As already related the chicanery of Bourgeois, the Frenchman, and of Fisher & Miller, the Americans, and the incapacity of those at the head of the German Emigration Company, the latter the inexcusable victims of land sharks, brought all of these fair promises to nought, and consigned the innocent immigrants to heartbreaking disappointment. Only a small per cent of the immigrants were provided with transportation to New Braunfels or Fredericksburg. No houses were provided, no supplies were furnished, and without funds the immigrants were dumped into the heart of a hostile wilderness. They had but few crude tools and implements with which they could provide shelter or produce crops. They had but few guns and but little ammunition with which they could protect themselves or kill game for sustenance. Texas, with all of its vast expanse of territory, had at that time less than 150,000 inhabitants, and these were for the most part, living in small, far separated communities. At that time there was not a city in Texas having to exceed 4,000 inhabitants. Large scopes of country had not been touched by the foot of whiteman. There was not a mile of railroad in the state, and only a few dim, winding wagon roads, many miles apart, connected the older settled communities. There was no place to which the German colonists could go; no neighbors to whom they could turn for assistance, counsel and sympathy.

Had the German Emigration Company (Adelsverein) listened to Count Boos-Waldeck and secured the land in advance of the immigrants, and have sent the colonists in properly regulated numbers, or had it listened later to the appeals of Meusebach and financed the colonists, how different things would have terminated. One cannot contemplate what these German colonists would have achieved, not only for themselves but for the entire country. When it is considered what these colonists have accomplished in spite of the hostile elements with which they had to contend, in spite of the deplorable and penniless condition in which they found themselves on arriving at the places where fate had decreed they should arrive instead of reaching the place to which they supposed themselves destined, there to receive a town lot and a ten acre tract instead of the 320 and 160 acre tracts for which they had paid, for the money they deposited was in reality purchase money, what they could and would have accomplished if given a square deal becomes in some degree apparent.

With these colonists were highly educated men and women, capable of teaching in any position from the kindergarten to the great universities, practical farmers, carpenters, stone masons, wagon makers, machinists, blacksmiths, cabinet makers and skilled artisans of all kinds. They had all the needed human equipment, and all these trained minds and hands needed was the material with which to work and a market for their products. With money and supplies provided as promised the colonists would have furnished abundant employment for the teachers and mechanics, and the farmers would have produced the necessary sustenance in the matter of farm products.

In many respects fortune favored them in the matter of location. They came to a country with vast natural resources. The land was fertile the water supply abundant, there was ample supply of the best building material, both stone and timber; sand and gravel of the right quality for mortar and limestone with which lime could be made, and they knew how to utilize all of these. They were perhaps the best equipped colonists that ever reached the American continent. Their work and achievements under the greatest of privations and disadvantages proves this. An ideal climate and a wonderful healthy country was especially in the immigrants favor. Had it not been a healthy country it is doubtful if the colonists could have survived the hardships, exposure and privations to which they were subjected for so many months, and even years.

Meusebach Makes Treaty with Indians.—Short Sketch of Meusebach.

When the Germans arrived at New Braunfels in 1845 and at Fredericksburg in 1846, they were in the heart of the Indians' favorite hunting ground. They made no treaty with the Indians until 1847 and the wonder is that they were not during all this time seriously molested by the Indians. Why the Indians did not resent this intrusion with a wholesale massacre and completely exterminate the colonists is one of the subjects on which not even legend throws any light. The Indians were not ignorant of the presence of the German settlers. In fact, the first Gillespie county colonists were met by a band of several hundred Indians between New Braunfels and Fredericksburg, and immediately on learning that these newcommers were Germans the Indians are reported to have given assurance of friendship. What agency had been at work with the Indians? How did they know anything about the coming of the Germans, and why did they manifest a friendly feeling for the Germans? Conjecture alone can make reply.

In the latter part of 1846 the colonial agent for the Adelsverein at Fredericksburg "Dr." Schubert, whose real name Professor Tiling says was Strohberg, "a bankrupt tobacco merchant from Cassel," Germany, made a rather rediculous attempt to visit the Indians and make some kind of treaty. He seems to have reached the Llano river and then turned back reporting to Meusebach that it would be impossible to go beyond the Llano river because of the myriads of hostile Indians. This report had no terrfying effects on Meusebach. He knew that some kind of satisfactory treaty must be made with the Indians, otherwise they were liable to attack and exterminate the colony. In January, 1847, Meusebach started on his treaty mission among the Llano and San Saba county Indians. Some authorities say he started from Fredericksburg January 22, others say it was January 26. But the undisputed fact is that he started in the latter part of January. It was one of the most remarkable visits ever made among the Indians by a whiteman. At that time war was underway between the United States and Mexico, and the Mexicans, always having direct communication with the Indians, were in every way conspiring to arouse the Indians against the whites. This fact made the trip of Meusebach the more dangerous, but he also realized that it made the trip the more imperatively urgent. Friendly relations must be established with the Indians before they were influenced to exterminate the little German colonies. With thousands of well armed warriors it would be an easy matter for the big chiefs to make a surprise attack on the colonies, particularly Fredericksburg, kill and scalp the men and older women, burn the buildings and carry the young women and children into captivity. Up to this time Meusebach had not had a moment's time to give the treaty matter his personal attention. He had been too busy trying to get the colonists from Indianola to New Braunfels and Fredericksburg, and then trying to sufficiently supply their wants to keep them all from dying. With three wagons, an interpreter and 20 men he started toward the Llano river, his destination being the heart of the Indian country, hitherto untraversed by whiteman.

Some days after its departure the expedition met a hunting party of Shawnee Indians on the Llano river. These Indians were of the friendly Arkansaw tribes and spoke the English language. Meusebach made a deal with them to go along with the expedition, do the hunting and provide the meat. Early in February the expedition reached the vicinity of the camp of Ketemoczy, one of the Comanche chiefs. Eight Indian warriors came riding toward Meusebach's camp, bearing a white flag, and Meusebach's Mexican interpreter was despatched to meet them. They informed Meusebach that their chief was well aware of his presence and travels through the country, and that the chief desired to know the purpose of his mission, whether friendly or hostile, and that in either event Ketemoczy was prepared to deal with them. The Shawnees had already advised Meusebach that though he had seen no Comanches they had observed his every move for many days. Then Meusebach through an interpreter convinced the Indians that his mission was one of friendship and that he desired to have counsel with the chief. It was perhaps the 7th of February when Muesebach reached the camp of Ketemoczy, this camp being near the San Saba river. Here he found the chief surrounded by more than five hundred warriors and a number of women and children, all on horseback and prepared to receive the great white visitor with royal ceremony. And here Meusebach displayed his wonderful courage and deep intuitive insight into Indian character. One requirement of Ketemoczy was that, as an evidence of good faith and peaceful intentions, Meusebach's party should fire their guns in the air. With this request Meusebach promptly complied, the Indians responding with a similar token. A less courageous and a less resourceful man than Meusebach might have suspected this request as a ruse by the Indians, for with their guns unloaded the visitors would have been hopelessly at the mercy of the Indians had they been in-

clined to take the advantage thus afforded them. Possibly
Meusebach had taken counsel from the Shawnees and his
Mexican guide and interpreter, but in any event he showed
that he was a man capable of dealing with emergencies.
Meusebach, like Sam Houston, was just the kind of man to
deal with the Indians. He was courageous, firm, honest
and fair.

Soon after Meusebach's departure from Fredericksburg
the news reached the governor of Texas. The governor was
greatly alarmed and immediately despatched Major Neighbors to overtake the intrepid German and persuade him to
abandon his wild mission. Owing to the hostile feeling of
the Indians toward the whites the governor was confident
the expedition would result in much harm. Muesebach
would probably be killed, together with his entire company,
and the Indians would be enraged to take the warpath and
wipe out many settlements. Major Neighbors and his party
came up with Meusebach at the camp of Ketemoczy. Major
Neighbors, who had long dealt with the Indians and thought
that he understood them, appealed to Meusebach to
turn back, but instead of turning back Meusebach convinced
Neighbors that it was necessary that he proceed to visit
the other Indian chiefs, and induced the major to join him
on the trip.

As a result of the conference with Ketemoczy arrange-
ments were made for a general conference with the other
Comanche chiefs, this counsel to be held on the lower
San Saba river. This meeting was attended by some twenty
of the big chiefs, principal among them being Santanna,
Mopechucope and Pochanaquarhip, a satisfactory agreement
having already been entered into with Ketemoczy. With
the chiefs attending the council a treaty was made between
them and Meusebach, by the terms of which the people of
Meusebach were to be permitted to come and go at leisure
and without molestation, and the surveyors and colonists
were not to be disturbed when they came to the land that
had been granted them. The people of Meusebach should
at all times treat the Indians with fairness, and should at

all times welcome them to their "wigwams," and Meusebach pledged himself to see that the chiefs and their warriors received presents to the amount of $3000.

In the main every feature of the treaty was lived up to by both the Indians and the Germans. No Community so exposed to Indian depredations suffered so little as did the German communities of Gillespie and Comal counties. Some mischief was done and some crimes committed by roving bands of Indians, but it was never positively proven that these depredations were committed by the Comanches, the tribes with which Meusebach had made his treaty. Even conceding that all the depredations from which Fredericksburg suffered at times was committed by Comanches, the fact remains that it was insignificant compared to what could have happened and doubtless would have happened had Meusebach failed in his mission. While general history has been silent on this matter old pioneers regard it as one of the greatest feats ever performed by a white man in dealing with the Indians of Texas.

Meusebach, a man of noble birth and high rank, accustomed to all the luxuries of royalty, had confirmed Robert Burns, "a man's a man for a' that."

Not even roving bands of Indians did any material mischief among the German colonists until after the death of Santanna in 1848. After his death the Indians in only small degree violated the terms of the Meusebach treaty until the government had established frontier forts, subjected the Indians to great restraints, removing them in theory if not in reality, from their hunting grounds to reservations. It was during the war and for some years after the war that the Indians did the greatest mischief.

Ottfried Hans Freiherr von Meusebach was born at Dillenburg, Nassau, May 26, 1812. His father was a man of prominence and held many important positions under the Prussian government. The son studied mining engineering and Forestry at Clausthal; natural science at Bonn; jurisprudence and state economy at Halle. After graduating his first position was with the superior court at Naumburg. He was later sent to Stettin to deal with the communistic uprising. He handled this serious situation with such masterful tact that he attracted national attention. In 1845 he was tendered and accepted the position of general commissioner for the Adelsverein, succeeding Prince Solms. In addition to founding the town of Fredericksburg he also founded the colonies of Castel and Leiningen in Llano county.

He was master of five languages, speaking English fluently.

He became a naturalized citizen of the United States soon after reaching Texas. When he took out naturalization papers he dropped all prefixes and became John O. Meusebach.

For the greater part of his life, after reaching Texas, his home was in New Braunfels, or in that immediate vicinity.

In 1851 he was elected to the state senate representing the counties of Comal, Bexar and Medina.

In 1852 he was married to Agnes Coreth, Countess of Tyrol, this marriage taking place at New Braunfels September 28, 1852. To this union eleven children were born, New Braunfels the birth place of them all. Four girls died in infancy. The eldest child, E. O. Meusebach, was born July 26, 1853; died in Torreon, Mexico, several years ago. O. C. Meusebach was born January 5, 1855; Max Meusebach was born March 2, 1857. Both O. C. and Max died in San Antonio. Four daughters are still living: They are: Mrs. Antonie Marschall (von Biberstein), born January 26, 1859; Mrs. Elizabeth Zesch, born January 18, 1861; Mrs. Lucy Marschall (von Biberstein), born July 12, 1865; Mrs. Emmy Marschall (von Biberstein), born June 6, 1869.

Mrs. Antonie Marschall now lives in Dallas, Texas; Mrs. Zesch lives in Oakland, Calif.; Mrs. Lucy Marschall lives in Llano, Texas, and Mrs. Emmy Marschall in Fredericksburg.

In 1854 J. O. Meusebach was appointed by Governor Pease to represent the state in the matter of issuing headright certificates to the colonists of the German Emigration Company (the Adelsverein.) Probably in 1854 he lived on a farm and served as justice of the peace at Comanche Springs, in

Bexar county. Later he lived for a short time at Waco Springs near New Braunfels. He also made his home for awhile at Llano and at Fredericksburg.

He owned a body of fine land between Fredericksburg and Mason. On this tract of land in 1869 he founded the town of Loyal Valley. Here for many years he ran a store, was postmaster and justice of the peace. He served as postmaster just as he served as justice of the peace at Comanche Springs and Loyal Valley, as a matter of accommodation. He was just the type of old time citizen that would hold any kind of position and render any kind of service to accommodate his friends and neighbors. At Loyal Valley it is said that he always kept two furnished rooms set apart to accommodate any friend or worthy stranger who might happen along in need of lodging.

He died at Loyal Valley, Mason county, May 27, 1897, at the age of eighty-five years and one day. He is buried in the Marschall family cemetery at Cherry Springs, Gillespie county.

His wife is buried at Llano, Texas, where she died December 15, 1909.

CHAPTER III.

FLASH LIGHTS OF HISTORY.

Statistics—Friction Arises—Independent Thought.

The first United States census of Texas was taken in 1850. In fact this was the first census of any kind that had ever been taken of the Texas population. Nothing more than a rough estimate as to the population of Texas had ever been made prior to 1850, and these estimates had varied to such an extent that they were of but little worth. The 1850 census gave the German born population of the state as 8191. According to Professor Tiling this was far from correct, and he certainly produces convincing figures in support of his contention. He says:

"Under the auspices of the Adelsverein alone there had come to Texas 7380 immigrants, while in 1847, 1848 and 1849 about 15,000 Germans arrived, and more than 10,000 arrived from 1830 to 1840. This makes a total of about 33,000 Germans."

Very few of the German immigrants left the state, and the death rate including the calamity of 1846 would not have been 25,000, this being the difference between the census report and the estimate of Professor Tiling. The birth rate would have certainly been equal to the death rate. Therefore it is conservative to estimate the total German population of Texas in 1850 at around 35,000, and the foreign born German population at around 25,000. At that time Texas was a very sparsely settled country, and on account of the Indians it was dangerous to travel from community to community, particularly was it dangerous to visit most of the isolated German communities. It is therefore reasonable to conclude that the census enumerators made an indoor calculation and estimate, and made a poor job of it.

The banner year of all history of German immigration to Texas seems to have been 1847, 8000 German immigrants reaching the port of Galveston that year, none of them under the auspices of the Adelsverein, however.

Professor Tiling says: "The Germans comprised one-fifth of the white population of Texas in 1850. Of these 6000 lived in eastern Texas, about equally divided between Harris and Galveston counties; 10,000 were in central Texas, in Austin, Washington, Fayette, Colorado, Milam, Bastrop, Travis and other counties, while more than 15,000 lived in western Texas in the present counties of Comal, Bexar, Gillespie, Medina, Guadaloupe, DeWitt, Victoria, Calhoun, Caldwell, Llano, Hays, Kerr and Gonzales."

Thus, according to Professor Tiling's figures, the total German population both native and foreign born, in 1850 was 31,000, which is certainly conservative. It is perhaps four to five thousand less than the actual number of Germans in all parts of Texas at that time.

No higher class citizenship ever immigrated into any country. Most of these immigrants were distressfully poor in money, but they were rich in brain and brawn, rich in energy and the highest purposes and noblest impulses. Out of this immigration Texas received many of its greatest educators, many of its greatest physicians, writers, musicians, artists and mechanics. Most of these immigrants were farmers, and the German farmers were then, are today and perhaps will always be the world's greatest farmers. In the matter of development every German community in Texas today speaks for itself. Their towns, their homes, their farms, their bank accounts reflect the embodiment of system, thoroughness, energy and close application. That which has been best for the German would have been, in a very great measure at least, best for the American, but the American would not observe, emulate and benefit. The American had a way of his own and the German had a way of his own. Early in the course of their relations there developed a coolness. This in time grew to mutual dislike and this in turn developed into bitter prejudice. An impartial analysis discloses the fact that the Germans were in very small degree responsible for this unfortunate status of relations. Like all highminded people the Germans are independent and sensitive, but they are not a people of high prejudice. They are strong and positive in their likes and dislikes. They have a high standard of honor to which they demand rigid adherence. They hate deception, and probably carry their frankness to an extreme. Naturally they are not diplomatic, since diplomacy is about ninety per cent deception. "Yes" or "no" is about the limit of the German's vocabulary in the art of diplomacy. This may not apply in the case of Germans trained in the school of diplomacy for the purpose of coping with the trained diplomats of other nationalities, but it does apply to all Germans brought up in an atmosphere of freedom, and who have had to battle the hostile forces of frontier conditions to attain that freedom.

During Texas' war with Mexico the Germans and Americans were in hearty accord. They fought and suffered and rejoiced alike. The war over and Texas' independence secured, friction arose between the Germans and Americans. The Germans had nobly done their part to secure this independence. They were opposed to chattel slavery. Even the half barbarous Mexican government had officially forbidden slavery, although it permitted open disregard of the law. After the war the Germans felt that they were treated very unfair in the matter of settlement and colonization of the lands. The American always got first choice. Persons who had contributed not one thing to the gaining of Texas' independence could come, into Texas and get concessions over a German citizen of the republic of Texas, although this German had been a veteran and a sufferer in the struggle for independence. Naturally such treatment didn't please the Germans, nor did it stand to the credit of the American. Back of it was the slaveholder's dislike of the German because of his anti-slavery sentiments.

As the slavery question grow more intense, and as German immigrants multiplied in Texas, taking whatever they could get in the way of homesteads and colonization permits, the bitterness of the slaveholders increased against the Germans, for they were nearly all abolitionists. The German haters never lost an opportunity to inflame the public against the German settlers.

In 1854 there was a convention in Vauxhall Garden, San Antonio, in which strong anti-slavery resolutions were passed, these resolutions declaring, among other things, that "slavery is a monstrous social wrong that should be abolished in conformity with the constitution of the United States." The convention also adopted resolutions, "demanding the abolishment of capital punishment, forbidding the speculation in land, and an income and inheritance tax." The leading participants in this convention were Ottomann von Behr, A. Siemering, Dr. Kapp, Dr. Adolph Douay and F. Thielepape. Commenting on the work of this convention Professor Tiling says:

"All these resolutions of the German convention are convincing proof of the radical progressiveness of the German pioneers in Texas, a progressiveness that was far in advance of the times, but somewhat utopian in character. While the participants in the German convention gave an unmistakable proof of their convictions, their public declaration in favor of abolishing slavery in a slave state must be termed an imprudent temerity, as it placed them in direct opposition to the majority of the Americans in Texas, and added materially to increase a feeling of distrust that the American slaveholders held against the German farmers and Germans generally."

Not caring to be openly insulted the Germans kept to themselves. For this they were pictured as a selfish, unsociable set, notwithstanding the fact that this self-isolation had been forced on the Germans by the very same people who gladly seized it as a pretext for industriously sowing slander.

While the Germans were abolitionists they were not opposed to states rights. But being above all things opposed to chattel slavery they didn't dodge the issue nor hypocritically dissemble about it. They spoke out boldly and for this many were imprisoned, many were killed by mobs and not a few were butchered by the armed military forces. The greatest tragedy of the civil war was the slaughter of more than fifty Germans who were attempting to legally and peacefully leave the United States and make their way into Mexico. This was the Nueces river massacre. This outrage alone was enough to embitter the German people even to the fourth generation.

The Germans sided with Houston in the matter of secession. Because of their views and attitude Houston was removed from office and the Germans were hotly hated and shamefully persecuted. Time and events have vindicated Houston and the Texas Germans, but it took a long time to overcome this bitterness.

Even before the war and anti-slavery engendered bitterness had subsided the prohibition question came up. The German was conservative in his drinking but radical in his personal liberty views. Again the German became the target for the fanatic, the hypocrite and the demagogue. The German had done nothing to justify the attacks made on his race. He just happened to be the victim affording the opportunity, serving the purpose and unable to vindicate himself before the world.

Then came the world war, bringing more unjustified and regretable bitterness. It was for the most part a matter of much noise about nothing. The trouble is not traceable to the majority of Germans nor to the majority of Americans. There were a few hot headed, indiscreet Germans, and a great many hot headed, uninformed Americans. Some of these hot heads were ignorantly sincere, but pitably indiscrete; many of them were ranting demagogues and hate breeding fanatics. Possibly it is best for the Germans and Americans of Texas, and the country generally, that it happened. The more false and absurd charges and rumors were investigated, the more the Germans were vindicated.

There exists a general but erroneous, idea that the German people implicitly follow leaders; that the masses do whatever these leaders suggest or command. Nothing is farther from correct, and nothing better serves to illustrate the degree to which the Germans of Texas, if not of all other countries or sections, are misunderstood. The Germans are the most independent people in the world, the Irish not excepted. ''Wherever you find two Germans you find three ideas,'' is an adage of more truth than exaggeration. It may be rather a misfortune that the Germans do not listen more to others of their own nationality. The American may rush off after some new political or financial fetish; spell binders, theorists and adventurers may lead the Americans but you have to show a German. They have a high regard for the person who has proven real worth in business, political or professional matters, and it doesn't matter with them whether such person be German, French, English or American or any other nationality. It is the idea and the proven merit of the individual that counts most with them.

They are great home lovers, and with them their own blood kin comes first and last. They provide for their families and plan for their descendants. This accounts for the fact that it is no uncommon thing to find even to the third or fourth generation of Germans living in the same farming community, and sons succeeding fathers in mercantile and banking concerns. With them the family tie and blood relation is nothing less than a sacredly dominant characteristic.

Germans not Strong for Secret Orders.—Great Believers in Physical Training and Lovers of Music.

The Germans are not much inclined to secret organizations. The first German society organized in Texas started with much promise but ended a failure, not because it was, in the strictest sense, a secret society, but because it attempted to be rather an exclusive society, drawing rank and social lines. This was the "Deutscher Verein fuer Texas" (German Society of Texas). This society was organized in Houston in November, 1840, with a charter, or rather an initial membership of 53. Many of these original members were afterwards prominent in the political, mercantile and financial affairs of the state, and this likewise applies to many persons who from time to time became members of the order. The main purpose of this organization, as stated in its constitution, was "the giving of assistance to the sick and needy, to promote the material and intellectual welfare of the Germans and to assist newcomers with advice and necessary aid and succor." According to Professor Tiling "the order was made up of several degrees. Admission to the second and third degree was conditioned on talent, ability and education. The less educated Germans were almost barred from passage beyond the third degree. The order existed only a few years. The foremost causes of failure was the evident class distinction between the different degrees and the difficulty of communication between settlements hundreds of miles apart."

The only secret German order is that of the Sons of Hermann. And this is not an exclusive German order. Membership in this order is open to any white person of good character and who is a native, or who must, before joining the order, declare his or her intention to become a naturalized citizen of the United States. Several Sons of Hermann lodges are composed of persons not even of German descent. This order has 456 lodges in Texas, with a total membership of practically 22,000, including men and women, is a mutual benefit and insurance order, chartered under the laws of Texas, and is one of the strongest orders in the state. It maintains a home for the aged at Comfort, in Kendall county. This is one of the best managed institutions of the kind in the United States.

The Texas lodge has assets in excess of two and a half million dollars. It has interest bearing and doubly secured real estate loans amounting to approximately two million dollars and has an interest bearing cash reserve of about half a million dollars. It makes no loans of any kind nor on security of any character outside the state.

The order is strictly American in origin and was named in honor of the great German chieftain, Hermann the Cherusker, or Arminius, as he was known to the Romans. The first lodge was organized in New York in 1850. It was purely a social and mutual aid organization. Its membership was limited for many years, and during these years the best it could do was to struggle along giving assistance to widows and orphans to the extent of its feeble but earnest ability.

The first Texas lodge of the order was organized in San Antonio in 1860. This lodge, like the New York lodge, struggled along until 1890 when it became affiliated with the national lodge. Some years ago the Texas lodge withdrew from the national lodge, the Texas lodge now functioning strictly to itself.

There are now 24 states in which there are lodges of this order, but only three or four of these state lodges have insurance features.

Principal German Societies.

It can be truthfully said that the Germans have taught the world to sing, and that they, more than any other race, have preserved the best elements of Grecian and Roman athletics. They have carried music and athletics into the homes, the school rooms, into the treeless wilds and the remote forests and before the greatest audiences in the world. If "music tames the savage breast," and athletics make a stronger and healthier race, then in these respects the Germans stand preeminent as benefactors of all mankind.

It is said that the first piano in Texas was brought here in 1834, by Robert Kleberg, who settled at Cat Spring in what is now Austin county.

The Saengerbund of Texas (united singing societies) is the leading German society in Texas. This society was first organized at New Braunfels, March 2, 1850, this date being San Jacinto Day. Singing societies were soon organized at San Antonio, Sisterdale, Austin and LaGrange. The first Saengerfest in Texas was held in New Braunfels in the summer of 1853, the New Braunfels, San Antonio, Austin and Sisterdale societies participating in this great singing convention. Six saengerfests, participated in by different societies, were successively held as follows: The second at San Antonio, the third, fourth and fifth at New Braunfels, the sixth at Fredericksburg and the seventh at New Braunfels. The saengerfest at Fredericksburg was attended by the societies from Austin, San Antonio, Pedernales, Grape Creek, by two societies from New Braunfels, these being Germania and Liedertafel, and by the Fredericksburg society. The seventh saengerfest held at New Braunfels March 26 to 29, 1860, was the last saengerfest held until August, 1869. As Professor Tiling says: "The threatening clouds that had been hanging over the United States for years had bursted, the unfortunate and destructive war between the states had begun, and song and music were replaced for years by tears and sorrow."

In August, 1869, representatives from the singing societies of New Braunfels, San Antonio, Austin and Boerne met at New Braunfels for the purpose of reviving the German State Singers' League. This was accomplished and the eighth saengerfest, perhaps the largest that had ever been held up to that time, met in San Antonio in September, 1870. State Saengerfests were held regularly, growing in general interest and increased membership, there being more than twenty societies represented at the great twenty-ninth saengerfest held in Houston in 1913.

The Saengerbund in Texas is at present composed almost entirely of membership from the larger cities. However, there are local and district societies throughout the state. Where-ever there are even a few Germans there you will find a local singing society and generally an orchestra.

In addition to the Staats Saengerbund there are local singing societies in every German community. They sing in their homes, in the church, in the parks, in their schools. Not only do they sing, but in even the most remote rural communities, as well as in the towns, they have their bands and their orchestras, it being nothing unusual for a German town of 3,000 or 4,000 population to have two or three first class bands and half a dozen good orchestras.

The Turnvereins, like the singing society, is a common and popular organization in all German communities. The first Turnverein in Texas was organized in Houston in January, 1854. Its cardinal principles, as first enunciated by the Houston club, this being in turn the principles upon which all turnvereins are based, are "for the practice of brotherly love and the promotion of physical and mental exercises and studies." Around the Turnverein revolves and from it emanates all that is best in physical training and exercise. It is the one great German society that has never, since the first meeting, been interrupted by the curse of war nor the scourge of epidemic.

CHAPTER IV.

CIVIL WAR TIME OUTRAGES.

The Nueces River Massacre—A Tragedy of War and Hate.

There have been many and conflicting versions of what is known as the Nueces River massacre.

The undisputed facts are: The question of secession was submitted to a vote of the people of Texas. A light vote was polled, and the proposition carried by a small margin. The Germans in Texas were opposed to secession because it carried with it the fundamental proposition of chattel slavery. The Germans were unalterably opposed to chattel slavery. The counties of Gillespie, Kerr, Kendall, Comal and perhaps the greater part of Bexar, Medina and other western counties, remained loyal in sentiment to the Union regardless of the results of the election. The outgrowth of this loyalty was the organization of the "Union Loyal League." The real purpose of this organization was to maintain neutrality and peace, and to take no part whatever in the war. About twenty persons attended the meeting at which the "Union Loyal League" was organized, but they seem to have been the duly accredited representatives of the different communities in the counties comprising the order. They declared and published that their intention was to prevent strife between the Union and Confederate partisans, to take such peaceable actions as would prevent the forced enlistment of Union sympathizers in the Confederate army, and to protect the homes and families within the area embraced in the limits of the "Union Loyal League" against marauding bands of Indians. Some time after this meeting there was another meeting in July, 1862, on Bear Creek, in Gillespie county, this meeting being attended by large delegations from Kerr, Kendall, Edwards, Kimble and Gillespie counties. At this meeting three companies were organized, not for the purpose of taking up arms against the Confederacy, but to protect the settlement from the Indians and from such outlaw bands as might invade the communities.

Notwithstanding the peaceful acts, protests and declarations of the "Union Loyal League" this was constructed by the Confederate authorities as a hostile action. The counties named were declared to be in open rebellion against the rebelling Confederacy, martial law was declared and one James M. Duff was assigned to take charge of the situation and apply such vigorous measures as he deemed necessary.

About the same time, or perhaps just prior to this military mix up, the governor had issued a decree announcing that all persons who refused to take the oath of allegiance to the Confederacy would be given thirty days in which to leave the state.

Soon after martial law had been declared, Major Fritz Tegener, who had been elected major in charge of the three companies organized by the "Union Loyal League," called a meeting of the advisory board, and this board issued an order disbanding the three companies as an assurance that it had no hostile intentions toward the Confederacy. The avowed Union sympathizers realized, however, that they must either join the Confederate forces or comply with the governor's oath of allegiance proclamation and leave the state. Accordingly on August 1, 1862, about eighty men met with Major Tegener on the head of Turtle Creek, in Kerr county, for the purpose of leaving Texas and going into Mexico. They were poorly armed, even for the purposes of killing game or protecting themselves against an Indian attack. At this meeting Major Tegener was recognized as commander of the migrating expedition. Of the eighty men at the meeting sixty-one joined in the expedition to Mexico. On August the 9th the company pitched camp in a rather open space near the west bank of the Nueces river. From the time they started until the fatal camp was made the men had drifted along leisurely. Had they been fleeing in fear they could have crossed the Rio Grande long before the day they camped on the Nueces. In the meantime Duff's men had been in hot pursuit, guided by one of the men who had attended the meeting on August 1, and knew about the movement of the refugees. It has been argued pro and con as to whether this betrayer was a spy or merely a weakling betraying his former companions to save his own life. About

2 o'clock in the morning, July 10th, Duff's men attacked the camp. In the fight that followed nineteen of the refugees were killed and nine were wounded. A few hours later these nine wounded men were murdered by order of Duff. No prisoners were taken, no quarters given, no mercy shown. Of the thirty-three men making their escape, seven were later overtaken and killed while crossing the Rio Grande river. Duff had more than a hundred well armed men under his command. He could have surrounded the camp of the refugees, and common sense would have caused them to peacefully surrender. But had they resisted and a pitched battle with a heavy death toll been necessary, no usage of war could justify the killing of the wounded and helpless men. More than one Confederate soldier who unwillingly participated in the affair has publicly condemned it as the blackest crime of all American warfare. Duff, the comander of the attacking force, according to the best authenticated history, was a Scotchman, an adventurer, a soulless soldier of fortune. It is claimed that soon after coming to the United States he joined the national army. Before the war he was charged with a rather serious offense, punished and dishonorably discharged. He later came to Texas. Owing to his military experience, political shrewdness and good address, and possibly with his bad army record a secret, he got into the good graces of the powers. and was given important position. Sometime after the civil war he went to Paris, France, and died there, and thus the land his savage crime had stigmatized was saved the further shame of having its soil polluted with his decaying carcass.

Chas. Bergmann the person that led Duff's men to the camp of the sleeping Germans, went to Mexico after the war, where he is reported to have been killed by a Seminole Indian Negro. Perhaps his last vision was that of a black face, wild with violence and dead to pity, black as the crime that will ever hover over the spot where the doomed refugees died, and black as the ghost of vengeance that ever pursued the betrayer. When killed Bergmann was reported as leader of a band of renegade outlaws and murderers.

During the battle following Duff's attack, 12 Confederates were killed and 18 wounded, according to official report. These added to the refugees killed makes a total of 47 men killed and 18 wounded. The list of killed includes those killed while crossing the Rio Grande, but several of the men who escaped were slightly wounded and this number is not taken into account in these figures. An unnecessary, inhuman butchery, by the directions of an imported adventurer.

It was a crime unjustified by even the rules of savage warfare.

Another barbarous feature of the Nueces massacre was the fact that not one of the bodies was buried by the conquering hero, Duff. The dead were left for varmints to tear and eat the flesh, the bones to bleach. Three years later these bleached bones were gathered by the friends and relatives and buried at Comfort, in Kendall county, and there a monument erected to their memory. And near that monument is a home for the aged, this home founded and maintained by the Sons of Hermann. A composit picture meriting deep consideration. In time of peace mankind pays deserved tribute to the victims of war, and humanity erects to its own merit a haven for the unfortunates in the battle of life—a home for the aged and needy.

The monument at Comfort bears the following inscriptions:

Inscription on the west side

Killed In Battle At Nueces, Aug. 10, 1862

Leopold Buuor,	Johann Geo. Kalenberg,
F. Behrens,	Heinrich Markwart,
Ernst Beseler,	Christian Schaefer,
Louis Boerner,	Louis Schierholz,
Albert Bruns,	Heinrich Steves,
Hugo Degener,	Amrey Schreiner,
Fritz Vater,	Wilhelm Telgmann,
Hilmar Degener,	Michael Weirich,
Pablo Dias,	Heinrich Weyershausen,

Adolph Vater,

Inscription on the north side

Captured (or taken prisoners) and murdered

Wilhiem Boerner,	Herman Flick,
Theodore Buckisch,	August Luckenbach,
Conrad Bock,	Louis Ruebsamen,
F. Tays,	Adolph Ruebesamen,

Heinrich Stieler,

Inscription on the east side

Treue der Union.
True to the Union.

Inscription on the south side

Killed at the Rio Grande, October 18, 1862.

Joseph Elster,	H. Hermann,
Ernst Felsing,	Valentine Hohmann,
Peter Bonnet,	Moritz Weiss,

Franz Weiss,

What a Confederate Soldier Thought of Duff.

R. H. Williams was an English adventurer, but a most
unusual man. He was honest and courageous, and had a
high sense of well balanced justice. He had acquired quite
a valuable ranch property when the civil war started, but
he abandoned his own business to join the Confederate army
and "whip the north because he believed the south was
right." Before it was over he had reached the conclusion
that the "whole thing was a foolish adventure—a rich man's
war and a poor man's fight." Some years after the war
this old pioneer and adventurer wrote a book dealing with
his actual experiences from the time he reached the United
States until the close of the civil war. This book was sold
extensively throughout the United States and England. This
is the most readable book that has ever been written with
war time conditions and frontier experiences as its theme. It
is ably written and deals only with subjects of vital concern.
There is no cheap dime novel nonsense about it. On the
whole it is a merciless condemnation of war, though it was

not specifically intended as such. Captain Williams, for he was at one time captain of a frontier force, plays no favorites. He exposes humbugs and frauds and war time rascality with a masterly sarcasm and directness. He was a great admirer of Lincoln, Grant, Generals Lee and Stonewall Jackson. He was an ardent believer in states' rights and the result of the war didn't change his views on fundamental questions, but how he did hate a brutal coward and a designing demagogue. Some things in his book are especially appropriate for consideration at present. There was so much going on during the civil war that goes on during all wars. So much lying, hate, intolerance, insane excitement and exaggeration, and big scares and wild reports about nothing. When the Captain joined the army he was assigned to Duff's Partisan Ranger company. He understood that this company was to do some necessary frontier service and then be sent into the regular army. In this he was disappointed, but to get the whole story you should read his book, "With the Border Ruffians," though the book was published many years ago, and is now rarely found.

Here are some rich extracts from the book, most of them having to do with the war time outrages in Gillespie county, but two extracts, aside from those dealing with Gillespie county, will serve as an introduction of this independent and forceful old character. In the opening chapter, "In the Confederate Service," he says:

"I enlisted of my own free will and against my interests, which should have led me to stay at home to protect my property, and my object was to strike a blow for the noble cause I had at heart. * * * I did not doubt then that it was a sacred one, and that the Southern States were justified in resisting to the death the oppressions of the North. But as to the representatives of that noble cause in Texas—the local nobodies who ruled the roost, and exploited us for their own base and selfish ends—I was very speedily disillusioned."

Elsewhere the Captain says his ambition and expectation has been to go to the "front, where the great leaders, Lee and Jackson were fighting their heroic battles," and then he gives a description of a "review of the army" held in San Antonio:

"At 4 p. m. we were all formed up in the Alamo Plaza in San Antonio, the force comprising four infantry companies and two of Partisan Rangers. The infantry was a mixed lot, dressed in all sorts and varieties of uniforms, or none at all. There were some queer specimens of humanity on parade that day, but the queerest of all was our own commander, who on foot resembled a bullfrog, and on horseback resembled Sancho Panza. We formed in double line, cavalry in front, and in the middle of the Plaza a wheezy civilian band discoursed such music as it could. Presently appeared our gallant general, surrounded by a heterogeneous staff, as ignorant and pretentious as himself, and followed by a small boy on a diminutive cow-pony, this boy acting as the general's orderly. The chief duty of the staff, aided by the small boy, seemed to be to keep back a crowd of about three hundred people who lined the square and wanted to fraternize with their friends in the ranks, while the performance was going on. This was soon over, for the general had ridden down the ranks, looking wise as he knew how. We marched past him once and then were dismissed. The whole thing was a farce, and I was thoroughly disgusted with the humbug of it; for the so-called general knew no more about soldiering than his boy orderly. He was a storekeeper who had been promoted by some back-door influence."

Speaking of a grand military expedition under Duff, this expedition going into Medina, Gillespie and other counties, the Captain says: "All we did was to bully and arrest a few inoffensive Germans." And, "next, on June 26, five of us were started off to catch seven armed niggers, supposed to be driving stolen horses into Mexico, and who had last been seen about 25 miles from our camp. I knew the thing was a humbug, but orders had to be obeyed. Three days we followed that will-o'-the-wisp, and then discovered the seven niggers had dwindled to two, and they were driving their master's horses.

"On July 19 the two companies of Partisan Rangers, one under our own Duff and the other under Captain Freer, marched out once more for Fredericksburg, in the vicinity of which it was reported that 1500 "Bushwackers," mostly Germans, had taken to the mountains and were plundering and burning the ranches of Southern loyalists. Furthermore they were said to be well armed and intended fighting their way north to join the federal forces. Those who, like myself, knew the country and the people, didn't believe one-tenth part of this yarn, but our leaders swallowed it whole, or professed to, and made great preparations to put down this formidable insurrection.

"Among the first steps to this end our redoubtable Captain Duff was appointed provost marshal with full powers to deal with the rebels. These powers, the sequel will show, he exercised to the fullest extent, committing atrocities that even his superiors in San Antonio would not have sanctioned.

"We marched by easy stages to Fredericksburg, and there found most of the inhabitants remaining quietly in their homes, though a certain number of misguided men had taken to the mountains, * * Their numbers were variously estimated, but as far as I could make out, they did not exceed a couple of hundred.

"The morning after our arrival we marched out fifteen miles to the west of town and pitched camp on a stream called the Pedernales, with the intention of remaining there about six weeks. Here Captain Duff issued his proclamation announcing his appointment as provost marshal, and giving the inhabitants three days to come in and take the oath of allegiance to the Confederacy; threatening to treat all those who failed to do so as traitors, who would be dealt with summarily at the discretion of the officer commanding * * * Presently, however, sinister rumors as to Duff's intentions began to spread, and it was said, amongst other things, that he had given certain of his followers to understand that he wanted no prisoners brought into camp. The majority of the men, especially those who were Southern born, were utterly opposed to such deeds; and many of us openly declared we would do all we could to put a stop to it. But amongst the command were many "whitewashed" Yankees, and even, I am ashamed to say, some Scotsmen, who were ready tools for Duff's infamies, and believed in converting Union men to the true faith by means of the halter.

"I soon noticed that neither I, nor any of those who thought with me, were sent out on scout. It was suspicious, as presently many parties were detailed to scour the country who rarely, if ever, brought in any prisoners, and were very reticent about their doings. Amongst these, two parties of twenty-five each were sent out with wagons to bring in from the scattered ranches the wives and children of those who had taken to the mountains, and, I fear, to harry their homes. In four days they returned with the wagons full of prisoners—four or five men, and eight women with their little ones. The latter were sent to Fredericksburg and the former confined in the guard tent.

"It was a pitiable sight to see all of these poor folks stripped of their property, such as it was, earned by hard toil and exposure on a dangerous frontier; and I could not but contrast their treatment with that of well known Abolitionists in San Antonio, who, because they were wealthy and made friends of the mammon of unrighteousness, were not only unmolested but specially favored in all sorts of ways.

" * * * Few of the outlaying prisoners came in to take the oath before the expiration of the three days; probably because they were more occupied with procuring a living, and protecting their families against Indian raids, than with politics. Possibly, too, many of them never herd of Duff and his proclamation until they were arrested."

The Captain next describes how the command started in pursuit of the Germans who had started to Mexico, and were later massacred on the Nueces. One incident of that pursuit, touchingly narrated by Captain Williams, merits reproduction:

"The first day's ride took us over a rather rough, prairie country, in which we passed several small homesteads, ruined and deserted. At sundown we reached what had been a well cultivated little farm, situated in a pretty, well watered valley. The owner, a Northern man, had gone to the mountains, but his wife, also from the North, had been brought into camp with her numerous children. I had felt very sorry for her then, for she bore her misfortunes with a quiet dignity that was very touching; but when I saw her desolated home, and how, in that out of the way place, they had made so prosperous a little settlement, all now wasted and destroyed, it was grievous. They had fenced and cultivated about twenty acres of good land on the side of the valley, cleverly irrigated by the stream running through it. Now the crops were trampled and destroyed and not a living thing was to be seen on the place; even the beehives in front of the comfortable log house were overturned and empty. The poor little furniture in the living room, and the loom in the kitchen, had been smashed; and all this had been done by some of our marauding parties by our captain's orders. It made one utterly ashamed to be serving with such men; but there was no help for it now!"

As a climax to these things came the Nueces river massacre. But such is war, and all wars are just alike. The innocent suffer most.

Waldrip and His Gang and Their Shocking Outrages.

From the beginning until the close of the war between the Confederacy and the United States the people of Gillespie county were subjected to the most shameful mob outrages ever imposed upon a community in a supposedly civilized country. All of the Indian troubles experienced by the citizens of Gillespie county pale into insignificance when compared with the crimes of an organized mob that rode roughshod over an unarmed, defenseless and inoffensive people Long before the civil war started the border toughs were a constant menace and nuisance, and with four or five exceptions every killing in the county from the time the German colonists arrived until 1859 was due to the blood debauches of these savage minded ruffians. Fortunately, in a majority of cases, at least, these characters would kill an equally worthless creature of their own species.

The Scotch renegade Duff opened the war time crime wave in Gillespie county and climaxed his infamy with the Nueces river massacre, but it remained for what was known as the Waldrip gang to reach the acme of infamy in so far as Gillespie county in particular was concerned. Most of this gang had a reputation in Gillespie county before the war started. What connection, if any, they had with the

Confederate authorities is not known. They claimed to have been in some way connected with the frontier service, but that is hardly probable. It was in reality an organization of renegades for the purpose of banditry and the committing of the most dastardly outrages. Possibly they had a thirst for military "glory," but not the courage to risk their own lives to attain such glory. They were of that type of characters common to the opportunities and environments of border days. They could hate and shoot and ride and hide. They could kill the defenseless without a tremor, and could face real danger with about the same degree of courage as a coyote. They rode in packs at night, and hid like wild varmints in the day time. It is said that at one time there were fully sixty men under Waldrip's command. Perhaps half of this number were refugees from other parts of the country, the original organization being composed of material supplied by this immediate section. Of this organization Waldrip was chief bad man and supreme commander, and all of his lieutenants were of his own choosing. It is said that he had a perfect spy system, and that every utterance of any citizen was promptly conveyed to Waldrip by masked villians posing as friends of the citizens. To criticise Waldrip or any of his gang, if the information reached the ears of the outlaw chief, was treason and meant death if the offender could be captured. The story of Waldrip and his gang is useful only to the extent that it reflects the dangers and terrors of mob law supremacy. What manner of men were these, do you ask, who treated the lives of others so lightly, and who were so dead to pity? They were the same in character and murderous motives as men of today who, with the same unlawful and unrestrained power to support their infamy, would not hesitate to inflict the same terrible punishment upon all who opposed them, even to the extent of mildly criticising their ghastly and cowardly conduct.

They were wild men, uneducated except in the ways of the jungle beasts and the nomads of the mountains. Like timber wolves they were most harmless and serviceable when dead; most desperate, dangerous and destructive when running in packs.

They had the animal instinct to flee from danger, to

flee from even the danger of equal combat. They would attack without fear and with pitiless ferocity when the victim of their vengeance was as a helpless fawn in the grasp of a hungry mountain lion. And yet they were men of flesh and blood; unborn to pity, devoid of all tender emotions, uneducated to any standard of justice. Many of them might have been good men if they had been civilized in infancy, and had never thereafter been exposed to temptation.

They transgressed and for awhile prevailed with all the glitter of infamous notoriety. Then came the hours of atonement; the hours of fear, flight, disgrace and death. There was no power to which they could honorably surrender; no deed to which they could point with pride. They could only die in agony; they could only live in terror as hunted varmints of a broken pack. The only legacy they could leave to posterity was the legacy of sin seared, crime smeared souls as a horrible adomition. Among Waldrip's gang were several mere boys, cubs educated to the ways of the pack, following by dumb instinct the paths of the leader. Banded together by animal fear for self protection, and not by the ties of love and friendship. They had not so much as the religion of the Indian to support them when alone, to console them in the hour of death.

I have talked with a gentleman who was well acquainted with a brother of two of the leading characters in Waldrip's gang, although this brother had no connection with the gang or its outrages. He illustrates the type of men comprising the gang. He, too, had something of a history, and he and his two brothers had grown up under identical conditions and environments. This older brother of the three had grown up in the mountains and on the frontier. He could neither read nor write, possessed considerable intelligence, but little knowledge, was of savage courage and lived according to his own code of honor. He differed from his brothers in that he ranged alone, while his less courageous brothers joined the pack. He knew the trails of the forest, the haunts of game, the ways of wild animals and the cunning of the Indian. He was neither man, beast nor Indian. He was a tribe unto himself, harmless so long as left to his own ways. At the age of seventy his greatest boast was that for sixty years he had never slept beneath a roof, and during the same time had eaten less than a dozen meals inside a house. Age alone perhaps kept him from responding to the call of the pack during the pandemonium of war, and adding himself to the untutored force that turned itself loose upon a community of civilized people. In the undeveloped minds and souls of such pitable creatures the hates and furies of wild fanticism finds its richest soil.

The human mind responds to the character of its cultivation, to the influences of its environment. The dwarfed intellect never reaches full bloom, no matter how great its inherent possibilities. As the slum feeds its mental filth it develops its own character of degenerate desperation. The border wilds produced another type. The one sneaks in dark alleys, its haunts the hovels of the poor; the other rode at night over vast areas, and its haunts were the mountain recesses. The animal in each was the same, though environment and the range of the pack make them seem different. Between the haunts of the two is the great plateau of civilization, inhabited by only a few great, developed intellects, perhaps lonesome and despondent in their isolation.

In the fall of 1865, after the close of the war, 25 individuals were indicted for these mob outrages, most of the indictments being in blanket form, or rather the indictments of several parties covered in one indictment for the same offense. The parties indicted by the 1865 grandjury were: Tom C. Doss, Bill Paul, John Hill, John Cadwell, J. P. Waldrip, Mac L. Neal, Jess Vaughn, Shepherd McDonald, John Benson, John Brown, —— Freeland, Sam Gibson, Bob Gibson, Joe Glenn, —— McNeil, Sam Doss, Sam Tanner, —— Blevins, Bill Williams, Bill Banta, Jake Banta (the last two names are also spelled Bente in the indictments,) and Bill Dixon (this name also spelled Dickson in the indictment.)

As already stated a number of these characters and members of their families had figured in the criminal history of the county prior to the outbreak of the war, and it was during the war that the mob crimes were perpetrated, and it was not until the close of the war that anything was done about these mob crimes.

Sylvester Waldrip was indicted for malicious mischief in 1857, but he skipped out and the case was dismissed in 1867. At a later date James B. Waldrip was indicted for stealing hogs, also for horse theft, but got out because indictment was defective. Neither of them were indicted for the mob outrages, but they belonged to the Waldrip tribe. J. P. Waldrip the mob chief who was indicted for the mob murders had also figured in lawless escapades before the beginning of the war. But the Doss bunch leads in the matter of criminal records. In 1854 John E. Doss and H. Doss were indicted for assault with intent to murder, the victim being W. Cass. Tom Doss was indicted for cattle theft in 1858. John E. Doss also indicted for assault in 1859. H. Doss and John Doss were not indicted as members of the mob murderers. Tom Doss, Bill Paul and others were also indicted for killing John Joy, and Tom Doss was one of a bunch indicted for assault with intent to kill Richard Joy, all of these indictments in addition to the mob murder indictments. Sam Doss and Sam Tanner were also indicted in 1865 for the murder of Peter Pletz in 1863. This was a typical crime for a mob murder outfit. Pletz had a little home and some fruit trees near town. It was hot weather and Pletz was sleeping under a tree near the house. Doss and Tanner invaded the little orchard late at night. Pletz was aroused and got up to see what was going on and was murdered. Sam Tanner had been indicted for murder in 1855. At least four indictments, aside from the mob murders, had been filed against the Dixons, these indictments being for cattle theft. The rest of the mob murder gang do not appear to have ever been indicted for any other crimes in Gillespie county

Bill Williams, Bill Dixon and the two Bantas seem to have been the only members of the bunch that were ever arrested and placed in jail. One night a mob took matters in hand and assaulted the jail. Dixon was killed and perhaps Williams and the Bantas were wounded. It was the wildest, most furious night in the history of Fredericksburg. Technicalities and court delays caused the wrath of the mob. Efforts were being made to get the mob members released on bond, and that meant that they would never be punished. Dixon and Waldrip were the only two to get their deserts, and they were both attended to outside the court room. The rest of the mob gang fled the country, most of them going to Mexico.

In 1867 Waldrip came to town, thinking perhaps he would not be recognized. He doubtless thought, as well he might, that to surrender would mean the same fate as that meted out to Dixon; so when he realized that he had been recognized he endeavored to make his escape. He got as far as the Nimitz Hotel when a bullet put an end to his career. It is said that the last words he uttered were: ''Oh, God! Please don't shoot any more.'' He probably memorized this exclamation from the heartrending appeals of mothers and babes whose fathers he and his gang had dragged from homes in the dark hours of night to hang, or perhaps had murdered in their own little homes or front yards. ''Oh, God! Please don't shoot any more,'' from the lips of a man who had never known pity, and who had met a fate perhaps too merciful. But he was more successful in his dying appeal than mothers and babes had been in their frantic appeals to him. His dying appeal was granted. He was dealing with civilized beings. They didn't shoot any more, and they buried him in a pauper's grave, the county paying the expense.

The only other member of the indicted gang that ever showed up was Blevins. He was a refugee for twenty years, then he came back and hired a lawyer by the name of Altgeld to defend him. It is reported that he paid Altgeld $1200 in gold, an exorbitant attorney's fee at that time. Many of the most important state witnesses had long since left the country or died. Very naturally none of the children or widows of the mob's victims could positively identify a man they had seen only once, if at all, and that under conditions of fear and terror, so Blevins was acquitted.

And so came to an end the rule of mob law infamy under the reign of Waldrip. They have gone, leaving only a record of crime and cruelty as evidence of the fact that they ever existed, but the civilized community they would have obliterated is something of which every fair minded man in the United States can and should be justly proud. To a large extent the great achievements of this magnificent commonwealth the night riders once despoiled with death and murder is the work of men and women whose frantic appeals fell on the pity deaf ears and the mercy dead hearts of an outlaw gang. They saw their fathers and their husbands shot down in cold blood or dragged from their humble homes, into the dark only to be returned to them on the morrow cold in death. Civilized beings had met the forces of mob spirited violence, and the honest effort, patient toil, though bathed in the tears of deepest sorrow and loaded with all the woes of frontier poverty, prevailed.

CHAPTER V.

HUMAN INTEREST HISTORY.

The Trails of a Pioneer Woman.

Accompanied by Mr. I. G. Wehmeyer the writer visited
Mrs. Clara Feller in her home in the southwestern part of
Fredericksburg. It is a simple, two room log house. The
walls and ceiling are as clean and white as fresh fallen snow.
The bed linen and everything within that home corresponded
to the walls and ceiling. The floor looked as though it had
at sometime been glazed and polished. This appearance I
learned was the result of years of use and owing to the kind
of material used. Mrs. Feller, ninety-two years old, is truly a
heroine of the pioneer days. She speaks but little English.
She is one of these people that smile a deep sincere smile
when they meet you. Unable to converse in my language,
and without knowing the purpose of my visit, she had a way
of making me feel heartily welcome. Mr. Wehmeyer interpreted the conversation, they talked direct to each other.
She talks rapidly, thinks clearly, only pausing occasionally
to recall some incident of many years ago. Her's is a soul
made divine by adversity, her life work a tribute to the
nobility of all that is highest and noblest in the realms of
motherhood. I was so impressed with her sweet disposition
that I particularly requested Mr. Wehmeyer to give as nearly
exact as possible her own words, but especially the exact
substance of what she said. This he has done. At only one
point did she show signs of sorrow and that was during the
recital of the killing of her husband. Never once was there
a tone or an expression of bitterness.

Here is her story:

"I was born in Heiligenroth, Amt Montebaur, Nassau
(a province of Prussia) December 12, 1832. My father was
John Peter Resseman. By a former marriage my mother had
one son, and his name was John Adam Rebeg. We left with
a ship load of immigrants in 1845, reaching Indianola in
September, 1845. I was then about thirteen years old. Our
party consisted of my father, mother, a brother, my half-

brother, one sister and myself, I being the youngest. Mother died soon after we reached Indianola. Father was a man of some means, so he purchased two mule teams and assisted in hauling immigrants to Fredericksburg. Brother assisted him in this work, sister and I being alone most of the time while they were away on these trips. While the teams were resting at the Fredericksburg end of the trips, father and brothers worked on our lot, finally getting a comfortable hut built. We remained in Indianola about eighteen months. When we reached Fredericksburg in the latter part of 1846 the awful epidemic had about run its course. There were only a few deaths from the cholera or whatever the epidemic was, after our arrival.

"Our home was in the extreme western part of the town. When we reached Fredericksburg a great many huts, shacks, tents and shelters had been erected. Immediately on arriving sister and I set about with considerable pride to make our new home as attractive and comfortable as conditions would permit. It was a great delight to us to get away from the miserable conditions, the lonesomeness and destitution that had surrounded us in Indianola. Father with his mule teams took up freighting again, making frequent trips to Bastrop, Indianola and other points. After we had been in Fredericksburg about a year, father started to Bastrop after a load of corn and died on the road, and thus we children were left without the assistance and protection of a father.

"About this time the Indians were just a little bit too friendly, especially after Mr. Meusebach had made his treaty with them. They seem to put in all their spare time coming to town, and they certainly availed themselves of that clause in the treaty specifying that the whites and the Indians should at all times be hospitably received in each other's "wigwams." My first vivid recollection of Indians dates from a short time after our arrival. A big chief came to town with about five hundred warriors, squaws and pappooses. They were all on horseback and rode into and all around town with much pomp and display. The chief's hair wasn't long enough to suit him for the occasion, so he had attached a horse tail to it. The pappooses were hung in baskets on the backs of the squaws. I have always suspicioned that the Indians' purpose was to impress us with their numbers and military efficiency. Maybe it was just an over played manifestation of friendship. After that they frequently made trading trips to town, usually coming in considerable numbers. Where it was honest exchange of the meats, hides, etc., that the Indian had, for something we could well afford to dispose of it was all right, but the rascals had a habit of taking whatever they could easily get away with and not even returning thanks for it.

"One day while I was at home alone in walked a big buck Indian. I had just made a successful bake of bread and was exceedingly proud of it. I had a real treat for the tired folks when they came from work. I was terribly frightened when the Indian deliberately walked in. I didn't know whether to scream or run and hide. The big scamp sized up everything, spied my bread, picked it up and walked off with it. My fear turned to helpless rage, to all of which the Indian paid no more attention than if I had been a bird chirping in a bush. If I had had enough physical powers I would have hung that Indians' scalp on the front door as a warning to others. The enormity of the crime can be imagined when the deplorable scarcity of bread in Fredericksburg at that time is recalled. It also sealed the fact that one white girl would never fall in love with the "noble red man" nor any of his kinfolks or outfit.

"I was married to William Feller when I was eighteen years old. He was an industrious, high minded young man. Soon after our marriage we purchased 200 acres of land from a party by the name of Ingram, this land being on what is now Dry Creek, and about fifteen miles from Fredericksburg. We moved on this land in 1853 and built a small house. By hard work we soon had much of the land grubbed, fenced and in cultivation. The price paid for the land was $2.00 per acre, making the total purchase price $400. We had our place paid for and were just as happy and contented as people could wish to be when the great tragedy of my life came.

"We had been married thirteen years and had seven children, the eldest twelve years old when this tragedy, or rather series of tragedies, befell us. My husband was a staunch opponent of slavery, and did not hesitate to express his views on the subject. He was also free in his denunciation of various outrages that had been committed in this community by armed mobs claiming to be state officials. Particularly had he criticised the Nueces butchery. He had been warned and threatened, and being a justice of the peace at the time was of some prominence and importance in our immediate neighborhood.

"The Indians never caused any real trouble until the war between the states started. Then they became an ever present danger. My husband and others had spent the day scouting for some Indians reported as having been seen in the vicinity. He had returned home late in the evening, had set his gun aside and we were at the supper table when a bunch of men rode up and asked if William Feller lived there and if he was at home. My husband perhaps not suspicioning the real danger, got up from the table and told them his name was Feller.

" 'All right,' replied the leader, 'you are under arrest.'

" 'What for and where is your warrant,' Mr. Feller inquired.

" 'Never mind about the warrant, and you'll find out what for when you reach the place to which we are taking you,' was the reply.

" 'By this time they had entered the house and taken hold of my husband.

"I was not too dumbfounded with terror to know what it meant, and resolved to make a desperate effort to render my husband all possible aid, or to at least unable him to defend himself. I managed to get to the place where Mr. Feller had placed his pistol, put it under my apron and was going to hand it to him. One of the men, a powerful fellow, saw what I was doing, grabbed my arm and wrenched the pistol out of my hand. I then begged and pleaded that I be allowed to go with my husband, but he insisted that I stay with the children, vainly endeavoring to assure us that everything would be all right, kissed each of us and rode away, surrounded by his captors. That was the last time I ever saw him alive. Late that night I received word that

Mr. Peter Burg had been shot through the back and killed, and that my husband and two other men, a Mr. Blank and a Mr. Kirchner, had been hanged from the limb of one tree not so very far from our home.

"It was a tragedy of war. The perpetrators of that crime were savages, their souls poisoned and their minds inflamed to insanity with hate. We had lived to the terms of our treaty with the Indians, but only because they felt that the government had wronged them they came back to rob, murder and harass us. We could defend ourselves against the Indians but not against these whitemen. When we saw an Indian we knew it was time to run, hide or fight. When we saw a bunch of whitemen we didn't know whether they were friends or foes until it was perhaps too late. I have never harbored hatred on account of these crimes. They were tragedies of the war, and women and children always suffer most when men indulge in hate and go out to fight. But even those murderers were not so mean as was the fellow from whom we supposedly bought our land. The fellow who, as it later proved, sold something he didn't own, was a deliberate, designing scamp. He was a man of good appearance and smooth of tongue. After the death of my husband I and the children went ahead, worked hard, made and gathered a good crop. And then along came the real owner of the land, and demanded that I pay him three hundred dollars for it. This I could not do. So he not only took the land, but all of the crop we had raised and gathered.

"Ingram had sold about two thousand acres at $2.00 per acre, dozens of poor people being victims. After selling the land Ingram left the country and was never heard of thereafter. Some of the purchasers, like myself, were unable or unwilling to pay for the land a second time and lost it. Others made the second payment. And later another claimant came along and demanded payment the third time. I think this claim proved a fraud, and that this third claimant failed to get anything.

"Soon after losing my farm and crop I decided to move back to Fredericksburg. All I had was my family of babies, the oldest one not thirteen, a few household goods, and a past due note for less than a hundred dollars left me by my father. Mr. Emil Wahrmund, Sr., gave me one hundred dollars for this note, which was really more than the note, including interest, amounted to. I don't know whether the maker of the note ever paid it or not. I only know that Mr. Wahrmund never said anything to me about it.

"With that hundred dollars I bought this house. Here I have lived ever since, educating and caring for my children as best I could, and I am not ashamed of the job. My children have been mighty good to me, and I feel that I have ample reason to be proud of them.

"I did washing and sewing and whatever I could get to do, and the children, even the little fellows, helped me in every way they could.

"What did we do for amusement? Well for my part I was too busy with my household duties, even when a mere girl, and with my family, my sorrows and my duties later to think about amusements, and I presume a majority of the girls who grew up during those early days would tell you about the same thing. Certain officials of the Adelsverein particularly a Dr. Schubert, used to have some gay times. They would engage in expensive revels while the rest of the people were suffering. I only heard the older people complain of this, but some of them complained very bitterly. It seems that Mr. Meusebach was very angry about these high doings, but he was unable to put a stop to it. These extravagent officials didn't remain here very long, and their doings were soon forgotten. I recall that the young people used to have dances and amateur performances, but I seldom had the pleasure of attending them.

"When I bought this house the floors were of hard packed earth. At that time my brother-in-law, Louis Wahrmund, owned a building used for a dance hall and amusement purposes. This building he extended, giving me the boards now in the floor of this house. You will notice that they are as good as new planks, and are not nailed down. You couldn't drive a nail into one of them they are so hard. They were sawed by the Mormons, who had a saw mill at the old Mormon colony south of Fredericksburg. These planks served in the dance hall for many years, and have been doing duty in this floor for nearly sixty years. They are postoak. As you see they are not worn but have a glaze, the result of long years of use and shoe sole polish.

"I was ninety-two years old in December, 1924, and can read or do needle work without the use of glasses. I was never sick until I suffered a stroke of appoplexy three months ago, which made me unconscious for several days, from which I have recovered and am myself again. I could do my own housework, but my children and grandchildren insist that I have a companion, and as she is a good companionable woman I like to have her around. I am glad the young people today do not have to go through with what I had to endure. I am glad they have their good homes, their churches, their schools, their means of amusement and hope we will never have any more wars and that every one will learn that the only way to be happy and useful is try to do something worth while, something that will make some one else happier and the whole world better."

Boyhood Reminiscences of Early Days.

No one can tell pioneer history and relate pioneer experience like the old pioneers themselves.

It was during a social visit to the home of Bernhard Fiedler, in Fredericksburg, that he related the following amusing, interesting and instructive story of early day experiences. It goes back to boyhood days and depicts in simple words the conditions of the people and the country:

"I am what you would call one of the younger set. I was born in Fredericksburg in 1857. I do not remember much about the early history of the town except in a general way from hearing the older people talk.

"I was a very small boy when my father Jacob Fiedler moved to our wilderness home fifteen miles west of Fredericksburg. My father and three other men bought a section of land from the state. I do not remember what the price was, but it was only a few cents per acre. The other men were: Charles Wahrmund, Wm. Juenke and Frank Peterman.

"I suppose these four families were at that time, about 1864, the farthest west of any settlement. Not so long after moving to this place my father died, leaving my mother with nine children, seven girls and two boys, on her hands. I don't think the eldest child, a girl, was fifteen when my father died. We lived in a one-room log house. That wasn't so bad in the winter time and during the dark of the moon, but in hot weather and moonshine nights it was the limit of discomfort. In dark nights during the hot weather we might leave a door open and sleep with only one eye shut, but during the moonshine nights we had to keep the door closed and bolted from the inside. The Indians always did their marauding during the moonlight periods. During the season of Indian raids we not only had to be in the house with the door bolted early but we had to stay close to the house during the day. The Indians were meanest during the war and for some years after the war. They got mad at all whites because the government had taken their hunting grounds away from them, established frontier forts and moved the Indians to reservations. Bands were continually breaking away from these reservations and marauding through the country. In fact, it was not until many years after the war that the government succeeded in getting all the Indians on the reservations.

"We had no money, no clothes, and we lived without bread. Few big boys or girls would have known what a piece of money was, and if you had handed a child a piece of bread I doubt if it would have known what to do with it. I am speaking for that little community only. I don't know how it was in other communities. We didn't have any horses, hogs nor chickens. The Indians wouldn't let us keep a horse, and hogs and chickens had not been introduced into the country. We had a good horse once. We built a log hut near the house, made a strong door out of logs and then fixed a heavy chain across the door. The Indians came along one night. They couldn't get the door open and the horse out so they just shot him full of arrows and killed him. The Indians seemed to have some kind of superstition about breaking into a house. It would have been an easy matter for them to batter down the door and butcher the family, for the average family barely had enough old guns to make a bluff. We had just one old muzzle loading gun. You could fire it and then it required several minutes to reload it. But we always kept the ax handy and anything else that could be used as an effective weapon in case Indians did break into the house. Doubtless the Indians knew this and were more scared of the clubs than they were of the old gun.

"The only teams we had were oxen and burros. The country was full of wild burros. The Indians didn't bother our burros but about the time we would get a burro broke to work, he would manage to slip away, get with a wild herd, and we would have to do our work all over. Having no horse with which to round up and capture burros we had to resort to strategy. We built a pen and fixed the gate to open toward the inside. We would put salt inside the lot and then some one would hide behind the gate and when the burros had drifted in to get the salt the gate would be closed. We would have some great times getting the particular burros we wanted and then we would have some more great times doing anything with them after we did get them roped. On one occasion we got an extra good burro in so far as physical qualities were concerned, but he certainly was a bad proposition in the matter of disposition. I never saw a burro that could pitch as high and as fast and land as hard as that burro could. But the emergency of the case required that the burro should be conquered. He repeatedly threw I and brother all over that lot, and I am not sure but maybe he threw us over the fence a few times. One of the neighbor boys came along in his shirttail and said he could ride the beast. But he didn't have any better success than I and my brother had. After getting two or three falls he gave it up. Then I resorted to a desperate measure. I had the two boys take a rope and tie me on the burro. They certainly tied me hard and fast, and as usual over did the thing. They not only tied me so the burro couldn't get me off but they tied me so that I couldn't possibly get off myself. They even tied the knot under the burro's belly where I couldn't get to it. Then they turned him loose. He pitched all over the lot, and you can imagine about how he punished me, with the rope cutting into my flesh and the jolting of the burro adding agony to misery. Just as the burro had given up some one erred and opened the gate, and away the burro went. He ran for more than a mile. I had no bridle, and the only

thing I could guide him with was a stick. I finally got him
back to the pen and the boys took me off. I was a badly
skinned up lad. The rope had almost torn through my legs.

"As stated we had no clothes in those days. The best
we had to wear was a shirt with a tail none too long. We
had only one shirt at a time, too. When it became necessary
to wash our shirts, the ladies would have to retire. It would
be worth looking at now, if I only had a picture of that run-
away burro skimming across the prarie, I pounding him over
the head while my one piece suit flopped in the air. Boys
were boys then just as they have always been and they had
their fun along with their troubles.

"Some one around that community had learned from
the Indians how to tan deer hides and maybe this person had
in turn taught the art of hide tanning to some of our
family. At any rate my mother got hold of some tanned deer
hides and made I and my brother a pair of breeches and a
kind of vest. We were mighty proud and had to go and strut
around awhile. The grass was waist high and wet with dew.
We got pretty well soaked. Not caring to go back to the
house in that shape we fooled around in the sunshine until
the suits were thoroughly dried. Evidently some one had
made a mistake in the tanning of those hides. They not
only got hard when dried but they shrank most shamefully.
By the time we got back to the house the skin was worn off
our bodies in dozens of places. We had ruined our brand
new suits.

"Even in those early days there was a wagon factory in
Fredericksburg. No better wagons have ever been brought
to this country than were made by Fritz and Henry Wilke.
We got one of those wagons to which we worked oxen. One
day we decided to break a pair of burros to work. We
didn't have any harness, so we yoked them up just as we
would a yoke of oxen. The result was a run-away and a
broken wagon tongue, but we fixed the tongue and taught
the burros to work under yoke just as oxen did.

"The country was full of game of all kinds. The wolves
and panthers and burros used to make night hideous. A herd
of burros would cut loose with their braying at any hour of
the night, wolves would set up a howl and maybe a panther

would chime in. The creek was full of fish, and we could catch more fish in the Pedernales with a hook in a few minutes then than could be caught with a seine today. We only killed game when we really needed it, and we tried to make every shot count, for ammunition was scarce. We could mold bullets but we couldn't manufacture powder, and we must always have on hand at least one loaded gun in case of an Indian attack. During the war and for sometime after the war the country was full of wild cattle, old bulls, cows, yearlings and calves unmarked and unbranded. They belonged to any one. Occasionally we would kill a fat calf for a change, but aside from the meat these wild cattle proved a blessing in the matter of milk supply. We would get hold of an extra good wild, long horned cow occasionally and would gentle her to milk. We would usually get the cow by getting the calf while it was very small. That involved no small degree of danger, for those fleet footed creatures with their keen horns, would fight on sight. Many was the trick we would work and the chances we would take to get the calf in the pen. With the calf in the pen we could rope the cow, for she would follow her baby into the pen. By kind treatment we would soon get the cow gentle. We would turn the cow out in the morning and she would always come to the calf at night. If the cow weaned the calf, or if the calf ever got out we would be be minus one milch cow.

"Our first crop was a two acre patch. This we planted in corn, pumpkins and potatoes. With plenty of fresh meat, dried meat, fish, milk and butter, plus pumpkins and potatoes we didn't need any bread.

"Physically the Indians were no tougher than we were, nor were they much wilder. They just had us bested in the matter of cunning and cruelty and in numbers. The wigwam of the Indian had just about as many comforts and provisions as our home had, and our home was just about like the rest of the homes in this country at that time.

"I never see a barefooted boy gingerly picking his way over rough ground that I don't think how different it was when I was a boy, and didn't know what a pair of child's shoes looked like. Our feet were as tough as a horse's hoofs. We could kick fire out of flint rock, figuratively speaking.

We could skate all day on the ice, without shoes and with only a short shirt of thin cloth, and not suffer from cold.

"When I was a boy there was an abundance of wild fruit. All along the creeks and ravines there were great arbors of wild grapes. We don't have any such wild grapes today. They were a deep blue and sweet as any home grown grapes you get today. There were great thickets of plums. Those plums were deep red when ripe, were large as a rubber ball and were sweet and mellow. No such wild plums any more. The red haw, the black haw and the pecan are the only wild fruits that have not deteriorated.

"Once or twice I remember destructive fires sweeping through the country. The dead winter grass was waist high and these fires were very destructive to all kinds of timber and growths, especially so with the grape vines and plum thickets. When the plums grew up they produced only small, inferior fruit. In many instances the grapes never grew again, and when they did the fruit was inferior—just the common mustang grapes. During the season we had plenty of fruit, and that doubtless contributed a great deal to our health. We couldn't dry nor preserve the plums and grapes, for the reason that we had no sugar to preserve them, and if dried would have been without sugar to season them.

"Sometime after the death of my father my mother married. My stepfather was an industrious and frugal man, and he accumulated a great fortune for those days. That fortune consisted of five Spanish mules and a work horse, a mare and a colt. He engaged in freighting from Austin, and was getting along prosperously. Once he returned from a freighting trip and made a visit on horseback to the Guadalupe river in Kerr county, leaving me to guard the mules, the mare and the colt. About middle of the day, there being not a single creature in sight except the stock I was herding, I went into the house, only a short distance away. I hadn't more than got into the house when a bunch of Indians began yelling. They were right after the stock I was herding. The mules were all hoppled and belled, and such a rumpus as those hoppled mules, jangling bells and yelling Indians made. With my old blunderbus gun and one load of ammunition I started after them. Two of the Indians were chasing two of the mules that had separated from the others. I took after these two, and was making a little better time than the hoppled mules were making. I guess the two Indians didn't have a bow and arrow or they were scared of that harmless muzzle loading blunderbuss. At any rate they tore away to join the other Indians and I got the two mules. A short way back toward the house I met my brother and directed him to take the two mules while I went after the others. Just then I glanced around and saw an object dashing across the prairie from the direction the Indians had gone. I promptly decided it was a bold, bad Indian coming after the two mules. I dodged behind a bunch of bushes, cocked my blunderbuss and prepared to get an Indian. My plan was to let the Indian run right onto me and then blaze away. I couldn't see the approaching object, but knew I could judge the distance pretty well by the sounding of the horses hoofs. When right at me I jumped up and was just in the act of shooting when a white faced horse charged up. I recognized the animal and my stepfather was riding it. Returning home he had almost ran into the Indians, and only escaped because he had the swiftest horse.

"A long time ago there was an old corn mill on Live Oak creek. If they had good luck they could grind two or three bushels of corn per day. One day a neighbor was taking a bushel of corn to mill and my mother permitted me to go along. I don't think I ever got so lonesome and homesick. A couple of customers with a bushel of corn each had beat us to the mill, and besides something went wrong, and we had to wait three days to get the grinding done. By the time I first went to mill I was a good big boy and the country was getting considerably civilized.

"I don't remember how we did keep track of time. If we had an almanac it was several years out of date.

"I was more than fifteen years old before I ever attended school. My mother had given us all the help she could, and we had applied ourselves to studying such books as we had. The school I attended was about seven miles from our home. It was the Pedernales school and was taught by a Mr. Weber. The lessons taught and the books used were all German. I boarded with a family near the school. I got a total of eight months at this school.

"I was nearly 22 years old before I got any more schooling. This was a night school, taught by Louis Hagen, and we were instructed in English. I attended this night school for three months. The total amount of my schooling was eleven months—three months in an English language school and eight months in a German language school."

A Great Genius That Turned Hermit.

Among the first colonists coming to Gillespie county was a young man by the name of Berg—later known as the "Hermit of the Hills." He was a skilled stonemason, a good musician, had a good education, possessed an artistic and inventive faculty, but seems to have been of sensitive temperament. Before leaving Germany he had dreamed and planned and became engaged to marry. He would come to Texas, select his tract of land, build a nice home and send for his bride-to-be. Although the company utterly failed to make good in the matter of delivering the land as per contract, Berg went to work to make good and send for his sweetheart. Even in those hard times he succeeded in accumulating enough money to pay the girl's passage to the United States, and she came as far as Indianola. There she was told frightful stories about the awful epidemic that had carried away hundreds of the colonists, and the present condition of the country to which she was journeying was depicted as something awful, infested with murderous Indians and uncivilized white people. Whereupon the fair one changed her mind and married another. That fickleness completely upset the sensitive, romantic, highminded young Berg. He charged his troubles to the whole human race and decided to disassociate himself from mankind by adopting the life of a hermit. He scouted around and found an ideal place for his hermitage in the mountain wilds about eight miles east of Fredericksburg. Here, near a fine spring in a deep ravine, flanked on all sides by rugged mountains, he built his hermit home. Berg did all the work himself. He burnt his own lime, quarried and dressed, hauled and placed the rocks in the wall, and did every piece of the woodwork. He built a two-story house, a masterpiece in design and workmanship. How long he was building this house no one knows, but persons fairly familiar with the history of the hermit think he finished it in a few months. In some way he got a large iron wheel and made a wheel barrow, and with this he hauled his rocks, and this same wheelbarrow was his only vehicle and means of transportation through his many years as a hermit.

In the walls and ceiling are many rocks weighing two or three hundred pounds. How he hauled these rocks and then placed them high up in the walls is another unsolved mystery. He had a kit of fine stonemason's tools and was well equipped to quarry and dress the rocks and by some process placed them perfectly in the walls.

The upper story of this hermitage has entirely disappeared, but the lower floor and the arched rock ceiling is still practically intact.

His home completed the hermit proceeded to give a further demonstration of the versatility of his genius. He made a bedstead, one chair and a pipe organ. This pipe organ was not a crude thing, but a real musical instrument and the hermit was an expert at playing it. And next he produced his masterpiece. This was a stone tower, several feet high, and on top of this tower he constructed a windmill, fashioned after the old style Dutch windmills. Then he provided sucker rods and all necessary connections and used this windmill as his power plant. He used it to crush corn and pump water. The mill completed he made a stone lined vat in the center of the lower room, made a copper coil and two old style stone mill burrs for grinding corn, and then he engaged in a limited way in the none too remunerative business of making a little whiskey. He made his own barrels and containers, and when he had a supply of whiskey ready he would load it on his wheelbarrow and, following a narrow, winding trail across a rough, mountainous country, would take it to Fredericksburg and sell it for perhaps thirty cents a gallon. In this way, and by occasionally doing masonry work for some of the settlers he eked out an existence. He was not what would be classed as a moonshiner, but, even if so, he was one of the most remarkable moonshiners the United States ever produced. An ordinary moonshiner would have selected some cave or at best have erected a rude hut.

No one ever thought of disturbing the old man in his occupation until sometime after the civil war. Then some revenue agents came along, arrested him and confiscated his still. But the court and prosecuting attorney, convinced that the old man was harmless and of no evil intentions, declined to press any prosecution.

It is said that the old man fell into the hands of the Government through his own simple minded honesty. He wanted to make a better quality of whiskey. He finally got the name of a distillery and wrote to them for some information. The distilling company didn't do a thing to their prospectvie competitor in the wilds of Gillespie county. They just passed the matter up to the government.

When the hermit selected the location and built his house he had no kind of title to the land. Finally William Kiehne bought a large tract of land in that section and the hermit's house was on this tract. Mr. Kiehne didn't dispossess the hermit, but gave him a life tenure to his hermit abode.

With the exception of the time he was taken under arrest to Austin, for a period of perhaps fifty years he never traveled farther from his hermit than to occasionally go to Fredericksburg or visit among his few neighbors.

After he was put out of the whisky business, and at an age when he was too old to do hard work, he had a hard time getting along, though he made his own clothes, which were few and savagely simple. A few months before his death the county granted him a pension of five dollars per month. After his death a search of the premises revealed that he had horded several dollars of this small pension, and had the money concealed in the lid of an old trunk. This money, with a small additional sum from the county, gave the old man decent burial in the Fredericksburg cemetery.

Every person that knew the old hermit speaks of him as a great genius, a man with a mind capable of great things, but a victim of his own eccentricities. Think what this genius might have accomplished under different circumstances and environments. A man who could go alone into the mountains, build as he did—a two story house of architectural beauty and soidity, provide his own power plant, make his own furniture, his own vehicle and a wonderful musical instrument—might have been an Edison, a Fulton, a Howe or a Mergenthaler, wasting his genius and his energies in the mountain recesses of Gillespie county. And there were dozens of such geniuses among the original German colonists, not only in Gillespie county but among all of the prominent German colonies. Berg was the only eccentric among the Gillespie county geniuses, and yet in the matter of skilled training and ingenuity he certainly had no superior, possibly no equal. His death was merely an incident, but his wasted life was perhaps a national misfortune.

His misery was the secret of his own soul. He lived without benefit to himself, without harm to his fellowman.

His pets were the turkeys, the deer, the squirrels, the birds and other creatures that came to drink from the spring feed pool a short distance from his house. At night, from the top of his windmill tower, he communed with the stars, or entertained himself with the music of his pipe organ and sang the old songs that soothed the anguish of his soul. The old windmill tower is gone, the old hand organ has disappeared, and the wonderful house he built is now an empty, dismantled relic in the lonesome ravine recesses of a rugged mountain country—a monument to a pioneer tragedy, the sad reflex of the misdirected energies and genius of a disappointed and soulsick man.

As a builder, a mechanic and genius he proved his capacity and possibilities, as a whisky merchant and manufacturer he was a total failure.

Many amusing and pathetic incidents are told about the old hermit by persons who knew him, although these people were young men and women or mere children when the hermit was an old man. The old hermit didn't have many intimate friends but among these friends were Wm. and Ed. Kramer, Ernst Althaus, Wm. and Ferd. Ebert, Wm. Kiehne and Gus Kuhlmann. From Otto Kramer, a son of William Kramer, and from Mrs. Adolph Lucas, daughter of Wm. Kiehne, the writer has gained most of the inside history of the life of the hermit. Mr. Kramer says the old hermit was considered harmless both in the matter of conduct and intentions. "He was very independent along with his eccentricities and didn't like to be under obligations to any one. In his old days, when feebleness of age and loss of health came upon him, the old man would occasionally visit some neighbor's to get something to eat, but he always insisted on paying for it. If he didn't have the money right then he would insist on paying for it later, and so far as I know he managed in some way to meet these obligations, never amounting to more than a few cents. He wouldn't receive anything as a gift. His honesty was considered unimpeachable; and yet, one day he was caught skinning a calf that belonged to Gus. Kuhlmann, notwithstanding the fact that Kuhlmann was one of his few intimate friends. When asked why he had done it the hermit made the simple but effective reply that he had to have something to eat. The neighbors would have freely given him enough to eat, but the trouble was that he was too proud and stubborn to accept it. Of course nothing was done with him for killing the calf.

"On one occasion some of us young people gave a dance, and we invited the old man, incidentally buying some of his whiskey, which was not of a very superior quality. After that he would show up at every dance we gave, and as a matter of courtesy and sympathy we would buy some of his produce."

Mrs. Lucas has some vivid childhood recollections of the old man and was familiar with his history through her father. Mrs. Lucas has a few, and they are perhaps the only remaining, relics of the hermit. Speaking of the old man Mrs. Lucas said:

"He was really a remarkable man, though an object of pity, and yet he asked no one for pity, and didn't seem to care very much for their friendship or assistance. I have frequently heard my father speak of him as one of the most expert stonemasons and mechanics in this country, and in those days there were some mighty good ones. In placing rocks in a building, or in building a long string of fence he never used a plumb line, a tape nor a straight edge, and yet his line or wall was perfectly straight and without defect. He could judge distance and direction perfectly with his eye.

"He would occasionally correspond with his relatives in Germany, and I have been told that he always wrote beautiful letters, teeming with love and kindness and good cheer, and that in these letters he never referred to his mode of living.

"Astronomy was one of his hobbies, and he used the windmill tower as his point of observation. The community finally came to rely pretty strongly on his weather prophecies.

"He was a man of diversified genius and talent. On one occasion some one entered his house and stole some whiskey. This might have been done as a joke, but it riled the old man, and he forestalled future depredations by rigging up a burglar alarm. This ingenius contraption was arranged to fasten on the outside of the lower room door, with a cord extending into the window of the upper room where he slept. The slightest movement of the door would cause the suspended weight to fall on the old man and wake him up. The fact of this precaution became well known, and as the old man always kept a gun, no one ever cared to experiment with the burglar alarm to see whether it would work or not. Every one took it for granted that it would work, and considering the hermit's perfection in the matter of making things that would work, this was doubtless the sane and proper conclusion to reach.

"I don't know what ever went with the windmill, the tower nor the hand organ. They seem to have just completely disappeared."

Like many a great genius he passed away "unwept, unhonored and unsung."

CHAPTER VI.

SCRAPS OF UNUSUAL HISTORY.

Old Fort Martin Scott.

Fort Martin Scott was established by the federal government in 1847, and was one of a chain of forts across the western part of the state. It was probably a two company post. It was abandoned in 1852 or 1853. The government had a commissary, barracks, officers quarters and a guard house on the reservation. The old guard house, slightly repaired and added to, is still standing. This fort was about two miles south of Fredericksburg, and just to the left of the present San Antonio highway. This old fort served a better purpose after the government took the soldiers away than it ever served before. This was during the few years that it was used as a fair grounds by the citizens of Fredericksburg and Gillespie county. The land is now owned by Henry Braeutigam. J. W. Braeutigam became the owner of the property soon after the government moved the troops, and in 1884 he was murdered.

Some authorities contend that Fort Martin Scott was both an infantry and a cavalry post, others that it was only a cavalry post, and this latter contention is probably correct.

The soldiers at this old fort, like the soldiers at all frontier forts in those days, were a "wild and wooly bunch" not very amenable to discipline, particularly when under the influence of whisky, and that was a very common occurance.

One one occasion a soldier came to town from the fort and proceeded to get drunk. In those days every character of business place sold whisky. There was an agreement between the business men and officers that no one would sell whiskey to a drunken soldier. J. M. Hunter was then the principal merchant in town. He was also county clerk, and had all the records of the county clerk's office in his store. The soldier, already well under the influence of whisky, endeavored to get into Hunter's store, although Hunter was closing up and warned the soldier to keep out. A struggle ensued, and the soldier was stabbed, dying a few minutes later. The killing was unintentional on Hunter's part, although he was justified and was never indicted for the killing. The soldiers learned of the killing and several of them came to town, probably got drunk and started out to get Hunter and wreak vengence. Failing to find Hunter they burned the store, and thus destroyed the first records of Gillespie county. Seven soldiers were indicted, charged with arson, but none of them were ever caught, and the cases were finally dismissed. It is probable that after burning the store the soldiers never returned to the fort, but drifted into the mountains, joining other outlaw bands and going on with their wild careers.

In 1855 some soldiers drifted into Fredericksburg, got drunk and pulled off a revolting killing among themselves. For this killing David M. Dean was indicted. The evidence of one witness to the killing was about as follows. This witness, A. B. McDonald, testified that "he was standing on the porch of his house and saw four men walking towards Hitzfeldt's grocery store. They were all very drunk, but walking with arms locked and there seemed to be no ill feeling among them. On reaching the place some of them tried to break in, pounding on doors and window shutters. One of the men was standing near the corner of the house with a rock in his hand and was threatening to tear the place down. Just then one of his companions raised a pistol and fired, although the man with rock had turned and was running away when the shot was fired." McDonald recognized the killer as Lieutenant David M. Bean of Travis company, "about 25 or 30 years old with black whiskers." The name of the murdered man was Carp. After shooting his companion Bean walked up to the dead man and examined the bullet hole in the back of his head. The case was continued from term to term. Finally Bean died in 1866, eleven years after the killing, and the case was accordingly dismissed. It is likely that Bean and the other three soldiers had formerly been stationed at Fort Martin

Scott. At any rate this escapade was typical of the frontier soldiers at that time.

The Mormon Colony.

About four miles south of Fredericksburg, on the Pedernales river, is a noted spot. This property, now owned by Charles and Frank Schmidtzensky, was at one time the site of a prosperous Mormon colony. Here, in 1847, about two hundred Mormons, including men, women and children located. They were industrious, and for those days, possessed considerable means. They had a big general store, a saw mill, a grist mill and a cabinet shop. In social and business matters the Germans and Mormons got along fine, but if the old records have been correctly interpreted they had a redhot political row. From the old saw mill came much of the lumber used by the early German citizens, and from the old Mormon grist mill the Germans obtained much of the first meal they used.

With the exception of the community gardens at Fredericksburg the Mormons were the first farmers in the county. Just how much land they cultivated is not known, but it certainly amounted to several acres.

Elder Lyman Wight was in charge of the Mormon colony. He served as chief justice of Gillespie county from September, 1850, to June 2, 1851. It appears from the old records that Wight was defeated at the election by J. J. Klingelhoefer, but Wight contested, and as Klingelhoefer had not been naturalized, the contest was decided in Wight's favor. At this time there were several other contests, the row evidently being between the Germans, Mormons and the element around Fort Martin Scott. To decide most of the contests a special election was held, the polls being kept open for a week. This election got all mixed up, there was more big fuss and another special election called. Just what happened is not known, but at the second special election the Germans won out in great shape. In fact, it was a one-sided election. Unable to run politics to suit them Wight and his adherents evidently got disgusted and would have nothing more to do with Gillespie county politics. Wight quit attending sessions of the commissioners court. Finally commissioners Schmidtzensky, Mosel and Jordan called themselves together, and the following significant entry appears in the minutes of the court: "Ordered by the court that the chief justice, Lyman Wight, be ordered to meet the said county commissioners at the chief justice's office this day two weeks, to-wit: on the 16th day of June, 1851, to settle the matters of said county; and it is ordered that Christian Gartner, constable for precinct No. 2, be ordered to see said Lyman Wight, and command him to attend said court and settle and close up all matters with the county as chief justice and probate judge." It is evident that said Wight was "sore" and hadn't been paying any attention to the court nor to the affairs of the county. What is more Wight didn't pay any attention to the summons of the court; whereupon the commissioners met again, declared the office of chief justice vacant and ordered a special election to fill the vacancy.

In the early part of 1853 the Mormons abandoned their colony. No one knows whether they practiced polygamy. Even then polygamy was outlawed in Texas. There has been some newspaper romancing about the Mormons nearly all dying during the cholera epidemic. There is no foundation for such stories. The epidemic was over before the Mormons came to Gillespie county. No one knows just why the Mormons left nor where they went. Their departure was doubtless due to a combination of circumstances and misfortunes. They had purchased a large tract of land, but the title proved defective and they lost the land, but as the colony was rich and land was then cheap they could have repurchased it. A flood destroyed much of their property, washing away the grist mill and saw mill. A third factor was the laws of the state against polygamy, and then came the political defeat. Such a combination of calamities would suffice to cause even a Mormon to move and not tell any one where he was going.

The Mormons still own an acre of land on which they had their graveyard for the old colony. It contains only a few graves and every two or three years some Mormon comes along and looks after it.

Except for this graveyard there remains taday scarcely a trace of this once prosperous colony. They left no such monuments as rock houses and rock fences to endure and serve for generations.

An Old Stone House and Hand Made Furniture.

Perhaps the first stone building in Fredericksburg was erected by Peter Tatsch in 1857. It is still standing in a perfect state of preservation and is occupied by Miss Caroline Tatsch, who, though she gets around by the use of a crutch, is practically an invalid.

This building is a fair sample of the stone homes built by the old timers many years ago. It has two rather large rooms and a side room running the entire length of the building. In one of the main rooms is a fire place of ordinary width. Across the east end of the side room is a chimney, the fire place extending across the entire width of the room. These wide chimneys are common to all the old rock houses built throughout the county fifty-five and sixty years ago, and probably all of them served in a measure the same purpose as did the broad fire place in the Tatsch home. There is an iron rod running the entire width and across the center of this fire place, and from this iron rod are suspended a number of large hooks. In the early days, and even in comparatively recent days, this fire place was used to cook the family meals, and it was also used for making syrup, cooking meat in large quantities and for curing meats. Much of the syrup and meats used by the entire community was made, cooked or cured in this big old fire place. The chimney was copecially constructed so as to carry away all soot and smoke and to regulate the draft. The building was a masterful piece of workmanship throughout, from the foundation to the top of the walls and the chimney. Owing to the scarcity of the tools, most of the rocks were picked to fit or chipped to fit. Few of them show any signs of dressing, except such as was done with a hammer. Yet every one of the stones fits perfectly, not a rough or unsightly place in the entire walls of either the house of the chimney. The walls appear to be about fourteen inches thick. The walls inside and the ceiling in the two large rooms are plastered snow white. Built into the wall of the main living room is a kind of closet, used as a medicine chest and as a place for keeping important papers and documents. The highly polished wooden door to this closet was hand made and fits air tight. In the two main rooms are two bedsteads. They are not only strong, but they are works of art. Nothing surpassing them in strength or beauty could be purchased in any city furniture store today. In the living room is a wardrobe that is certainly a masterpiece. It appears to be about six feet high, four feet wide and two feet deep. Because of its artistic finish it would attract attention in any display of the most beautiful furniture, for it is a work of art. The bedsteads and the wardrobe were made by Mr. Tatsch after his house was finished. There is much delicate carving and the work was all done by Mr. Tatsch. One of the bedsteads was made of hackberry, another of black walnut and the wardrobe was made of cherry. All of the timber was procured from the forests in the vicinity of Fredericksburg.

Only the most painstaking experts could have constructed such a building, and only a master artist and cabinet maker could have made such furniture.

Miss Tatsch has refused fancy prices for every piece of this furniture, but not being in need of the money and because of the endearments attached to it, refuses to sell it for any price. There is a great deal of this kind of old hand-made furniture in the old homes of Fredericksburg and Gillespie county.

This old house and this furniture is evidence of the thoroughness, the art and efficiency of these old timers in all things, while the big old fire place reflects the system and proficiency they applied in all things.

Miss Tatsch still cooks in the old fire place, using a skillet or oven for baking bread.

The lime used in this building was made in a kiln still standing on the east bank of Town creek, just a few blocks east of the courthouse. This old kiln was built and operated by Julius Splitgerber. There are dozens of these old kilns scattered throughout the county today, for the old timers not only used lime in building their rock houses, but in many instances in building rock fences. Not only are there dozens of old rock houses built years ago, but many miles of rock fence, and seldom does one see where one of these old fences has given way in a single place. They built them across mountains, creeks and blackland flats, but regardless of soil, surface or destructive forces they are standing intact. Some of them were built seventy years ago.

Neighbor helped neighbor, for in those days their principal medium of exchange was co-operation. They built their own lime kilns, burned their own lime, quarried their own rock and hauled their own sand and cut their own timber, and whether it was building a log hut, a lime kiln, a rock fence or a stone house they helped each other. Nowhere else will you find door locks and latches such as you find on the doors of these old homes, cribs and barns in Fredericksburg and Gillespie county. They were handmade, and they were made to serve and to last.

As early as 1847 there was a wagon factory in Fredericksburg run by two brothers Fritz and Henry Wilke, one a wheelwright, or a wagon maker, and the other was a blacksmith. Between the two they could make every part of a wagon, and the only thing they had to import was the iron used, and they could make a good wagon without iron. It is said that some of the best wagons ever made or used in Texas were made by these brothers.

A Wartime Gun Cap Factory.

During the war between the states the scarcity of ammunition became a serious matter throughout Texas, and especially in Gillespie county. Particularly was there a scarcity of caps for guns and pistols, all guns at that time being of the cap and ball make. The citizens of Gillespie county must procure game for food and they must have firearms for protection against the Indians. Without caps bullets and powder were useless. Two men, Captain E. Krauskopf and Adolph Lungkwitz, met the emergency. Captain Krauskopf was a gunsmith and Lungkwitz was a silversmith, and both were endowed with a high degree of mechanical skill and inventive genius. They first made their own machine for rolling the copper to proper thickness and a machine for cutting out or stamping the caps. They made both the hat caps and percussion caps for guns and pistols. For loading and priming the caps both saltpeter and quicksilver must be used. From the bat caves in the mountains around Fredericksburg they got the material for the saltpeter and Captain Krauskopf made a trip to Galveston to get the quicksilver. They not only saved the ammunition situation in Gillespie county, but in time found a considerable market for their caps throughout this section of the country.

Mr. Oscar Kruskopf, son of Captain E. Krauskopf, still has a box of the old caps. This is a paper box with the name of the maker of the caps and the number 1400 on it, this number doubtless indicating the number of caps in the box.

This was perhaps the only gun cap factory ever established in Texas.

As a gunsmith and a gunmaker Captain Krauskopf rendered a conspicuous service to the gunmaking industry not only of Texas but of the nation. He made dozens of guns of different patterns and calibers in Fredericksburg. He had the bored barrels shipped in but did the rifling and made the stocks, hammers, triggers and sights himself. The officers of the different government posts in this part of the state were among his principal patrons. In those days the government issued the same kind of guns and pistols to the officers as were issued to privates. The officers would bring these to Captain Krauskopf to have them silver mounted, initialed and made in keeping with the officers' ideas of propriety. But hundreds of the guns he made were sold to citizens in all sections of west Texas.

Captain Krauskopf got the agency for the Winchester rifle when it was first placed on the market. This gun was at that time an improvement over any other gun. While agent for this gun company Captain Krauskopf worked out an improvement in the matter of a dust proof loader and discharge. He also invented the automatic cartridge and hull extracter. The district agent promised the captain a handsome remuneration for his inventions, but the upshot of the matter was that the Winchester company procured the patent, and Captain Krauskopf never so much as received thanks for his work and great inventions. While agent for the company Captain Krauskopf sold 1000 rifles, and for this record the Winchester people presented him with a silver barreled winchester. After the company appropriated his inventions he dissolved relations with the concern, and in disgust gave the silver barreled winchester to a friend.

Oscar Krauskopf has a real curiosity shop in the matter of old guns. In this collection are guns of every type and size and ancient make. Among the number is a beautiful muzzle loading double barrel English made shot gun at one time the property of General Robert E. Lee. Before the civil war General Lee was for several months stationed at Fort Mason, and made frequent visits to old Fort Martin Scott, near Fredericksburg, and on these visits would always stop at the Nimitz hotel. General Lee was a close friend of John M. Hunter, a Kentuckian and the first county clerk of Gillespie county. General Lee finally made Hunter a present of this gun. When Hunter died he gave it to Captain Krauskopf, and he in turn gave it to his son Oscar. In some way Hunter broke the stock of the gun, and this Captain Krauskopf mended with a beautiful German silver band. This gun is a treasured heirloom. Oscar Krauskopf doesn't need the money and wouldn't sell it for any price.

Santanna, the big Comanche Indian chief, was a friend of Captain Krauskopf. One day the chief gave the Captain a beautiful combination pipe and tomahawk. A few days later a sport from San Antonio came along, spied the beautiful gift and planned to procure it. The sport had a fine bird dog, to which Oscar Krauskopf took a fancy. The sport offered to trade the dog, for the combination pipe and tomahawk, and the deal was closed with record speed. When the family learned what had been done there was great wailing and lamentation. The family has made liberal offers to get the Indian chief's present back, but to no avail. It now decorates the lodge room of the Redmen in San Antonio. The dog is dead.

SUNDAY HOMES.

Gillespie county is perhaps the only county in the United States where the people, or at least, many of the people have "Sunday homes." This is a most unique and sensible system. Just when it first started is not definitely known, but it was several years ago. George Zenner and John Baumann were among the first persons to build a "Sunday home." Mr. Zenner doesn't remember just when this house was built, but thinks it was fully twenty-five years ago. He doesn't think it was the first home of this kind, but is sure it was among the first. There are dozens of these "Sunday homes" in Fredericksburg, a few in Harper and possibly a few in the other towns of the county, but the custom started in Fredericksburg.

A few of these homes are two stories and contain four or five rooms, but most of them are neat one-story, two room houses, furnished with all conveniences for light house keeping. They are owned almost exclusively by people who live on their farms and ranches. Every Saturday these country people can come to town, take their time to do their trading, remain over Saturday night, attend church and Sunday school and leave for their homes Monday morning, and in the meantime they have been perfectly and comfortably at home. In fact they can come to town any time they like, stay as long as they wish and be at home all the time. While they are used principally on Saturdays and Sundays, it is not infrequently the case that the farmer or ranchman preferring to send his children to school in town, can use the "Sunday home" during the school term. The houses are not expensive, though substantial, the furnishings are simple but ample, and altogether it is one of the most convenient, sensible and economical customs imaginable.

When Whiskey Was Fifteen Cents Per Quart.

At one time, in the pre-Volsted days, Fredericksburg had fourteen saloons, and there were as many more scattered throughout the county, and yet it was one of the most law abiding and best behaved towns in the country. They had high standards of conduct and any saloon man who didn't live up to those standards didn't remain in business long. At their dances, and at all public gatherings, drunkenness and misconduct was the rarest thing, and this was due to established standards of conduct more than it was to legislature enacted laws.

A prominent old timer was telling the writer some time ago about the early dances and cheap whiskey. The music for these early day dances was furnished chiefly by an old time fiddler. Sometimes this one piece orchestra would get as much as a dollar and a half for playing for an all night dance, and then again maybe he wouldn't get more than four bits. But be the amount what it might he was always satisfied, and everybody would be well behaved, and everything would pass off in the most enjoyable manner. But this fiddler couldn't get down to business unless he had a drink occasionally, so they would take up a collection and go out and buy a quart and present it to the musician. This was the very best of homemade whiskey and the price was 15 cents per quart. The old fiddler would get liberal with his donation whiskey and pass it around, and if there was a big crowd present maybe they would have to take up two or three collections before the dance was over. But they never bought too much and the fiddler nor any one else ever got too much.

Fredericksburg never had a distillery except in a limited way, but at one time it had two of the biggest breweries in the country. Frederick Probst put up a brewery in Fredericksburg many years ago, and for years it was a great money making institution, but the big combined brewing interest finally put the local brewery out of business. Maurer Bros., perhaps representing the Lone Star Brewing Co., put a brewery in Fredericksburg in competition with Probst, but this brewery was finally converted into an ice factory, and then went broke, or at least went out of business.

Of course there has been bootlegging and illicit distilling in Gillespie county since national prohibition. But the same is true of every county in the country, and there has been less of it in Gillespie county than in any other county in the country, population considered, and people who think to the contrary don't know what they are thinking about. The Germans were always ardent anti-prohibitionists, but they are strong on law enforcement, and they have less respect for a bootlegger than they ever had for the most fanatical prohibitionist. They regard the bootlegger as a menace and a nuisance.

Before prohibition a drunken bum was a rare thing among the Germans. They enjoyed their beer, but they enjoyed it with a marked degree of sense and moderation. It was seldom that one of them became the slave of the alcoholic habit, and today, denied the right to enjoy their beverage openly and legally, they are perhaps the most abstemious people on the American continent.

An Original Dispenser of Justice.

One of the most original of the old time characters was J. P. (Peter) Mosel, for many years a county commissioner and justice of the peace. He was honest, just, independent and original. When it came to dealing out justice or handling a judicial matter Mosel didn't permit statutes and technicalities to interefer. Many amusing incidents are told about this popular old timer, these anecdotes illustrating the kind of man he was and his methods of dealing with emergencies.

On one occasion a man missed a bunch of milk pen calves. He scouted around and found the calves in a neighbor's pasture, bearing the neighbor's mark and brand. Possibly some boys had done the mischief just to see what would happen. The owner of the calves hastened to Mosel with his troubles, and Mosel settled the matter in short order. He sent for the neighbor, who stoutly denied any knowledge of the business. But Peter was obdurate, and advised the neighbor to bar out his brand, put the rightful owner's brand on the calves and have them in the owner's pen by noon the next day, or he, the said Peter, would send the defendant to the penitentiary for not less than two years. Mosel went on the theory that it was up to the neighbor to find the parties who had played the joke, just as it had been up to the owner to find the calves, but that in the meantime the justice of the peace could deal only with the situation "as the law directed."

On another occasion a merchant had extended credit to the amount of more than $100 to certain parties. Finally these parties were preparing to leave the country without paying the debt. To Mosel went the creditor with his troubles. Without the formality of filing a suit Mosel issued an attachment for a bunch of cattle owned by the debtors, and directed the constable to go get the cattle or the money. The parties raised a mighty roar and undertook to convince the constable that the attachment wasn't any good, but the constable convinced them that he wasn't going to waste his time trying to explain matters to Peter Mosel, that orders were orders, and that he would have to have the money or the cattle or fight Mosel, and that he didn't propose to get in bad for contempt of court. The result was that the parties paid the debt, including cost and "attorney's fees." And Peter had an equally effective way of dealing with people who came bothering him with something that didn't amount to anything.

Mosel was a man of considerable education. He didn't believe in phrenology, but the gang, none of whom believed in phrenology any more than Mosel did, would argue long and loud in favor of phrenology as a wonderful science. They were designedly paving the way for a practical joke. Finally a stranger came to town. As per arrangement this stranger posed as a great phrenologist. And in due time Mosel also came to town. The gang told him about the wonderful "phrenologist." They urged Mosel to test it out and see what he thought about it. If Mosel wasn't convinced that there was something in it, then they would all agree that phrenology was a fraud. To please the gang Mosel agreed to have his head examined. Of course the "phrenologist" had been told all about Mosel, that he was a great mathematician, had a wonderful memory, and was otherwise fully informed as to Mosel's traits and peculiarities. The reading was progressing fine, and Mosel was agreeing that the "phrenologist" was exactly right about everything, and had confessed his own error in doubting the science of phrenology, when his sister, an elderly and sensible lady, who was at the hotel where the "phrenologist" was stopping, happened along, saw the gang off to one side trying to keep from laughing so loud as to give the scheme away. Whereupon the good lady seized a broom and chased "phrenologist," duped brother and the whole gang off the premises. Except for this uncalculated interruption Mosel would have soon been a confirmed believer in and convert

to phrenology. As it happened he left town more firmly
convinced than ever that phrenology was a humbug, and that
several of his closest friends could not be depended on when
it came to making scientific tests.

Some Indian History, Mixed English and Stray Stock.

One of the fine old early day Gillespie County characters
was H. Ochs, who was county clerk from 1859 to the fall of
1869. In German, Latin and mathematics he was one of the
best scholars in the entire country. He was a highly refined
and thoroughly conscientious gentleman. He taught school
in Fredericksburg for many years and many of the leading citizens of Fredericksburg and Gillespie county were at
one time scholars in Ochs' schools, and all of them venerate
the name of Ochs. But the fine old gentleman had a way
of getting the English language compounded in a most ludi-
crous manner. Three extracts from the old records during
Ochs' encumbency as clerk are rich and amusing, and at the
same time they are of moral and historical interest and importance. They reflect the honesty and the simple but practical and just methods the old timers applied in dealing with
business matters.

A stray steer had been troubling Ernst Schaper for sometime, and finally on account of the steer being a rogue and
fence break it became necessary to dispose of him in short
order, and here was the way the court did it, according to
ver batim extract from the records:

"April 13, 1863: In relation to a certain steer of white
color with blue spots, which is running at large in this county
for 3-4 years without having been estrayed; it being a bad
beast, breaking down fences and obnoxious to the public;
the county commissioners had been required at a late session
to estray the same and till today they did fail to so do.
Now, whereas, new complains were shown to the court in
that concern, and it was apprehended that said steer might
be killed useless and unlawful by some body whose fields he
would hurt. Therefore the court determined that said beef
should be butchered, its beef fat sold, then the proceeds
delivered to the county treasurer. The county clerk shall
give notice of that fact publicly that the concerning owner

may have an opportunity to a just claim to be found out by examination of the skin of said animal, which is to be preserved to that purpose.''

And further in relation to said wicked steer, the following was written in the minutes at the next term of court:

''In relation to a certain steer having been obnoxious to the public, as mentioned in the last foregoing session, Ernst Schaper made report to the court that he was butchering the same, and that the realized money after covering the resp. expenses is nine dollars. The court ordered the clerk to instruct the County Treasurer to collect said amount and to account for at proper time.''

In another entry in the old court minutes Ochs says: ''Judge Schuchard got his assignation for the salary of office of one quarter of a year.''

It will be noticed that the old clerk's spelling and punctuation are beyond criticism. He just got his English twisted. But even at that he didn't leave any room for doubt as to what he meant and being in dead earnest about it.

A Dishonorable Outrage.

Back in the early days a couple of inebriated roughnecks played a mean trick on the deputy county clerk by putting the deputy in the old jail, bolting the door from the outside so the prisoner couldn't release himself, and then going away. The deputy clerk was a highly educated, sensitive man, and was justifiably indignant because of such coarse, ungentlemanly treatment. His degree of wrath is reflected in the following complaint he filed with the county court relative to the matter;

The State of Texas,
County of Gillespie,

To the Hon. County Court of Gillespie County:-

''This afternoon, between the hours of two and four, the usual hours for performance of official business of the County Clerk, Thom. Smith and Cameron locked me in the county jail, and after doing so went away and left me inclosed there for the space of about a quarter of an hour, and by these means they kept me away from my official duty, which I was charged with by the County Clerk. Said T. Smith and Cameron did not open the jail door for the pur-

pose to let me out, but I am only obliged to the inter-
vention of a strange gentleman who opened the door and
released me.

"Now by these presents I in duty bound complain to
your Hon. Board the above mentioned dishonorable outrage,
inflicted to my person to the whole Hon. Court, and I expect your Hon. Court will make use of all lawful means to
cause the said outrage to be punished and prevent for future
such offences.

Respectfully,
Your obed. serv.

Deputy County Clerk
Fredericksburg, March 15, 1860.

The Sheriff and Prisoner Made a Trade.

Many years ago, when John Walter was sheriff, J. C.
McGrew, a Mason county ranchman, killed another man.
McGrew, a typical old time cowman, was brought to Fredericksburg for "safe keeping." A few days after the prisoner was brought to Fredericksburg a friend chanced to be
passing along and saw McGrew sitting in front of the jail
reading a newspaper. Curious to know how the prisoner happened to be enjoying freedom, the friend walked up to in-
quire about it.

"But I ain't out of jail," the prisoner replied in answer
to the question. "No, sir, I'm very much in jail. Just usin'
the streets for a run-around."

"How come?" inquired the friend.

"Well, I made a trade with the sheriff. He's a fine man
and mighty busy. I decided to help him out all I could, so
one day I says to him: 'Say, sheriff, you needn't be pester'n
with bringin' my meals to me. You just leave the door
unlocked and when it comes time to eat I'll go to the bordin'
house and come right back, and when bed time comes I'll
turn in, and you can bet on me doin' just what I say I'll do.'
So the sheriff agreed to it and that's the way we've been
workin' it ever since. I've fudged on the sheriff a little, for
once in awhile I step over to the saloon and take a little nour-
ishment, and I've moved by bed on the outside on account of

hot weather. Don't know whether the sheriff's in town or not. I ain't seen him in a week."

And when court convened in Mason the sheriff and the prisoner got in a buggy and drove over. McGrew was tried and acquitted.

Lott Shot Schultz and Paid the Board Bill.

In the minutes of the October term, 1880, the following entry appears: "In the matter of Schultz, a wounded person now in the care of Matthew Zenner, the said Schultz being without means or property, and his wound of a dangerous character, requiring proper care and attention, expense of which may finally fall on the county, it is ordered that Wm. Wahrmund be instructed to supervise the matter. And A. Lott, the person who inflicted the wound on said Schultz, being present in court, agreed to this order, and gave his promisory note to refund all expenses, if able to do so, in the course of time. And said A. Lott further deposited with the court the sum of $25.00 to defray immediate expenses, the sum so deposited to be deposited with the county treasurer." The facts in the case are that Lott and Schultz were fooling with an old cap and ball pistol. It wasn't loaded, of course, but nevertheless it went off and Schultz' knee happened to be in the path of the bullet. Schults later lost his leg, but just how much Lott paid on his "personal note, in the course of time, if able to do so," the records fail to disclose.

F. Brodbeck and His Flying Machine.

One of the original colonists was F. Brodbeck. He was an educated man, of an inventive turn. He designed and constructed an airship. He had the principal correct and his airship would rise from the ground and sail around in the air for several minutes, until the power was exhausted, or until the unguided ship model collided with some material object. He provided rudder, propeller, wings and body, but he lacked sustaining power. That was long before the days of gasoline engines, so this airship artist used spring coils as motive power. So long as the springs were wound up the power was there, but when the springs ran down, the power was exhausted and down came the machine. He finally, as he thought, solved this problem by building a machine big enough to carry a passenger, he to be the first passenger, of course, this passenger to keep the springs wound up, thus supplying power and keeping the ship afloat. The day for the great trial test arrived and the ship sailed away. It eclipsed Darius Green's record by several seconds. Then the inventor discovered that a spring will not wind up and run down at the same time. He was several feet higher than a tall tree when he made this discovery. The inventor survived the crash, but the machine didn't. The stockholders declined to stand any further assessment for repairs, rebuilding and further experimenting, and Brodbeck, whose only income was his meagre salary as a school teacher, was not financially able to carry on the work himself. Lack of a gasoline engine years ago was doubtless all that kept F. Brodbeck from becoming one of the world's famed inventors, and incidentally kept Fredericksburg from becoming famous as the home town of the invention.

Tax Troubles—Rancid Bacon and Weevily Wheat.

And they had tax burdens and revenue raising troubles in those good old days. They didn't have much to pay taxes on, but they had still less to pay taxes with. In 1858 they levied a considerable occupation tax on all kinds of mercantile business, including saloons and ten pin alleys: 12½ cents on each hundred dollars worth of real and personal property, 10c on each hundred dollars worth of merchandise, 10c on each hundred dollars loaned at interest, and a 25c poll tax. A dollar then was worth about ten at present, which makes it comparatively easy to calculate their actual tax burden. But during the war cash was so scarce that they substituted country produce for cash in payment of taxes. Here is an interesting extract from the minutes of the commissioners court of February 15, 1864: "Owing to the liabilities of the county in providing for indigent persons, the extraordinary tax of 12½c tax on each hundred dollars value of property, which is to be used for soldiers families and is unavoidable, shall be collected either in specie or in grain, and shall be receivable for taxes as follows: 1 bushel of wheat, $1.50; 1 bushel of corn, $1.00; bacon, 12½c pound." But collecting taxes in country produce didn't keep the commissioners from having trouble. On one occasion they discovered that some one had worked off on them a considerable quantity "of old, impure, rancid bacon, and some wheat all full of weevils." They instructed the treasurer to sell the stuff at any price, and warned other tax payers to not try the same trick.

But about this tax business their was a serious side. In the county were dozens of indigent families of Confederate soldiers. And at nearly every meeting of the court there is some reference to this pathetic feature. The commissioners were doing their best to keeping any one from actually suffering, but they were having a hard time to do so. In one instance the minutes say that "a great many soldiers' families were applying for clothing and bread stuff," and "as the Gillespie county soldiers families are entitled to a share of the million dollars to be distributed by the state in treasury notes, and to their share of penitentiary made cloth," a committee consisting of Wm. Kook, C. Marschall, C. Wehmeyer and C. Althaus was appointed to look after the matter. A few days later they were advised by state authorities that their share of penitentiary made clothing would be forthcoming, and they posted notices for the families to come forward on July 25th and get their share. The hungry, half clothed mothers and children came as advised, but the state failed them—the promised relief didn't arrive. And the mothers took their babes back to the cabin homes, where there was little to eat and less to wear. In 1863 they directed the treasurer to pay the sheriff in Confederate treasury notes, and the sheriff wouldn't have it, and as a result he didn't get anything, but in the long run what he did get was worth as much as a hundred dollars in Confedrate money would have been worth.

Places of Scenic and Historic Interest.

The Enchanted Rock, about twenty-two miles north of Fredericksburg, is one of the natural wonders of the United States. It is a great globe shaped, solid granite formation, the base of which covers more than a section of land. It is several hundred feet from the base to the top. The slope from the base to the top is so gradual that it is easily climbed, except along parts of the north side where there are a number of rough places and perpendicular bluffs. Along the north side are a number of great fissures or caves. The full extent of some of these caves have never been explored. It is a place of endless wonders, and persons who have spent weeks exploring about this great formation are constantly finding something new and wonderful. No picture or pen description of this giant rock can convey an adequate idea of its magnitude and mysteries.

Its history is enveloped in volumes of legend. The Indians believed the caves were inhabited by destroying demons, and that witches and supreme spirits guarded its summit. They believed that any one venturing into the caves would be destroyed by the demons, and that any one venturing to the top of the mountain would be destroyed by the guarding spirits. The Indians held the great rock mountain in reverential awe, and never dared to profane it by explorations or investigations. They made sacrifice of captives to the gods, spirits and demons of the Enchanted Rock, and this fact gave rise to many romantic legends. Not only the Enchanted Rock, but all the canyons, mountain sides and creek valleys in that entire area have their buried treasure legends and to unearth these bags and bushels of gold, many an hour's hard labor and weeks of secret search have been made. It stands as a monument to the dawn of creation, and smiles on the foolish, feverish efforts of men to dig hidden wealth from recesses where only myth and imagination had planted it.

It is an authenticated fact, however, that in more than one instance the superstition of the Indian has been the salvation of whitemen who, possessing no such superstitions, scaled the mountain to its top. The Indians, confident that the enraged spirits would destroy these desecraters would go on about their business, and when the coast was clear the whitemen would descend and perhaps go about their business of digging for treasure that had never existed, led on in their search by the vodoo spirit of legend with wealth as the promised reward.

There are numberless natural marvels throughout the mountainous portions of the county. But perhaps next in importance to the Enchanted Rock is the Indian cave, near

Lange's Mill in the northwest part of the county. In ancient times this cave was perhaps used as a dwelling place by prehistoric man, and later as a burial ground and place of refuge by the Indians. Its full extent has never been explored, though men have crawled and crept for hours into its deep, dark recesses, and have brought forth nearly every kind of souvenir that Indians would leave about their places of abode or burial grounds.

The Balancing Rock, only a short distance from Fredericksburg is a remarkable freak of gelogical formation. This is an egg shaped granite rock, weighing hundreds of tons, supported by two frail pieces of granite—mere little thin wedges—which in turn rest upon another giant boulder. But the enormus strength of these two little wedges is proven by the vast weight they have sustained throughout the ages. But by what process of creative formation, of wear, decay and erosion did that giant boulder get itself balanced on these two frail supports?

The Mount of the Holy Cross, just on the outskirts of Fredericksburg, is interesting mostly because of the history, whether real or legendary, that surrounds it. It was doubtless a landmark and place of meeting between the Missionaries and the Indians in the Mission Period of Texas. Long before the Germans reached Gillespie county the Mount of the Cross was a noted landmark in the topography of Texas. On its summit stood a great wooden cross, roughly hewn out of native timber, and here the Indians and missionaries are reputed to have held frequent council. In later years the wooden cross has been replaced by a great concrete cross, visible from a long distance on a clear day. The present cross is arranged with electric lights, which are lighted on big festival and other special occasions. When lighted the cross is a beautiful sight, and can be seen for many miles. Present day science can send its brilliant rays for miles across the country, and make as bright as day the top of the mountain where not so many years ago the fathers and the Indians could hold council only by the glare of the signal fire or the light of the moon.

A Pioneer Irrigation Project.

Here is the brief story of what was certainly one of the first attempts at irrigation in Texas. In April, 1861, diverse citizens appeared before the commissioners court and complained that Gerhard Rohrig, H. Kothmann and Heinrich Stiehl "did, in the years 1860 and 1861, irrigate their land with the waters of Baron's Creek, taking all of the water out of said creek, and not only depriving the complainants of said water, but doing other damage in that such use of the water by said defendants is injurious to the health of the neighborhood." In response to this complaint the commissioners ordered a full investigation, and set May 6 as date for final hearing. But the date had to be continued as "high waters prevented the attendance of A. Siemering, attorney for complainants." On July 3 Siemering appeared and announced that the case would be dropped in accordance with agreement reached by all parties. But on July 21 Adam Reiger and others came before the court and made complaint, requesting that the defendants be prevented using the waters of Baron's creek for irrigating their lands. On August 2 the court heard both sides to the controversy and "ordered and decreed that the defendants cease to use the waters of Baron's creek for irrigation purposes," and directed the constable to see to it that the decree of the court was enforced.

And They Didn't Incorporate in 1868.

Here is a historical extract from the commissioners court minutes of November 9, 1868. (It was then called the police court): "Court convened to investigate contests concerning an election on the 20th day of October, 1868, in the matter of incorporating the town of Fredericksburg. The court, deducting the illegal votes illegally polled, found the result in favor of non-incorporation, and gave decision accordingly." Some ten or twelve years ago an election was held to vote on incorporation, but the proposition was defeated. In the fall of 1924 another election was held and the proposition was defeated by approximately three to one, and as this is written, and perhaps for a good many years after it is printed, Fredericksburg can boast of being the biggest unincorporated town in Texas, if not in the United States.

First Wheat, Cotton and Gin.

The first wheat crop was raised in Gillespie county in 1849. Perhaps in the late summer of early fall of 1848 a Mr. Nebig picked up a few handfuls of wheat at Indianola, to which place he had doubtless gone on a freighting trip. This wheat he brought to Fredericksburg and it was later sowed in rows. It was gathered by hand, for every grain was valuable, and was threshed with a stick. One bushel was ground in the old Mormon grist mill, and this was perhaps the first flour bread eaten in Fredericksburg. This information is obtained from an old letter, preserved by Mr. I. G. Wehmeyer, this letter having been written by Peter Schandua, Sr., in 1850. Mr. Schandua also states in his letter that Theodore Specht received specimens of wheat and rye from the agricultural department, but the letter fails to state what Mr. Specht did with these specimens. Mr. Schandua had kept a great deal of valuable data, but one day he decided to burn "a lot of old rubbish." The stuff he destroyed would be of great historic value today.

There is no record as to when the first cotton was raised in the county. Sometime before the war Frederich Lochte built a gin in the south part of Fredericksburg. It was a very crude, one-stand affair, and was entirely homemade. The cotton was carried from the gin stand to the bale packer, into which it was poured and then tramped down. After two or three heavy men had tramped on and packed the cotton as tight as possible they would take hold of a pole lever, march around the bale packer, and a big wooden screw from the bottom did the pressing. The first big cotton crop planted in Gillespie county was by John M. Hunter. This crop was on what is now the Joachim Hohn place. There is no record as to the number of acres planted by Hunter, but the gin books show that eighteen bales were ginned from this patch. During the same year five more bales were raised by other parties in the county. Hunter died before his crop was gathered, but before planting it he had Captain E. Krauskopf agree to put in a gin, the Lochte gin havig been long since abandoned. This second gin stood where Oscar Krauskopf's residence now stands, and like the Lochte gin, was a very crude affair. At first

Krauskopf had a horse or man power gin, but the second year he bought a boiler and engine from the government, this boiler and engine having been installed in a government saw mill at San Angelo. What kind of timber the government found to saw in that country history fails to disclose.

Krauskopf hauled his boiler and engine to Fredericksburg, but one season was enough to disgust him with the undertaking and he sold out. It is not known what finally went with the outfit.

CHAPTER VII.

FROM THE OLD COUNTY RECORDS.

County Organized—Court Houses Built.

Gillespie county was created out of Bexar county by an act of the legislature. The county was organized by vote of the citizens and the first officers elected in the summer of 1848. This was more than two years after the arrival of the first colonists. Prior to the creation and organization of Gillespie Fredericksburg was in Bexar county. When Gillespie county was organized it covered much more territory than it does at the present. Its boundaries were changed when in later years new counties were created and given parts of Gillespie, Mason county in particular, getting a big slice of Gillespie county. As late as 1876 Kimble county was attached to Gillespie for judicial purposes. Gillespie county was named in honor of Captain Gillespie, a Mexican war hero.

What is called the old court house, a two-story rock house, was built by Jacob Arhelger in 1855, at a cost of $2,200. This building now has three rooms downstairs and a large room up stairs. The upper room was the court room, and one of the lower rooms was added some twenty-five years ago. In this old court room many of the most important civil and criminal cases in the history of the country have been tried. In its day this old building has faithfully served in many essential matters. It has been court house, school house and post office and doubtless in its early days served occasionally as opera house, otherwise it wouldn't be in line with the history of other pioneer court houses.

The present court house was completed in November, 1882, at a total cost, including furniture, of approximately $27,000. It would probably cost $75,000 if built today.

The most sensational incident in connection with the history of the present court house was the attempted assassination of county judge Wm. Wahrmund by a school teacher. This occurred Nov. 24, 1885. The teacher who was mentally unbalanced, became incensed over a trival matter in connection with the approval of a voucher. Judge Wahrmund was in his office when the teacher appeared and fired two or three shots at him, all of which missed the judge. The county judge at that time occupied the office used at present by the tax collector. The assailant rushed to his room and was followed immediately by the sheriff. The prisoner was returned to the court house, and died there a few minutes later. He had taken a deadly poison, either before leaving the court house and following the shooting, or as soon as he reached his room, which was only a short distance from the court house.

They had Lots of Trouble with the Old Jail.

But they had some history making experiences in the matter of building jails. For the first four years they got along without a jail, but in 1852 they built a stone jail with thick walls, this building being 14x14 feet. But that jail proved too small to take care of the transient business, for every now and then some tough would blow in and shoot up the town. The new jail was 14x18 feet. The contract was let to a local stonemason and a local blacksmith, and the total cost was $413, payable within two years. It was strictly a homemade affair, built on the installment plan.

But business kept increasing, and in January, 1859, they contracted with Ludwig Schmidt to build a jail 18x30 feet, with thick stone walls, four rooms above and cellar beneath. Three months later the county had a new jail, at a cost of $900.

But some tough was eternally getting out of it, so something had to be done. They decided to put in a steel cage, but had to abandon that idea; first, because the cost was prohibitive; and second, because the cage was bigger than the jail.

So they decided to borrow $2000 and build a new jail, this being in the spring of 1871. The clerk advertised, but money lenders didn't respond, so the commissioners decided to use part of the public school fund, "to be paid back as soon as possible." The contract was finally let and then the "fun begun." They got into a lawsuit and had all kinds of trouble, and finally decided to settle the matter by a special election, "the polls to be kept open for a week." The election went all right, but the money couldn't be raised. In the meantime the district judge and every grandjury was getting after the commissioners about that old jail. Finally, in August, 1874, they decided to build the jail or "bust." The contract was awarded to Louis Doebler for $1645, and four months later the jail was completed. But the jail was to have more strenuous and tragic history. In the latter part of November, 1884, it burned, and in it burned Bill Allison. The supposition is that Allison tried to burn his way out of prison, and that the fire got beyond his control.

Nov. 17, 1884, Wm. Allison, Jack Beam, Wesley Collier and Jim Fannigan, or Flannigan, were indicted for killing J. W. Braeutigam. This case attracted considerable attention throughout the country. There were no witnesses to Braeutigam's side of the killing. Braeutigam had a small store and sold beer, his place of business being at the old Fort Martin Scott grounds. Beam was the only man known to have made any statement in regard to the killing. According to his story the four men went to Braeutigam's place, all four of them got drunk, and some of them got very boisterous. Braeutigam ordered them to leave and all of them except Fannigan went. Then Fannigan and Braeutigam got into a row and the killing resulted. The general presumption has been that the motive was robbery and murder. The murderers made their escape and rangers and peace officers were put on the case. Collier, Beam and Allison were captured. Fire destroyed the jail while Allison was confined therein and he was burned to death. Collier's case was dismissed as there seemed to be insufficient evidence that he participated in the killing or was instrumental in causing the trouble. Beam was sent to the penitentiary for a short term, but Fannigan, the man who actually did the killing according to Beam's statement and the defense of Collier, made his escape. It was reported that he was later killed somewhere in the northwest, but this report was never verified. Braeutigam had many friends in Gillespie county and other parts of the state, and was known as a peaceable citizen.

The present jail was completed in December, 1885, at a total cost of $9446.

Records Burned—A Political Row—Historic Gems.

Practically all the public records of Gillespie county covering the first two years of its organic existence were destroyed by fire. The records as they now exist begin with date of July 15, 1850. There is nothing in these records showing just when the first records were destroyed, but from such reference as these records do make of destroyed books and documents, it appears that the first records must have been destroyed sometime between the 1st of January and the 15th of July, 1850. The fire was a tragedy then and has a double significance as a tragedy at present. What may be termed the old records consists of three books, and cover the period from July 15, 1850, to June, 1880. The first and third books are in excellent condition, but the second book, being of a much cheaper binding and make is in bad shape. All of them are small books, of about the same size and material of an ordinary ledger commonly used by merchants of today. They contain approximately 300 pages each. There is perhaps not a neater or more correctly kept set of old records in existence. Of course they do not compare with the record keeping system at present, but they do surpass the records kept by other counties during the same period. There is lots of history in these old records, and abundance of material for comparison and reflection. The first thing that looms up in these old records is what appears to have been a redhot campaign.

They had a general county election in August, 1850, and immediately following the election the court had its hands full of contests. The court ordered a special election to settle the matter. But the special election didn't settle it. In fact, the special election seems to have made matters worse; whereupon the court declined to declare the result of this special election and ordered another special election.

The second special election seems to have gone to suit the court.

In those days they would keep the polls open for several days at a time, and pull off an election whenever it suited them to do so. By keeping the polls open for several days every one was given an opportunity to vote at his own convenience. Legend also says that maybe a fellow would vote, and a day or two later change his mind and come back and vote different. Those old timers had a genuine democracy of their own, and they didn't substitute formalities and technicalities for principle. Everything had to be on the square, and they held that a man had a perfect right to vote as he pleased and change his mind when he got ready. They didn't think it was necessary for a man to quit his business and come to town just to vote on a particular day and between certain hours. And when you come to think about it there was some mighty sound sense and practical democracy in their methods of holding elections. In all of its long history only one county officer, a sheriff and tax collector of many years ago, has defaulted, his defalcation amounting to about fourteen hundred dollars. So they must have had pretty clean politics and clean men all along.

On March 24, 1851, John Leyendecker submitted a report covering his two years term as county treasurer. The report showed that during the two years from 1848 to 1850 he had paid 21 accounts, totaling $445.80. The biggest item for the two years was the salary of the chief justice, amounting to $200, or $100 per year. The sheriff and the county clerk received the next princely sums. They each got $50 per year. For his two years services the treasurer got 8 per cent amounting in all to $35.66. On August 12, 1851, Daniel Weiershauser submitted his report as treasurer showing that covering a period of twelve months he had paid out for officers' salaries and for all other purposes a total of $199.15, and that during the same period he had received from all sources a total of $238.25, out of which he had deducted his commission, leaving a cash balance in the treasury of $27.20. Weiershauser's salary for the entire year amounted to $11.91.

At the January term of court, 1852, Fritz Pape presented an account for $3.00 due for services rendered as deputy sheriff in 1849, and the account was paid three years after the services had been rendered, and this was doubtless just as soon as the county was financially able to pay it.

In 1856 F. Vander Stucken presented an account for $6.50 for "iron hobbles or handcuffs." These hobbles were doubtless shackels to be used on the legs of bad prisoners, and must have been considerably in demand in those days of bad men and poor jail facilities, for during a period of three years the county bought about three dozen pair.

In 1856 the commissioners received a kick from John Kleck. Kleck's bill amounted to $25, for which amount he had received an order three years prior thereto. He had been paid $5.00, and he wanted the balance of it. The matter was satisfactorily compromised by paying Kleck $10 cash in full settlement. Another party had done $25.00 worth of work on the jail. He owed the county $30 for a fine and the court settled in full with him, by which settlement the offender got $30 instead of $25 for his work. Many years later a mere boy was sentenced to jail for failure to pay a fine, assessed against him for a minor offense. This vexed the sheriff greatly, for the boy was a harmless kind of a chap. The result was that the boy was "put in jail," but the sheriff left the door open.

In August, 1858, the court paid Peter Itz $25 for making coffin for one Tom McAdams who had committed suicide on the premises of Itz. The court held that Itz's bill was very reasonable, considering the fact that he had had much worry and trouble with the decedent.

In November of the same year the sheriff of Bexar county presented the court with a bill for $7.00 for "keeping and releasing" two prisoners from jail. The court held that in view of the fact that said sheriff had allowed the prisoners to get away his bill was exorbitant; so they paid him only $3.00.

The next term of court got extravagant and instructed the sheriff to hire a janitor, and set apart $1.00 per month to cover said expense, but the next term of court they repented of their extravagant action and decided to not hire a janitor.

In the matter of a transient pauper a druggist presented a bill for $51.30, the doctor's bill was $38.25, and the party who boarded the pauper presented a bill for $48.00. The court allowed $15 for medicine, $10 for doctor's bill, and

$10.00 for board, and then took a rap at the druggist, the doctor and the boarding house man. They also unreservedly declined to pay a $10.00 whiskey bill for another pauper, the court giving as a reason that the amount of whiskey furnished was far in excess of all reasonable requirements, and served notice that hereafter persons furnishing whiskey to paupers must first see the court about it.

In November, 1874, the court paid Charles Basse $10.00 "for burying Waldrip in 1867, said account having been transferred to Basse by F. Kiehndeutsch." The burying of Waldrip was one of the most meritorious achievements of the county, but just why they delayed paying the bill for seven years the records fail to disclose.

About this time a law was passed requiring all butchers to make report of marks and brands of all cattle slaughtered by them during certain months throughout the year. H. Henke was the first butcher to make such report to the county. Two of his sons, Henry and August, have a butcher shop in Kerrville; another son, Richard, has a butcher shop in Fredericksburg, in which a fourth son, Hugo, is employed. Two of his grandsons, Louis C. and Walter R. Henke, have a butcher shop in Fredericksburg.

In July, 1861, the commissioners appointed a committee to visit different parts of the county and ascertain number and amount of arms and ammunition in hands of persons other than members of volunteer companies, in order that such report could be made to state authorities. The committee found a few old antiquated guns and about the same number of old worthless pisols, but no ammunition. About the same time the chief justice was authorized to issue scrip notes to the amount of $300 same to be in 1200 notes of 25c each.

In November, 1863, the county was advised that the state could provide 218 pairs of cotton cards at $10.00 per pair. In July, 1864, the court sent Matthias Schmidt to Austin to get 72 pairs of cards, but he failed to get any, the supply having been exhausted. But they got the cards later and in November, 1864, the court ordered that 72 pairs of cards be distributed among families of indigent soldiers, and the remainder be sold for $2.50 per pair.

In February, 1872, the sheriff came into court and reported that a horse belonging to one Goff had got away. Goff had been committed to jail for a criminal offense, and had turned the horse over to the sheriff as security for a fine Goff owed amounting to $25.00, and the sheriff had turned the horse out where he could get some nice green grass and grow fat, and about that time Goff broke out of jail, and there was a well defined suspicion as to what had become of the horse. The court released the sheriff from all liability in the matter.

In September, 1876, came James Kiechler and presented a bill of $281.85 for transcribing field notes of land in Gillespie county in 1859, with interest on said amount. But the court was of the opinion that Kiechler need not have waited 17 years to get his money, so they allowed him interest at eight per cent for three years and paid the account.

In November, 1876, C. C. Callan tendered his resignation as county attorney, and here is what the minutes say: "He saying that such action was necessary in justice to himself and his creditors, whom, he further says, are very numerous." Resignation was accepted.

In October, 1878, G. Seiter presented an account of $3.00 for blacksmithing and was paid "in old iron and $1.00 in U. S. currency."

First land and town lots sold in county for taxes in August, 1873. Nearly 20,000 acres was sold for $276.95. Practically all of the land belonged to non-residents and the amount it sold for represented the taxes and court costs.

Nov. 12, 1853, on application of the Fredericksburg Hook and Ladder company, it was ordered, "that said company be permitted to build an open shed between the old court house and jail, as a shed and a place to keep tools and apparatus."

In June, 1888, J. T. Estill presented an application praying that D. E. Moore and John Freeman, sureties for H. C. Dalton in the sum of $200 be released from such obligation. At the March, 1888, term of district court Dalton had failed to appear and answer to an indictment for assault with intent to murder. In the meantime Dalton had killed Wm. Moore, a brother of D. E. Moore, and had left the country.

In view of the fact that Dalton had skipped out for the murder and not for the assault charge, the court reduced the bond
liability to $75. Dalton was later captured and sentenced to
life imprisonment.

In February, 1902, the commissioners ordered a local
option election for the Harper precinct, and designated Klein
Branch School House as the place for holding the election.
The election was held March 11, and resulted in 44 votes
for prohibition and 9 votes against it.

At the same term of court in February, 1902, the Kerrville Telephone Co. was given a permit to erect its lines in
Fredericksburg and in Gillespie county. The Willow City
Telephone Company seems to have been given a county
permit in 1893. The Fredericksburg Electric Light Co.
received its permit in 1903.

Willow City voted on local option June 12, 1917; result,
23 votes for prohibition; 15 against. And Harper and Willow
City were the only two local option precincts in the county
prior to the Volstead act. In voting on the prohibition
amendment in 1887 the vote of the county was: 59 votes for
amendment, 1186 against it. Harper and Willow city cast
8 more votes for local option than were cast for the prohibition amendment by the whole county. And there was
very little change in the vote of the county at any of the
prohibition amendment elections held after 1887. The
records show that the voters of Gillespie county have voted
overwhelmingly against practically every constitutional
amendment of any character. Only two or three exceptions,
and the vote on amendments has generally been heavy.

Court Order Demolishing the Old Coffee Mill.

June 14, 1897. "A petition was presented to the court
signed by more than ninety residents of the town of Fredericksburg and Gillespie county generally that the remains
of the round church in the center of San Saba street and San
Antonio and Mason public roads may be removed. Said
petition having been fairly considered and it being evident
that said church building has long since been abandoned by
all the religious church communities, and ever since being so
shamefully desecrated by affording an offensive herding
ground for cattle and horses contaminating the same, and

being a disgaceful sight to the public, besides it appearing from an examination that the sleepers and other parts have rotted and lost cohesion, rendering it unsafe and dangerous to enter same. And there being no protest against such action, though full notice had been given, the court decreed that said structure be demolished and removed in order that the San Antonio and Mason road, in which it is now an obstruction, may be straightened. It is further ordered that notice hereof be given by posting for twenty days in three places in Fredericksburg inviting parties who will undertake to remove said building, and for what price, the material to be counted in, except foundation rocks. The material and debris to remove within twenty days after commencing work of demolishing." And thus passed the Vereins-Kirche, "the Old Coffee Mill," the Alamo of Fredericksburg.

One other item is of sufficient interest and importance to justify another reference to the old records. Perhaps no county in the United States, population considered, has spent more money taking care of indigent and unfortunate persons than has Gillespie. So long as it was taking care of deserving persons the court didn't complain, but professional bums and toughs learning of Gillespie county's liberality, made a habit of coming to Fredericksburg, and getting on the charity list. The county had poor jail facilities, and toughs also took advantage of this fact. Finally, many years ago, the court got enough of such foolishness, and put on a real clean up campaign. As usual they went about it in a practical and effective way. They offered the sheriff a reward of five hundred dollars to chase all "the bums, deadbeats and vagabonds out of the county." But the records fail to disclose whether the sheriff got the reward.

CHAPTER VIII.

HISTORIC OLD MILLS

Lange's Mill.

Only a short distance from the picturesque little town of Doss, in the northwest corner of Gillespie county, is Lange's Mill. This old structure, standing on the west bank of Threadgill creek, embowered among stately trees and near where a spring fed mountain rivulet empties into Threadgill, occupies a most conspicuous position in the history of this county, and deserves an equally conspicuous position as a landmark in the history of Texas.

The property was first owned by Doss Bros. In 1849 these men built a house near where a fine spring breaks from the hill side. Below this house they built a dam and below this dam they built a rude corn or grist mill. The building near the spring was used as a distillery and most of the products ground in the old mill was mash for the distillery. The first dam was not built until 1852, at which time Doss Bros. also put in a saw mill, a very crude affair compared with present day improvements, but a saw mill that rendered great service in its day. In 1854 the old saw mill was washed away and the old grist mill was almost destroyed by the worst flood in the history of that section. In the meantime the builders had erected a fine home on a high hill just south of the big spring and the old distillery. This home was destroyed by fire some time prior to 1859, but the exact date is not known. In 1859 Wm. F. Lange acquired ownership of the property, and made several improvements, tearing away the old distillery, and making additions and improvements to the old mill. In 1862 he made it both a flour and corn mill. The product of this old mill was famed throughout the surrounding country, and in order to take care of the increased demand the dam was built higher in order to increase the power. At that time an overshot wheel was used. The new trouble was too much power and the shaft of the overshot was broken. Then a turbine was installed. This called for more power, to obtain which the dam was again rebuilt. A few hours later this dam broke. Julius Lange and his brother were bathing in the reservoir, and the dam broke only a few seconds after they climbed onto the bank on the north side of the big pond. The breaking of this reservoir dam gives some idea of the mighty volume of water that flowed into the pond from the main spring and from the smaller springs along the ravine supplying the reservoir. This was a calamity not only to the mill owner but to the country then dependent upon the mill for breadstuff. And again the old mill was almost destroyed by the avalanche of water that surged against it when the dam broke. With rugged determination Lange set about to rebuild it. He started on this dam in 1872 and completed it in 1875. It is one of the most remarkable pieces of workmanship in the country, and was built to serve through centuries. The present dam is perhaps thirty feet high, about forty feet wide at the top and is several times that wide at the bottom. Above this dam is a deep pool of crystal water, fed by the nearby mountain springs that constantly flow into it. This pool is stocked with fish, and here flocks of geese and ducks swim and sport and gracefully float, oblivious to the history that has been made by human genius in its sacrifices and struggles to provide them with this ideal play place. And the water still flows down the old mill race, but it no longer gives power to an important industrial institution. Hydraulic rams now pump water to different parts of the premises, but the old mill and the old race and spillway merely stand as monuments to pioneer struggles and achievements and as masterpieces of masonry.

Three years after the present dam was completed Wm. F. Lange died. Julius Lange then took charge of the property and operated it until 1888. For many years after the present dam was built the old mill did a flourishing business. Then it came in competition with the products of roller mills. No roller mill ever made flour equal to that of the old burr mills, but they produced in greater volume, had ample financial support, and the burr mill was doomed. The Lange Mill was one of the last of the old burr mills to quit business in Texas, and it is perhaps the only one of these old mills now standing in a perfect state of preservation, with practically all of its machinery just as it stood the last hour it ground grain. Mrs. Wm. F. Lange died in 1910, and Julius Lange acquired and still owns the property, the ranch consisting of about 1000 acres.

On the side of the steep hill overlooking the old mill and the reservoir is the comfortable home occupied by Julius Lange and his wife. Part of this old house was built in the days when Indian raids were common moonlight night occurrences. Julius Lange and his brother had many narrow escapes and thrilling adventures with these marauding Indians. Near the original home is a nice and substantial two story residence, built of stone quarried from the nearby mountains. This house was built by Wm. Lange and his sons years ago and was originally intended as a stable, but was later converted into a dwelling.

About the whole place there is a most unusual blending of history, romance, beauty and rural contentment. It represents the struggles, the achievements, the sore disappointments and the unyielding determination of hardy pioneers, plus the achievements of highly skilled geniuses and workmen. It is now a beauty spot of productive utility, environed by a highly civilized and progressive community.

The Indian cave near this old mill is mentioned in the article on places of scenic and historic importance.

Guenther's Old Mill on Live Oak Creek.

Mills formed a big part of the early day industrial history of Gillespie county. As a general thing these mills were combination corn mills, feed mills and saw mills. This was a matter of practical economy. While the power might not be sufficient to operate the corn and grist mill and the saw mill at the same time, it was sufficient to operate the one when the other was idle. In this way one of the mills could be kept in operation with the same power. This was true of the old Mormon mill, of the Lange mill when it was first put in, and it was true of the Guenther mill on Live Oak during its entire period of operation in Gillespie county. The following historic sketch of this old mill is contained in a letter from Mr. Erhard Guenther, president of the Pioneer

Mills, of San Antonio, to Mr. Robert Blum, of Fredericksburg:
"The old Live Oak creek mill in Gillespie county was
really the cradle of the Pioneer Mill, now located in San
Antonio.

"At the time, in 1851, when my father built the mill in
Gillespie county, on Live Oak creek, it was customary for
millers to look for a location on some creek or river where
there was sufficient water power to run the mill, as engines,
electricity and steam turbines had not been sufficiently developed to furnish power profitably.

"Live Oak creek, as well as many other creeks in West
Texas at that time, had a great deal more flow than the same
streams now have. At that time they were beautiful streams
with flowing water and deep clear pools, the banks lined
with large trees. But since the cultivation of the fields
above and in the watersheds of these streams, many of them
have been filled, or partially filled, with sand carried from
the fields, so that a great deal of the water is now absorbed
by the sand and gravel, or disappears and runs underground,
thereby diminishing the general flow.

"In order to get a sufficient fall for the Live Oak creek
mill a dam had to be built away up the creek, on the old F.
Pape farm, and a canal, or millrace, was dug on the west
bank to carry water to the mill.

"At that time there was a general rainy season. Almost
every afternoon, for months, heavy, black, thunder clouds
would gather and form into rain, and there were almost
daily rises or floods in the creeks as well as in the Pedernales
river below. These rains and these small floods came with
such regularity that when the clouds would bank up the
farmers would rush their milch cows back across the creek
before the expected rise of the water.

"In those days the rains filled the mill ponds with
water, but the ponds have been filled with sand, and thus
all of the storage reservoirs have been destroyed and rendered
useless by having been filled with sand and gravel instead of
water.

"The water wheel was a large wooden structure and
furnished enough power for a corn mill, grist mill and a
saw mill.

"When the dry season began to set in the power diminished and was not sufficient for C. H. Guenther's idea of energy, so he sold the mill and the adjacent farm land to his father-in-law, Mr. F. Pape, and found his way to San Antonio, where he located at the present site of the Pioneer Flour Mills, on the San Antonio river, which was considered a very formidable and steady stream. But even the San Antonio river, with all of its water, could not keep pace with the growth of the Pioneer Mills, so auxiliary steam engines had to be installed, and now their latest power consists of a 1000 horse power steam turbine that revolves 3600 revolutions per minute, and is connected with a generator that furnishes the Pioneer Flour Mills with power.

"By simply throwing a switch either one of their large flour mills are thrown into operation. Another switch, from the same generator, throws all the cleaning, separating, elevating and conveying machinery in their twenty-story fire proof, concrete and steel elevator into operation."

And here you have the forceful story of an old Gillespie county mill's wonderful, progressive evolution.

Conrad Bierschwale Had Trouble with His Mill.

One of the historic relics near Fredericksburg is the remains of the old Bierschwale mill dam. In January, 1853, Conrad Bierschwale was given permission to build a corn, flour and grist mill near Baron's creek, conditioned that he would not build a dam. Later Bierschwale discovered that he had to have a dam to provide water power for his mill. But in July, 1854, eleven citizens appeared before the court and protested against building the dam, contending that the building of the dam would cause sickness and would interfere with certain springs from which the complainants and other citizens obtained their drinking water, "and the court instructed the sheriff to notify Bierschwale to not build the dam." Later Bierschwale's attorney appeared before the court and asked permission to build a mill race across the creek, but still later Bierschwale came into court stating that he could not build the mill race, but in view of the fact that complaint had been made that the construction of the dam would cause overflow that would destroy certain valuable springs, he would gladly compromise the matter by drilling a well to take the place of the springs. Another hearing was set, and then came numerous citizens citing the fact "that a well which said Bierschwale proposed to dig would not be equivalent to the springs, and that said dam being on the south side of town would cause much sickness and would be a great damage and detriment to the town," whereupon the commissioners refused to give Bierschwale permission to build the dam. They finally got into a lawsuit about it. How it ended the records fail to disclose, and no one living knows. Parts of the old ditch is the only remaining trace of this old mill. It was a typical old time burr mill, operated entirely by water power, and probably went out of business before the war, or soon thereafter. With the exception of the old Mormon mill, the Lange mill and the Guenther mill this was the first mill in Gillespie county.

The Henke, Maier and Vander Stucken Mills.

Three other mills have played their parts in the history of Gillespie county, these being the Henke mill, the Maier mill, and the Reliance mill.

The Reliance mill was established by Frank Vander Stucken in 1862. It was a burr mill with steam power, with the old time cylinder boiler. About 1867 Frank Vander Stucken returned to Europe, and his brother, Felix, became the owner, and some time later his son Alfred became associated in the ownership and management. In 1889 the mill was converted into a roller mill, and considerable improvements made to the building. Perhaps in 1911 or 1912 it was closed and remained idle for two or three years, when it was sold to Ernst Wilke, and he operated it until some two years ago when it was sold to the present owner, Albert Moellendorf. Henry Cordes was the first engineer for this mill, and was connected with it as engineer for a total period of more than twenty-five years. R. L. Rodman, the present miller, has also been connected with this concern for more than twenty years.

What is known as the Old Henke Mill, has a rather tragic history. This mill, still standing on the bank of Barons creek, was built perhaps about 1868, by a joint stock company composed of farmers. Some years later it got into

financial troubles and passed into other hands. Henry
Henke finally had to pay some notes which he had signed as
surety, and took the mill over to satisfy his claim. The
mill passed into Henke's hands probably in about 1876.
Sometime after Henke got the mill the boiler exploded,
killing the fireman and injuring a few others. Among the
seriously injured was Henry Henke, Jr. As a result of
severe scalds he was confined to his bed for several months.
After the explosion a new boiler was put in and the mill was
operated until about 1886, when it was closed down forever.
It was an old time burr mill, and rather than go to the great
expense of equipping it as a roller mill, Mr. Henke closed it.

Another early day steam power mill in Gillespie county
was put in by Edward Maier. This old mill stood where the
Zimmermann hotel now stands. In 1874 Maier also put in
a cotton gin, this gin being on the back part of the lot now
occupied by Gus. Malchow's Second Hand Store. In 1884
a disaster befell the gin. The boiler exploded. John Becker
was instantly killed, Edward Maier received injuries from
which he died a few hours later, and another man was
seriously scalded, but recovered within a few weeks. The
force of this explosion was the most terrific shaking up the
town ever received, and the wonder is that the damage was
not far greater than it was. After the destruction of the gin
and the death of Edward Maier, Richard Maier and August
Sembritzky continued to operate the mill until about 1884,
when it was closed. The gin never was rebuilt.

CHAPTER XIX.

SKETCHES OF LESS ANCIENT DAYS.

Dietrich Rode and Cherry Spring Church.

A short account of this noted church is given in Rev. Bracher's history of Lutheranism in Gillespie County. Dietrich Rode, founder of this church, was a noted character in the early day history of the county. He was a deeply religious, austere man, and would at present be deemed severe in his enforcement of discipline and adherence. He was frugal, practical and farsighted in business matters. Any one visiting his home would be hospitably entertained and liberally exhorted. He had a custom of providing free dinners on certain occasions, to which the entire community was invited, it being in a measure compulsory for his own members to attend these dinners. These meals, and all others, for that matter, would be preceded by prayer. After the meal he would read the bible, then have singing of religious songs, followed by a closing prayer. He educated, as best the conditions of the times would afford, many children, for which he made no charge, except that the pupils attending the school, of which he was teacher, must work when not in school. He didn't believe in sparing the rod and spoiling the child, and he abhorred extravagance and idleness.

In the long ago John Stehling and his brothers, Christian, George and Adam, did a regular freighting business from Austin and San Antonio to different towns and communities in this section of the country. They hauled most of the lumber for Rode's buildings at Cherry Spring, this lumber being hauled from Austin, nearly 100 miles. It took an average of twelve days to make the round trip, the time required depending on conditions of the roads. At first Rode paid them $10.00 per thousand feet for hauling, but he finally raised the price to $12.00 per thousand. Twenty-five hundred feet of lumber, condition of roads in those days considered, was a big load. They could make a round trip every twelve days. John Stehling figures that they could

clear about six-bits a day or nine dollars per trip. But
Stehling says he could have gotten rich at it if he had only
used good business judgement. Land was then 25c an acre
and he could have paid for three acres of land with each
day's earnings. The poorest land he could have bought
would now be worth $15.00 per acre, and by taking his own
choice he could have bought land that would now be worth
$100 per acre. In later years he paid considerable more
than 25c an acre for the land he now owns.

Rode was not only teacher, philanthropist, financier and
preacher, but he was a missionary, and made frequent visits
to different localities in that, as then, thinly settled country,
and it is said that he would accept no kind of compensation
for his services, but that he usually treated the community
he visited to a feast and paid the bill himself.

Dietrich Rode had three brothers, Fritz, Charles and
Joachim. Joachim was an eccentric bachelor and lived the
life of a hermit on the ten acre tract awarded him by the
German Emigration Co., and would have nothing to do with
his other relatives. Fritz and Charles were among the substantial farmers and citizens of the county.

A Remarkable Handmade Book.

No town or county in the United States could supply a
museum with a greater quantity of rare, interesting and
instructive material than could Fredericksburg and Gillespie county. Old handmade furniture of different kinds and
of the best workmanship and most artistic finish; old guns,
homemade spinning wheels and cloth making looms; homemade wagons, war time homemade gun caps and dozens of
other things would "glowingly adorn a tale and point a
moral." Among the most remarkable of these souvenirs
would be a book in two volumes, the work of James Larson.

Larson was born in Fredericksberg, Denmark, in 1837,
and died in Fredericksburg, Texas, April 21, 1919. He came
to the United States in 1850. The first volume of the book,
79 pages, deals with his experiences in the great forest of
northern Wisconsin from 1854 to 1859. The second volume
deals with his experiences as a soldier for a period of seven
years, four of these years being spent in the hardest cam-

paigns of the Union forces, Mr. Larson holding the rank of
1st sergeant Co. H 4th U. S. cavalry when the war ended.
Larson had only the advantages of a common school education, but by hard application he became a finished scholar.
Both volumes are written in English, the composition excellent and the style forceful. It is a work from which a great
novel could be produced. In fact, it is a great historical
novel within itself. Larson never expressed to any one his
intention to have the book published and all indications are
that he merely put in spare time on the work and left a most
unusual heirloom to his family. Aside from the interesting
manner in which Larson handled his subjects the books are
masterpieces. Both volumes are hand bound, and no book-
bindery could do better work. The matter is all single
spaced, written on both sides of each sheet, the margins on
every sheet are perfect and exactly the same throughout
both volumes. With the exception of chapter pages there
are exactly fifty-six lines on each page of the small volume
and exactly seventy-one lines on every page of the large
volume. There is not an erasure on a single page in either
book. There are in the two volumes 33 hand painted, full
page colored illustrations. These illustrations were made
with pencils, and over most of the illustrations is tissue
covering, nicely pasted down around all edges. These illus-
strations are real works of art, and yet Mr. Larson never had
a lesson in art. He did every bit of the work, writing, binding and illustrating.

Mr. Larson came to Gillespie county in 1870. In 1871
he was married to Miss Susanna Zenner. They had two
daughters. One daughter, Miss Emma, died in Fredericksburg in 1892. The other daughter, Mrs. Robert Blum, now
lives in Fredericksburg. Mr. and Mrs. Larson also raised
two orphan children, Frank Baker, who now lives at Morris
Ranch, and his sister Miss Minnie Baker, who died in San
Antonio some years ago. They also educated Mrs. Willie
Juenke for a teacher. Mrs. Juenke now lives in Tivydale,
Gillespie county.

Mr. Larson farmed in the Cave Creek community for
eleven years. He taught school at Cave Creek for eleven
years, and served as postmaster in Fredericksburg for eleven

years, or from 1903 to 1914. He was for many years a county commissioner and justice of the peace.

He started to work on his books in 1893, and did the last work in 1916.

It is doubtful if there is another similar piece of work in existence.

Oldest County Fair in Texas.

The first county fair held in Texas was held in Fredericksburg in 1881. This fair was held under the auspices of the farmers Verein, on the old Fort Martin Scott army reservation about two miles south of town, this land now owned by Henry Braeutigam. For eight consecutive years county fairs were held there. In 1889 the fair was moved to town and held where the Turner Hall now stands. Two fairs were held at that place. In 1891 the fair association was incorporated as the Gillespie County Fair Association, forty acres of land was purchased from Peter Bonn, and the fair held in that year on the present fair grounds, where it has been held every year since. Some years ago about eighteen acres of the original forty acre tract was sold in lots and small tracts for railroad uses, residence lots and other purposes, the Fair Association having at present about 22 acres of land, all inclosed and well improved.

From 1891 until 1905 the association continued to operate under the name of the Gillespie County Fair Association. In 1905 there was a kind of reorganization and the name was changed to the Gillespie County Fair and Improvement Association. In 1921 there was another reorganization and the name was again changed to the Gillespie County Fair Association, and is now a fixture under that name.

In all there have been forty-four consecutive fairs. The catalogues for the 1924 fair referred to it as the 38th annual fair, this in conformity with the number brought down from former fair catalogues. This is perhaps due to the fact that all fair catalogues date from the fair held in 1886, in which year the fair was in reality made permanent, although prior to 1886 there had been five successful fairs held, but they were not held under what might be termed a permanent organization. If there has been a failure in holding the annual fair since the first one in 1881, there is no record of it, either in book records nor the memory of man.

The records of the first fairs are lost, if any records were really ever kept. Emil Wahrmund and Oscar Krauskopf served as president and secretary of some of the fairs prior to 1891, and Mr. Krauskopf served as secretary at least one time after the fair was moved to its present grounds.

One remarkable thing about the Gillespie County Fair is the number of men who have served for many years in official capacities.

For 1905 and 1906 the officers were: Herry Wahrmund, president; C. H. Nimitz, vice-president; Henry Hirsch, secretary; H. B. Meckel, treasurer.

For 1907, 1908 and 1909 the officers were: Wm. Bierschwale, president; C. H. Nimitz, vice-president; Henry Hirsch, secretry, H. B. Meckel, treasurer.

From 1910 to 1916, both years inclusive, the same officers served with the single exception that Adolf Gold succeeded H. B. Meckel as treasurer in 1910.

For 1917 the officers were:—Wm. Bierschwale, president; C. H. Nimitz, vice-president; Harry Schwarz, Secretary; Adolf Gold, treasurer.

1918:—Henry Hirsch, president; E. H. Riley, vice-president; Harry Schwarz, secretary; Adolf Gold, treasurer.

1919 and 1920:—E. H. Riley, president; F. W. Arhelger, vice-president; Henry Hirsch, secretary; Adolf Gold, treasurer.

1921:—E. H. Riley, president; Adolf Gold, vice-president; F. W. Arhelger, secretary; Henry Hirsch, treasurer.

1922:—Wm. Bierschwale, president; A. F. Moursund, vice-president; Henry Hirsch, secretary and treasurer.

1923:—A. F. Moursund, president; R. L. Kott, vice-president; Wm. Schneider, secretary; Max J. Bierschwale, treasurer.

1924:—Wm. Schneider, president; R. L. Kott, vice-president; J. E. Bell, secretary; Max J. Bierschwale, treasurer.

1925:—Same officers as 1924.

The Hill Country Poultry Association.

The Hill Country Poultry Association, composed of the counties of Gillespie, Mason, Kerr, Blanco and Llano,

holds an annual poultry show in Fredericksburg. This is
one of the leading poultry associations in the state, and its
shows take first rank.

The first show was held in Fredericksburg December
8 and 9, 1922. Willis Lee, of Eckert, Gillespie county, was
elected president and B. L. Enderle, of Fredericksburg, secretary. About 450 birds were exhibited at this show, of
which about 250 were standard bred. While this first show
was not extensive in the number of exhibits it was a success and insured the permanency of the organization.

The second show was held in December, 1923, and 890
birds were exhibited, of which 800 were standard bred. One
important feature of the 1923 show was the organization of
a boys and girls poultry club. At this meeting H. V. Heyland
was elected president, George Moneyhaur, vice-president,
and B .L. Enderle was re-elected secretary.

The second show was held at Fredericksburg December
6, 7 and 8, 1924. While the number of birds exhibited were
not so numerous as at former shows, it was really the most
satisfactory and successful of all the Hill Country poultry
shows. Only standard bred birds were exhibited at the 1924
show. The silver loving cup for the best showing made by
a boys and girls club in the judging contest was won by
Harper club. The association also took up in earnest the work
of organizing egg circles in Gillespie county. The rules to
govern this circle were drawn by Mrs. Christian Mathisen,
and a committee of seven, one member from each community,
was elected to handle the work of this organization. The
officers of the Hill Country Poultry Association elected at
this meeting were: H. V. Heyland, president; George
Moneyhaur, vice-president; B. L. Enderle, secretary.

One of the special, and most important, features, of this
association's work is to educate and induce people to raise
a standard variety of turkeys throughout the territory embraced within the scope of its territory.

But They Finally Got a Railroad.

Every town in Texas has had its experiences in the
matter of railroad promotion propositions, and Fredericksburg is no exception. All told perhaps a hundred promoters

have submitted railroad propositions to Fredericksburg. Finally, in 1888 the town and county tackled a proposition out of which it got around $27,000 worth of experience, but no railroad. The chief promotor of this proposition was W. A. H. Miller, a lawyer of Llano. His proposition was to build a railroad from Fredericksburg Junction, where the present railroad connects with the Fredericksburg & Northern, to Llano and elsewhere by way of Fredericksburg. He got approximately $27,000 out of Fredericksburg, and several thousand out of Llano. Miller went to work in good faith and honestly spent every dollar he received on his impractical project. He graded some twenty miles out of Llano, about twelve miles from Fredericksburg north and about three miles from Fredericksburg south. But he never got any further with his project than these several miles of dump on which no ties or steel was ever placed. Future generations may speculate on what manner of ancient civilization constructed these mysterious and winding mounds of earth, for most of the old dump is still there, grass covered, and is liable to be there for archeologists a thousand years hence to dig into in attempts to fathom the mysteries of some lost civilization.

But long before Miller came, and long after his failure. railroad promotion propositions came thick and fast to Fredericksburg. The Frisco and other roads surveyed proposed routes across the county in different directions.

Finally, perhaps early in 1911, R. A. Love appeared on the scene. The result was that a bonus of $200,000 was raised in Fredericksburg and Gillespie county and in San Antonio, Fredericksburg and Gillespie county raising $150,-000 of the amount. Comfort was also interested and possibly promised a considerable bonus, as it was originally planned to build the road from Fredericksburg to a connection with the San Antonio & Aransas Pass at Comfort. Love started to survey his road from Comfort to Fredericksburg. He hunted all through the mountains for a route, and finally had to wind around, go within eight miles of Kerrville and then down either Bear creek or Meusebach creek to get to Fredericksburg. Love had already experienced considerable trouble in getting a bond company to finance his project, but finally got this trouble, as it seemed, satisfactorily arranged. When the proposed line went within eight miles of Kerrville powerful interests in that town took a hostile hand. The Kerrville interests did not object to Fredericksburg getting a railroad, but they did object to the road coming within eight miles of Kerrville, and owing to the Kerrville interests having heavy stock in the bond company behind the projected Fredericksburg railroad, the Kerrville interests won out. As a result of this complication and the refusal of the bond company to finance the project Love had apparently lost out and went away. A few months later he returned to Fredericksburg, accompanied by a contractor named Foster Crane. Crane gave ample proof that he was financially able to handle the job of building the road. On October 9, 1912, the Gillespie county railroad committee entered into another contract with R. A. Love to construct a railroad from Fredericksburg to a connection with the San Antonio and Aransas Pass at what is now Fredericksburg Junction. The committee making this contract and signing the guarantee was composed of Chas. H. Nimitz, chairman; R. G. Striegler, secretary; August Cameron, treasurer; Oscar Krauskopf, L. F. Kneese, Adolph Lucas, Jacob Weinheimer and John Knopp. (The contract was signed by Jacob Knopp as representative of the John Knopp estate.) A. W. Moursund was the attorney representing the citizens committee. This contract was practically the same as the first contract, Love to get a cash bonus of $200,000 and right-of-way, Gillespie county again putting up $150,000 and San Antonio $50,000. The route was surveyed to Fredericksburg Junction, and the road was incorporated under the name of the San Antonio, Fredericksburg & Northern railroad. Actual construction work was started in December, 1912, and was completed in November, 1913. The contract with Love specified that the bonus was to be paid in monthly installments, no installment to exceed $15,000. The contracts were immediately assigned by Love to Crane, who contracted to build the road and gave bond in the sum of $200,000 for faithful fulfilment of contract. Crane operated the road until June, 1914, when he conveyed it to the San Antonio, Fredericksburg & Northern Railway Co., of which R. A.

Love was president. In October, 1914, the road went into the hands of a receiver, former governor Joseph D. Sayers being appointed master in chancery; M. H. Trice, receiver. The report of the master in chancery made June 16, 1916, showed the total indebtedness of the road to be $228,668.47. Of this amount the receiver recommended that $41,060.21 be not paid, leaving an approved indebtedness of $187,608.26. The principal creditor was the State Bank and Trust Co., of San Antonio. Its bill amounted to $128,000, and added to the $200,000 bonus, represented the amount actually spent in the construction of the road, a total of approximately $328,000, or practically $14,000 per mile, as the road is approximately 24 miles long.

In December, 1917, the road was sold at receiver's sale, the purchase price being about $80,000. The original stockholders were the purchasers and J. L. Brown became president. Under the reorganization following the sale the name of the road was changed to the Fredericksburg & Northern.

Considering the character of country traversed the cost of the road was reasonable. It is built across a mountainous country, passes through a tunnel 910 feet long, the only railroad tunnel in Texas, and crosses a gorge over Block creek on a very long and high trestle, and is in many respects one of the big railroad engineering feats of the entire country. In granting permission to fund its debt, the interstate railroad commission valued the road, together with rolling stock and other property and improvements at $429,966.34.

One unusual feature about this road is the big per cent of the $150,000 bonus that was subscribed by Gillespie county farmers. There is perhaps not another railroad in the United States where such a big part of the bonus money was subscribed and paid by farmers. And every farmer promptly paid every cent he had subscribed.

The present officers of the road are: J. L. Brown, president; H. A. Ries, vice-president and general manager; T. P. Russel, vice-president; O. H. Judkins, secretary; W. W. Collier, treasurer.

And the Railroads Got the Land.

In October, 1879, the commissioners court had a tabulated report prepared showing the railroad lands in Gillespie county, and set apart by the legislature in July, 1879. The report was prepared and showed that there were 223 such tracts of railroad land in the county, the total acreage being 103,575, to be assessed at $1.00 per acre, which was about the tax value limit at that time. The railroads hadn't fought any Indians, endured any mob outrages, nor done one thing to develop or aid in the development, of Gillespie county. The lands were in due time sold to the citizens of Gillespie county for a price much in excess of $1.00 per acre. The lands were given to "railroads" for the purpose of encouraging railroad construction, or at least such was the pretext. Many years later the people of Gillespie county, who had never received a single gift from the state as a reward for what they had done to develop the country, forced by necessity to have a railroad, had to raise a cash bonus of $150,000 to get the road.

An Early Day Publicity Stunt.

In the minutes of the commissioners court, October term, 1878, the following entry appears: "Court considered the petition being circulated for contributions for a statistical report of Gillespie county, presenting the advantages and inducements for immigration, wherein Messrs. Gifford & Winters, editors and proprietors of the Texas Sun, published at Houston, Texas, offer to furnish Gillespie county 1000 copies of said paper for $100, and it appearing to the court that same will probably benefit Gillespie county and Texas generally, it is ordered that the sum of $50.00 be contributed and paid by the county, or so much thereof as may be necessary to make up the sum of $100, same to be paid upon delivery of the 1000 copies." And even in those days the hotair merchant and advertising specialist was abroad in the land with a plan to make everybody rich by the use of printer's ink.

County School Lands Sold.

At a very early date the state awarded Gillespie county its share of land set aside by the legislature for public school

purposes, Gillespie county's allotment being four leagues, or
17,704 acres. In 1877 the commissioners made a deal with H.
R. Bieberstein to survey the land and subdivide it into tracts
of 320 acres each. For his services Bieberstein was to receive
one-tenth of the land amounting to practically 1770 acres. A
few months later Bieberstein asked the court to relieve him
from the contract, he stating that the land was in a wild, arid
country, inhabited by hostile Indians, that there would be
no demand for it in small tracts, and suggesting that it be
sold in a body. The land was described as located in
Young county, but when first sold in 1880 it was described as being located in Scurry county, fully 150 miles
west of the present line of Young county, but in 1873 Young
county covered a territory extending to the line of New
Mexico, more than 250 miles west of its present western
boundary. At that time there were no farms or enclosed
pastures and but very few settlers between Young county
and the line of New Mexico. And Bieberstein was right about
the land being in a wild country, covered with buffalo and
inhabited by hostile Indians, and all people thought it would
take centuries and not a single generation to see it a thickly
populated and highly developed area. The commissioners
generously released Bieberstein from his contract.

In December, 1880, the county contracted to sell the land
to J. S. Daugherty for 75c per acre, one-tenth cash, balance
in ten years at 6 per cent interest per year. Daugherty
evidently got sick of the deal, for he failed to put up the
required amount of money. The commissioners then decided
to fix the price at one dollar per acre and hold the land
until it could be sold for that amount. In January, 1882,
they again contracted a sale at $1.00 acre to T. L. Smith, of
Hall county, Ill., but Smith backed out. Then the commissioners raised the price to $1.25 per acre, "unless P. A.
Booker, who had previously made an offer of $1.00 per acre
wanted it," but Booker didn't want it. In June, 1882,
the land was sold to R. E. Montgomery for $1.25 per acre,
one-tenth, cash, balance ten years at six per cent interest
per year. Montgomery had a hard time meeting his
payments, and on three or four occasions had to get the

county to give him an extension, and at least twice it looked as though the county would have to foreclose its lien, but Montgomery finally got it paid for. But $22,130 plus the interest each year, was an awful load to carry in those days.

CHAPTER X.

OFFICERS—SCHOOLS—REMARKABLE STATISTICS.

County Officers from Organization of County to Present.

It has been practically impossible to get a complete list of all county officers, beginning with the organization of the county. During the first few years changes were constantly taknig place. The offices paid but small salaries, and frequently men elected would not qualify, or would soon resign. This was especially true of sheriffs, surveyors and county attorneys. No attempt has been made to compile the names of surveyors and county attorneys, for at best the list would be incomplete.

Until after the war the system of county government was considerably different to the present system. Instead of a county judge they had a chief justice. From 1866 until 1876 the commissioners court was known as the police court, and was composed of five justices of the peace, the justice of the Fredericksburg precinct presiding, and acting in the capacity of county judge.

The chief justices have been: Wm. Keidel, Lyman Wight, J. J. Kllngelhoefer, Wm. Wahrmund, A. Maier, F. Vander Stucken, Theodore Bucholz, Julius Schuchard, R. Radeleff. In 1876 Wm. Wahrmund was elected county judge, being the first man elected to the office under that title.

The county judges have been: Wm. Wahrmund, 1876 to 1890, in which year he died and H. R. Bieberstein was appointed to fill the term; Henry Wahrmund from the fall of 1890 to February, 1894, at which time he was appointed postmaster and J. T. Estill was appointed to fill out the term, Estill being elected in November, 1894. Then came F. R. Loudon, one term; then Estill, one term; then Loudon for one term; Max Blum, five terms; A. H. Kneese, 1914 to April, 1920, when he resigned to become postmaster, a position he still holds. Hermann Usener appointed to fill out term, re-elected in 1922 and 1924.

Sheriffs: Lewis Martin, Richard Cloudt, F. Oestreich, Charles Gartner, George Freeman, J. M. Hunter, Louis Weiss, Francis Kettner, H. Schulz, Edward Maier, Philip Braubach, Julius Splittgerber, Ernst Schaper, H. P. Garrison, Ferdinand Ohlenberger, Wm. Wittneben, Francis Jung, Sylvester Kleck, Alf. Hunter, F. C. Radeleff; John Walter, fourteen years; J. J. Hagen, 1888 to 1892, when he died in office, and Frank J. Morgan appointed to fill term; George B. Riley, 1892 to 1900; John Klaerner, 1900 to 1910; Hermann Ochs, 1910 to 1918; Alfred Klaerner 1918 to 1920; Alfred Petmecky, 1920 to 1924; Alfred Klaerner again elected in 1924.

County clerks: J. M. Hunter, F. Wrede, Hermann Ochs, ten years; H. Comparet (appointed by governor) H. Bier-schwale, 1870 to 1898; Wm. Bierschwale, 1898 to 1906; Hermann Usener, 1906 to 1920; Albert E. Klett, elected in 1920 and re-elected in 1923 and 1924.

When the county was first organized, and for some years thereafter the district clerk's office was a separate office, then it was consolidated with the county clerk's office, and so remained until 1902, at which time George E. Wright was elected and held the office until 1918, when A. D. Stahl was elected, and holds the office at present.

From the organization of the county until 1871 the tax assessor was also tax collector. In 1871 the sheriff became collector, and so it remained until 1920, at which time August Jung, present collector, was elected.

Tax assessor: R. W. Cecil, A. Erlenmeyer, George Max, Charles Feller; then B. Blum, 27 years; August Cameron, 12 years; Louis Kordzik, 8 years; Charles Schmidt, 4 years; Henry F. Kirchhoff, present collector, elected in 1922.

Treasurer: Daniel Weiershausen, John Leyendecker, Fritz Pape, Conrad Wehmeyer; Bernhard Meckel, 1869 to 1882; Daniel Ludwig, 1882 to 1894; Max Wahrmund, 1894 to 1896; Henry Evers, 1896 to 1902; Samuel Krueger, 1902 to 1908; Henry Evers again, 1908 to 1912; Albert J. Schmidt, 1912 to 1924; Alfred Crenwelge elected 1924.

From the organization of the county until 1868 the following men served as county commissioners: Peter Bickel, John Peter Keller, Fred Kiehne, Peter Schandua, Henry Jordan, John Schmidtzensky, J. N. Mosel, Wm. P. Eldridge, Irwin F. Carter, G. B. Starks, E. Frantzen, H. Hoerster, J. N. Mosel, F. Kneese, F. Vander Stucken, Julius Luckenbach, Stephen Peters, John Leyendecker, Jacob Doering, I. W. Cadwell, F. Fresenius, Wm. Marschall, Wm. Feller, John Metzger, Peter Mosel, John Dietz, Daniel Weiershausen, Christian Althaus, J. F. G. Striegler, Casper Marschall, Charles Koenig, George Goehmann, Theodore Bucholz, F. Lochte. From 1868 to the present time the commissioners have been:

1868 to 1870:—F. Vander Stucken, F. Welgehausen, Conrad Ernst, C. Brockman.

1870 to 1872:—C. Ernst, F. Welgehausen, H. Langerhans, August Duecker. Langerhans and Duecker were really appointed in May, 1869, at which time Vander Stucken and Brockman resigned.

1872 to 1874:—Chas. Feller, Wm. Schumann, August Koennecke, Christian Kothe.

1874 to 1876:—Same justices, except that on July 19, 1875, James Larson succeeded August Koennecke, who had ceased to be a justice, but whether he died or resigned the records fail to disclose. In this connection it may not be digressing too much to state that at one time Julius Schuchard was presiding justice, superintendent of schools and deputy county clerk.

1876 to 1878:—F. Kneese, J. P. Mosel, James Larson, Jacob Brodbeck.

1878 to 1880:—J. P. Mosel, John Dechert, John Weinheimer, James Larson.

1880 to 1882:—F. Kneese, John Dechert, J. P. Mosel, James Larson.

1882 to 1884:—John Weinheimer, John Dechert, J. P. Mosel, James Larson.

1884 to 1886:—John Weinheimer, J. P. Mosel, Jacob Kusenberger, G. D. Laxon.

1886 to 1888:—John Weinheimer, J. P. Mosel, Green Harrison, Jacob Kusenberger. Harrison resigned; succeeded by A. J. Knox.

1888 to 1890:—John Weinheimer, August Arlt, Jacob Hoelzer, J. D. Harrison.

1890 to 1892:—John Walter, Jacob Hoelzer, J. P. Mosel, Peter Schuch.

1892 to 1894:—J. P. Mosel, Jacob Hoelzer, G. F. Harper, Clark Lee.

1894 to 1896:—Henry Kordzik, Jos. Hoelzer, G. F. Harper, C. J. Lee.

1896 to 1898:—John Jordan, H. Brodbeck, C. Welgehausen, Henry Kordzik.

1898 to 1900:—Henry Kordzik, P. L. Staudt, Joseph Spence, C. J. Lee.

1900 to 1902:—Peter Baumann, Jacob Hoelzer, Y. J. Delavan, John L. Durst.

1902 to 1904:—P. Baumann, Adam Metzger, August Lange, Daniel Rode.

1904 to 1906:—Chas. Kiehne, F. J. Morgan, J. A. Luckenbach, C. J. Lee.

1906 to 1908:—C. Kiehne, F. J. Morgan, Julius Luckenbach, Daniel Rode,

1908 to 1910:—George W. Grobe, Lorenz Wendel, Julius Luckenbach, D. Rode.

1910 to 1912:—George W. Grobe, W. L. Brandon, Louis Heimann, Daniel Rode.

1912 to 1914:—W. Pfiester, W. L. Brandon, Felix Jenschke, Daniel Rode.

1914 to 1916:—Mathias Berg, Joseph Moritz, Alfred Sauer, C. H. Laurence.

1916 to 1918:—Peter Roeder, Mathias Berg, Alfred Sauer, C. H. Laurence.

1918 to 1920:—Chas. Lehne, Henry H. Rahe, Mathias Berg, C. H. Laurence.

1920 to 1922:—Chas. Lehne, Lorenz Wendel, Mathias Berg, Ira W. Lee.

1922 to 1924:—Chas. Lehne, R. B. Moore, Mathias Berg, Ed. Gold.

Elected in 1924:—Adolph Gerhard, R. B. Moore, Joe Heep, Ed. Gold.

It is interesting and important to note the number of years many of these officers have served, and in most cases the men ceased to be in public office because they declined to stand for re-election. This is where a display of common sense and business judgment comes in. The Germans care nothing about rotation in office. What they want is efficiency. The excellent condition of their public records and the condition of their county is evidence of the fact that they have been getting the right service. They demand that an officer be capable and honest. His religious faith and his political party affiliations doesn't enter into the question.

It has been impossible to give anything like a complete list of precinct officers, aside from commissioners; but one instance may be mentioned. A. W. Petmecky, present justice of the Fredericksburg precinct, has, with the exception of one term, served continuously for thirty-four years. He is the dean of Gillespie county office holders, and it is doubtful if this record is surpassed in Texas.

Gillespie County's Progress in Education.

It would be to a great extent uninteresting and unnecessary to deal at length with the present educational advancement in Gillespie county, and particularly in Fredericksburg. In Fredericksburg is one of the leading parochial schools in Texas, and the public schools of the entire county are unsurpassed by any county in Texas. They are just as perfect and proficient as the school law limitations of the state will permit. With the Germans education is a universal and cardinal principle. When the improvished colonists first reached Fredericksburg they were absolutely without educational facilities except in the matter of teachers. Among the pioneer colonists were some of the most highly educated men and women in the United States at that time. They were qualified to teach in any university or other educational institution in the world. But they had no houses in which to teach, few books with which to teach, and there was no money in the community to pay them for their services as teachers or to provide school equipment of any kind. The history of these pioneer teachers is one of the finest examples of self-sacrifice and patriotic devotion in the history of America. The argument has been advanced that the Germans stayed in this isolated community because they couldn't get away, and that they have prospered for the reason that they had to stay. It is true that the Germans had no place to go and no money with which to pay the expenses of going, but the fact of their having to remain here is not the secret of their success. In order to exist it was not necessary that they should progress. They could have adopted the non-productive life of the Indian and the outlaw. They could have lived on wild game and wild fruits. They could have raised their children as ignorant barbarians. Instead of teaching and building and planting they could have lived in huts and hovels, but they had the inherited and cultivated impulse of progress, advancement, improvement. Admitting the argument that the colonists remained because they couldn't get away and progressed because they had to stay; yet, such admission, though only in small part true, does not apply in the case of the pioneer teachers. The majority of these educated people were finished Latin, English and French scholars as well as being thoroughly educated in German. There was at that time a demand for such teachers in all parts of the United States. They could have gone elsewhere and have obtained lucrative employment, and to go elsewhere they could have obtained the money to make the journey. The institutions that would have gladly given them employment would have advanced the money to make the move. But they remained in Gillespie county and gave their services for practically nothing. Such loyalty is sublime. They were handicapped in every way except in the matter of devotion and grim determination. The people of Gillespie county rank far above the most advanced counties in the matter of practical education and general information, and the old patriotic pioneer teachers are in great measure entitled to credit for this condition. They laid the foundation, and others have improved upon the work they did. The pioneer school teacher, though crude his methods and limited his means, was the force that first impelled civilization to move to its present status. He lives on in influence and effect, though his name be forgotten, the place of his burial unknown, his grave unmarked. This humble tribute applies not only to the poorly paid pioneer teachers of Gillespie county, but to those who have rendered like services for any people in any community in any nation at any period in the history of the world, but the pioneer teachers of Gillespie county deserve their conspicuous position among the benefactors of mankind.

It is possible to give only a brief sketch of the pioneer school history of the county, for the reason that only a limited amount of data is available.

One of the first public movements in Fredericksburg was taking up a subscription for building a school house. This building was the two room rock house now used as a fire station. It was used by first one teacher and then by another, but never was used for what would be termed a public school house, unless it was so used after the war. Even then there was considerable muddle about it. From the old records of September 7, 1857, this excerpt is taken: "In response to numerous requests of citizens of Fredericksburg permission is given for holding school in one room of basement of courthouse, provided same shall be vacated during holding of district court." There was no basement, and school was taught in one room of first floor. In 1854 five school districts were created in the county, and the total available school money, amounting to $258.54, was prorated among the five districts. This was an average of less than $52.00 for each district. In 1856 $963.98 was prorated among seven districts in the county, the average per district being $137.71. But in 1857 the same districts received only $843.87, and in 1859, the same districts received only $610.00. Thus the school matters dragged along until the war started, and during the war the teachers got practically nothing. In 1857 the commissioners appointed the first board of school examiners, this in accordance with an act of the legislature approved Nov. 12, 1866. The first certificates issued in the county were issued to H. Ochs, court house; R. B. Dangers, school house; F. Stein, Catholic school; John J. Weber, Lutheran school house; Rev. Mumme, Methodist church; Christian Kraus, Friederichsthal; G. H. Gombert, Live Oak Creek;

Theodore Hulsemann, Pedernales; A. Erlenmayer, Crab Apple, and H. Ohlensberger, Grape Creek. Among the early day teachers whose names do not appear in this list, were P. Donovan, A. Siemering, A. Schultz, F. Brodbeck, H. F. Schiermitz, H. Hohenberger, W. Kelly, Christian Kraus, John Leyendecker.

And even then they had school rows, just as progressive, up-to-date communities have at present. Here is an extract from the records of Nov. 13, 1869: "The police court having been informed that upon the demise of Pastor Dangers, who having lately occupied a certain building upon the public square of said county, built by donation for a school house; and the court having been further informed that it has jurisdiction over said house, heretofore used by Pastor Dangers as a school room, but now occupied by H. Ochs as a place for having school, without having made proper application to this court, it is therefore ordered and adjudged by the court that said court take immediate possession of said school room, and to notify said Ochs to vacate said building."

This court order must have "started something," for during the same month Carl Weyrich, "foreman" of the school board appeared in open court and reported that the school board would have nothing more to do with the public school house. Later the building was rented to F. Vander Stucken for $2.50 per month. But rents were advancing, for in February, 1870, "the north room of said building was rented to F. Vander Stucken for $2.00, specie, and the other room was rented to Mr. Grote (parson) for $2.10 per month." At the April term the court called for bids to "repair said building, including a bath." In September, 1873, the building was rented to H. Ochs and L. Hagen "as a school house for $4.00 per month until such time as a public free school shall be established regularly and in conformity with the present school law, at which time it may then be let to the highest bidder." And thus it will be seen that the present fire hall has played its role in the school history of Fredericksburg.

As late as 1884 there were only 31 school districts in the county, one of them "a school for negroes in the lower part of Fredericksburg," a school that is still maintained. Today there are 39 school districts, not including Fredericksburg, in the county, these thirty-nine schools employing forty-eight teachers. Thirteen teachers are employed in Fredericksburg public schools, making a total of sixty-one teachers employed in the public schools of the county.

As this book goes to press the following is a list of the schools, together with the teachers, in Gillespie county:

Big Flat, Miss Alice Stovall; Live Oak, Miss Antonette Bracher; Luckenbach, E. H. Baethge; Cave Creek, Miss Velma Renick; Rocky Hill, E. L. Schmidt; Palo Alto, R. E. Weber; Pilot Knob, Miss Myrtle Mathisen; Crab Apple, Miss Lizzie Rumsey; Meusebach, A. C. Heimann; Pedernales, Miss Veleska Moellering; Young's Chapel, Miss Velma Burrier, Grapetown, Miss Vera Schoenewolf; Junction, Miss Viola Sager; Cherry Springs, Miss Cora Petmecky; Honey Creek, Miss Ruby Adams; Stonewall, M. A. Wiemers, principal, Misses Cora Hahn and Catherine Kimbrough, assistants; Hayden, Miss Hedwig Ludwig; Wrede, Miss Dora Kott; Lower South Grape Creek, Herbert Merz; Reingold, E. C. Fiedler; Knopp, Charles J. Ott; Doss, Clarence St. Clair, principal, Miss Alice Braeutigam, Miss Irene Flachmeier, assistants; Tivydale, Miss Edna Young; Cherry Mountain Miss Annie Rae Ottmers; Onion creek, Miss Emily Dechert; Pecan Creek, Miss Nellie Feuge; Nebo, A. C. Lehne, principal, Miss Clara Lehne, assistant; Bear Creek, Miss Elsie Pfiester; Klein Branch, Miss Marguerite Fussel, principal, Miss Mabel Fussell, assistant; Nebgen, Miss Leslie Burch; Pocket, Miss Tille Brieger; Flat Rock, Cordia Hamilton; Klein Frankreich, Miss Clara Kott; White Oak, Miss Julia Knopp; Williams Creek, Miss Ottilie Immel, principal, Miss Anna Wilke, assitant; Petersburg, Miss Hattie Crocker; Morris Ranch, L. E. Brodie, principal, Miss Monnie Turner, assistant; Cain City, F. A. Renick; Willow City, Morel E. Burch, Miss Flora Mueller.

Fredricksburg:—C. W. Feuge, superintendent; E. M. Bittner, R. W. Klingelhoefer, B. L. Enderle, Miss Julia Estill, Miss Merle Hudson, Alfred Neffendorf, Miss Helen Wallace, Miss Alma Hoffmann, Miss Dora Conrads, Miss Elsie Kolmeier, Miss Flora Eckert, Miss Esther Mueller.

And some of these teachers have remarkable records for having taught school in Gillespie county for many years. In the Fredericksburg schools Professor Bittner has taught for 29 years, Miss Estill for more than 20 years, Professor Enderle more than ten years, Professor Klingelhoefer and Miss Conrads for more than six years each, while Professors Feuge and Neffendorf each have a record of five years.

Professor Brodie, at Morris Ranch, has been teaching in Gillespie county for 26 years and Professor Heimann, at Meusebach, has a record of seventeen years.

The total value of public school property in the county at present, including buildings, real estate and school equipment is, at a most conservative estimate, $200,000. The school census of the county shows 2575 children within the scholastic age. The salaries paid teachers is in excess of $44,000 per year, the average school term for the county being nine months. Thre are four independent school districts in the county, these being Fredericksburg, Harper, Willow and Cain City.

Compare this with 1854 when five districts received a total of $258.54, and school was taught wherever the teacher could find a shack of any kind in which to teach.

Remarkable Statistics of Births, Deaths, Marriages and Divorces.

It has been said that statistics are dry, uninteresting reading, but Rev. K. Konzack has, with much labor and painstaking research, compiled statistics of births and deaths in Gillespie county that are interesting and educational. Beginning with 1847 these statistics, subdivided into ten and eleven year periods, embrace the church records of every denomination in Gillespie county, and they are particularly important because they start at a period many years prior to the Texas law requiring filing of births and deaths in the office of the county clerk. During the period covered by this record, there were but few births or deaths that were not put of record in some church.

From 1847 to 1860 there were 697 births and 60 deaths in the county; the total age of all persons dying was 1315 years, only two of these persons being over 60 years old, and the average was 22 years. However, the death record for this eleven year period is by no means complete.

From 1860 to 1870 there were 864 births, 220 deaths; total age of all persons dying, 3557 years; average age at time of death, 16 years and 2 months. Of the deaths during this period 144 were under 14 years, and 2 over 70.

From 1870 to 1890 there were 902 births, 249 deaths; total age of all persons dying, 7132 years; average age, 28 years and 8 months. Only 85 persons dying during this period were under 14 years old, while 23 were over 70 and 15 were over 80.

From 1880 to 1890 there were 1088 births, 241 deaths; total age of all persons dying, 7530, average age, 31 years and 3 months. Only 95 were under 14 years, while 26 were over 70 and 11 over 80.

From 1890 to 1900 there were 901 births, 226 deaths; total age of all persons dying, 8259 years; average 36 years and 6½ months. Only 72 were under 14 years, while 29 were over 70, 11 over 80 and 2 over 90.

From 1900 to 1910 there were 1035 births, 188 deaths; average age of all persons dying, 7750; average age 41 years and 3 months. Only 41 were under 14 years of age, while 29 were over 70, 19 over 80 and 2 over 90.

From 1910 to 1921 (this period covering 11 years) there were 1339 births, 324 deaths; total age of all persons dying, 12,444 years; average age, 38 years and 5 months. Only 87 persons died under 44 years of age, while 39 were over 70, 34 were over 80 and 5 were over 90.

Three things are worthy of especial notice in this connection, viz: The decrease in birth rate, and the decrease in the death rate, population considered, and the increase in the average age at time of death.

From 1847 to 1860, when the county had but a small population, there were 697 births. From 1910 to 1921 there were only 1339 births, and yet the county had practically five times the population from 1910 to 1921 that it had from 1847 to 1860.

As previously stated death statistics are not complete from 1847 to 1860. So compare the ten year period from 1860 to 1870 to the period from 1910 to 1921. From 1860 to

1870 there were 864 births, 220 deaths. The average age of all persons dying during that period was 16 years and 2 months, and of the 220 deaths 144 were under 14 years. From 1910 to 1921 there were 1339 births, 324 deaths. The average age of all persons dying during this period was 38 years and 5 months, and only 87 of the 324 persons dying were under 14 years of age.

You will also note that the age at time of death increases from 16 years and 2 months during the period from 1860 to 1870 to 38 years and 5 months during the period from 1910 to 1921. Sanitation, good clothing, plenty to eat, wholesome living and medical service easily accounts for the increase in the life period, and particularly for the decreased death rate among children. The decrease in the birth rate is another problem.

The figures regarding persons 70, 80 and 90 years old at time of death is also worthy of attention. This may be accounted for by the fact that there were very few persons past middle age among the first colonists, and doubtless few of them had passed the 70 year mark as late as 1870.

The average age of persons dying between 1900 and 1910 was 41 years and 3 months. From 1910 to 1921 the average age at time of death was only 38 years and 5 months. This considerable decline in the life period is easily acccounted for. During the period from 1910 to 1921 there was a considerable immigration of Mexicans to the county. The deaths among them at an age under 41 years accounts for the decline in the high average ages during the period from 1900 to 1910.

There is material for interesting study in these figures Reverend Konzack has assembled.

Reverend Konzack has also compiled some interesting statistics showing the number of persons who have lived to a very old age in Gillespie county. The list does not include all persons who have lived to a very old age in the county, but only those as shown by the church records. As shown by Reverend Konzack's statistics out of 366 persons dying in Gillespie county from 1887 to 1924 inclusive, 57 were more than 80 years old. Here is the list, the figures following each name indicating that the person had lived more than that number of years:

Wm. F. Meier, 98; Mrs. Christine Braeutigam, 96; Mrs. Wilhelmine Pfiester, 95; Heinrich Hotopp, 94; Christian Behrens, 91; Henry Welge, Sr., 91; Vincenz Wahl, 91; Mrs. Maria Specht, 90; Mrs. Maria K. Schuch, 90; John H. Dietz, 90; Frederick C. Ruebsamen, 89; Heinrich Mueller, 89; Adam Klein, 89; Katherine H. Crenwelge, Karl Weyrich, George Goehmann, Henry Welge, Albert Molsberger, each more than 88; Mrs. Maria Goehmann, Mrs. Eva C. Marshall, Mrs. Margarite A. Schaper, John Christian L. Meyer, Mrs. Auguste Grona, each more than 87; Adam Zimmer, Mrs. Anna Maria Pletz, Mrs. Henriette Hotopp, and John P. Mosel, each more than 86; Mrs. Dorothea Meinhardt, Jesajas Pahl, Karl Barsch, each more than 85; Mrs. Henriette Itz, Mrs. Sophie Dietz and John F. W. Teschner, each more than 84; Heinrich Bierschwale, Heinrich P. Dapperich and Christian Fahrenhorst, each more than 83; Philipp Kirchhoff, Mrs. Maria K. Schmidt, Mrs. Caroline Grobe, Mrs. Auguste Wahrmund, Mrs. Eleonore Weinheimer, Mrs. Anna E. Hopf, each more than 82; Mrs. Caroline Jordan, Mrs. Katherine C. Eckert, Mrs. Ilse Ernst, Peter Gold, Louis J. Gardner, Wm. Walter, Sr., Daniel Ludwig, each more than 81; Mrs. Katherine Schmidt, Heinrich F. A. Schlueter, Mrs. Charlotte D. Langerhans, Mrs. Margarethe Weyrich, Jacob Schmidt, Sr., Matthias Bonn, Adam Rodenbusch, each over 80.

Can this record for longevity be equalled or surpassed by another community in the United States? Of 336 persons dying during a period of 38 years, 17 per cent of them were over 80 years of age.

The marriage records of Gillespie county are equally interesting. In 1824 the United States department of commerce made a report on the marriages and divorces of each state in the Union, this report being compiled from the official records of each county. For Texas, likewise for every state in the Union, the figures were little less than astounding. The report, covering the years of 1923-24, shows that in Texas during the two years there were 130,973 marriages and 27,169 divorces. According to this report for every 100 marriages there were practically 21 divorces. For each of the 252 counties in the state there was an average of 111 divorces against a marriage average record of 516 for each county. Some of the smaller counties in the state had a divorce record exceeding 39 per cent, and at least one of the most heavily populated counties had a divorce average of nearly 40 per cent. Gillespie county heads the list with its showing of small per cent of divorces. For the two years there were 218 marriages in the county and only two divorces, less than one per cent. Kendall county comes next with 194 marriages and 5 divorces, or less than 2½ per cent for the two years. Lynn county, one of the most westerly of Texas counties, is next with 184 marriages and 5 divorces, or less than 3 per cent for the two years. No other county in the state approaches the marriage and divorce record of Kendall and Lynn, and Gillespie county beats either of them by more than fifty per cent. In fact, Gillespie county has the lowest divorce record of any county in the United States, having an equal population and an equal number of marriages. Most assuredly the divorce evil cannot be charged to Gillespie county.

CHAPTER XI.

AMUSING, ROMANTIC AND TRAGIC HISTORY.

A Noted Hotel and Some Practical Joke Artists.

Fredericksburg has two of the most noted hotels in Texas. They are not only noted for their relation to the history of Fredericksburg, and of this section of Texas, but likewise for the excellent service they have always given. Both of these hotels are conducted on the American plan.

The Ostrow Hotel was originally a saloon, owned by Charley Dietz, but some thirty, or thirty-five years ago, the saloon was converted into a hotel, and was named the Dietz. Dietz conducted the hotel until some ten years ago when he sold out to the present owner, John Ostrow, and the name was changed to the Ostrow Hotel.

The Nimitz is unquestionably one of the oldest hotels in Texas, and it is doubtful if there is another hotel in the United States that has been so long conducted continuously by the same family.

Among the first colonists to Fredericksburg was Charles Nimitz. Prior to coming to this country Nimitz had been a sea captain. In 1846 he built the first section of the Nimitz hotel. This was a one-story frame building. Some years later he built another one-story addition, this second addition being stone, and was used as a saloon. Some years later he added the "steamboat" addition, this two-story addition being the model of a river steamboat.

The story has gone the rounds to the effect that a rich old sea captain came to Fredericksburg, made his home at the Nimitz, died there and left a large legacy to the elder Nimitz, and that the legacy was used in building the "steamboat" addition as a memorial to the benefactor. An old sea captain did come to Fredericksburg at an early day, made his home at the Nimitz, died there, and left as a legacy a small tract of land, not enough, perhaps, to pay his bar account and hotel bill. The "steamboat" addition was undoubtedly one of Charles Nimitz' own original ideas.

Nimitz, Mogford, and Judge O. A. Cooley were original characters. They never tired of loading a tourist or stranger with "big windies," playing practical jokes on each other, and any one else that chanced to be available.

For instance, there is the joke that has traveled considerably about the dead man. This hoax was probably worked up in retaliation for some equally ridiculous joke Nimitz had pulled on some other member of the old crony crowd. This story was to the effect that a man died at the Nimitz, and his relatives sent a message to Nimitz requesting that the body be embalmed and shipped to some distant point for burial. There being no embalmer available, and Nimitz being anxious to comply with the request of the bereaved relatives, removed the entrails, smoke cured the body as one would the carcass of an animal and then shipped it. This hoax was in keeping with the dozens of jokes these old cronies played on each other, but this one went over in great shape.

On one occasion one of the joke playing bunch came to town and got well tanked. Cooley had, not so long prior thereto, been the victim of a joke played on him by this particular member of the bunch. The party who had just reached town was the owner of a horse to which he was dearly attached, and upon which he placed a very high value. Cooley made a sneak, got the horse, changed saddles and then did some transformation work. He painted one or two of the horse's feet white, painted a streak down his forehead, and maybe daubed a little paint or soap suds on the horse's flanks and hips. He then hitched the horse on the opposite side of the street and proceeded to hunt up his considerably intoxicated friend, and informed him that he had found and bought a perfect match and mate for old "Jim," just what the intoxicated friend had been hunting for. The drunk proceeded to stagger across the street to take a look. He objected to the white feet and blazed face, but otherwise he was delighted. He finally decided that he would never find a better match for "Jim" and made a cash deal with Cooley. The saddle was removed and the purchaser of the horse proceeded to go get "Jim." But there was no Jim. The old scamp had got loose and was gone. But Cooley was kind enough to let the owner of the missing animal have his saddle to ride the newly bought horse home. He arrived well after dark, but was sorely perplexed when he learned that "Jim" hadn't showed up. The next morning he discovered that he had bought "Jim" from Cooley, and what was more Cooley had let him have his own saddle to ride home. Whereupon he came back to town, got his money, set 'em up a few times and bided his opportunity to get even with Cooley.

The army officers stationed at Fort Martin Scott, at Mason and other early day federal forts in this section made the Nimitz their regular stopping place. Cooley, who was a bachelor, made his home there. In its earliest day the Nimitz possessed a set of table silverware, used almost exclusively by the army officers. One day a lot of these officers passed through and stopped for dinner. After dinner some of the silver spoons were missing. Cooley appeared on the scene. He didn't like to turn informer, but his sacred friendship for Nimitz compelled him to do it. He had noticed one of the officers handling the spoons, and later had seen the same officer suspiciously putting something in his valise. Some spoons had been put in the officer's grip, all right. The officer didn't do it, but Cooley knew exactly who had done it. The sheriff was sent poste haste after the spoons and overtook the officers near Cherry Spring. The accused officer was dumfounded when the sheriff stated his business, and gladly produced his valise for examination. There were the spoons. There was nothing to do but bring the officer back, and of course his brother officers came with him. Cooley had put some of his friends wise, and they appeared and explained everything. Then everybody got full, the officer, Nimitz and Cooley taking a leading part in the festivities.

And thus they passed time merrily in the days of long ago.

Charles Nimitz, senior, died in 1911. His son C. H. Nimitz then took charge of it. In fact, the younger Nimitz had been in charge of the hotel for sometime prior to the death of his father. The younger Nimitz, now past 73 years, still runs the hotel. The hotel has been conducted by father and son for a period of nearly seventy-nine years.

For the first twenty-five years of its existence the Nimitz kept no register. During these years some of the most distinguished statesmen and military men were guests of the Nimitz. The old register started in 1871, is an interesting document, but the old ledger is the most interesting. This was the book in which Nimitz kept his saloon and hotel accounts.

Not so many years ago a good old man living in the south part of town owned a gray horse. He was very much attached to this horse, looked after him carefully and attended to him regularly, and for this reason the horse ranged pretty close to home and was always on hand at feeding time. The gang got the horse and painted him black. For several days the old gentleman distressfully hunted, enquired and offered a reward for his horse and all of this time he was sorely troubled and beset by a black horse hanging around his place. He finally got wise to what had been done, and the gang got wise to keeping out of his way for several days.

Some Noted Old Ranches

There never were any really big cattle ranches in Gillespie county. There were and there are yet, a number of ranches consisting of a few thousand acres, but the county was never a big ranching county in the broad sense of the word. It is today one of the leading stock raising counties in the state, particularly in the matter of sheep and goats, and nearly every farm and ranch is stocked with good cattle, mules, horses and hogs, but this industry has been gradual in its growth and development. The early German settlers were primarily a farming people, starting with nothing, acquiring land as they could, and getting a start of livestock by slow degrees. It is this fact, more than anything else, that gives the big historic interest to every community and to every old home in the county. These early German settlers made permanent history, history that grows greater as the years pass. Practically all the ranching history of Texas was romantic, but transitory. But in Gillespie county there was a permanency about the early ranches, something entirely different to the ranching history of other counties.

Perhaps the most famous of the early day ranches in this county were those along Crab Apple creek and around the Enchanted Rock. Doubtless the first ranch located in this part of the country was the Davis ranch. This ranch is in the northwest corner of Blanco county, though part of the land is in Gillespie, but for all practical purposes the history of this ranch belongs to the history of Gillespie county.

This ranch was established by A. C. Shelley in 1855. Soon after locating the ranch Mr. Shelly died. Sometime later Capt. Alfred Davis married Mrs. Shelley, and the ranch was thereafter known as the Davis ranch. Captain Davis was a most remarkable man, one of the very highest type of pioneer citizens. He was broad minded, well educated, and a thorough gentleman, a man who left a big influence long after he had passed away. In the very early history of this country he taught school, not as a profession, but in order to give his own children and the neighborhood children as much schooling as possible. This old ranch has never passed out of the hands of the Davis and Shelley ownership. Tom Shelley, now nearly eighty-three years old, and his sister, Miss Sarah, now around seventy-five, still live on the old, home place, and the ranch consisting of more than ten thousand acres, belongs to the grandsons of Capt. Alfred Davis. These grandsons are Alfred, Pike, Virgil, W. O. and Hiram B. Davis. Captain Davis died in 1901, and Mrs. Davis died in 1920, being nearly 100 years old at the time of her death. This writer has met a great many remarkable and high class old timers, and incidentally, a good many of the other kind, but he has never met two higher minded, more intelligent people than Mr. Tom Shelley and his sister, Miss Sarah. And persons who are intimately acquainted with the grandsons of Capt. Alfred Davis, speak of them as being the same type of people.

Here is material for a real big and beautiful story—too much material for a necessarily short sketch.

There stands the old, substantial ranch house built more than seventy years ago. Around it towers cedar covered mountains, separated by winding valleys, skirted by a little

stream, and in that old house live two people who have seen
and lived and made pioneer history in its fullest and best
measure.

On the old ranch is four miles of cedar rail fence, built
in 1857, still serving its purpose, and in this fence are more
than 25,000 rails. In addition to this old rail fence is more
than six miles of rock fence. Men now past middle age were
not born when that old fence was built. Comanche Spring,
one of the noted landmarks in the primitive history of this
section, is located on this ranch. At one time it was the permanent camp and council capital of the powerful Comanche
tribe of Indians. It was later a prominent way-station of the
state and federal government frontier forces. It is still a fine
spring, but not the wonderful spring it used to be. Its history
is the same as the history of hundreds of water courses in this
part of Texas. Modern improvements have changed the land-
scape around this old spring. Near it stands a nice home, and
for conveying water a windmill has taken the place of the old
cedar bucket.

At the old Davis ranch headquarters there used to be a
post office by the name of Blowout. The post office was dis-
continued many years ago, and the ranch together with the
rest of the community, is now served by a rural free delivery
mail route. The post office derived its name from one of the
most remarkable bat caves in Texas, this bat cave being about
a mile from the old ranch house. In this cave thousands,
perhaps millions, of bats make their regular roost and winter
quarters. It is a wonderful sight to see the vast swarm of
bats leaving or returning to this cave. In conection with this
bat cave is a thrilling legend. There are two entrances to
this cave, which winds through a mountain for more than a
mile. It is said that there was originally but one entrance.
According to the legend about 1850 the Indians chased a
bear into the cave. The Indians had many torches. When
they departed they threw the torches away and left them
burning in the cave. The gas and refuse in the cave caught
fire and burned fiercely for several months. Finally there
was a terrific explosion, and thus was made the second
entrance to the cave. Mr. Shelley says that the first settlers
in Fredericksburg stated that this was a fact, and that the

report caused by the explosion was heard in Fredericksburg, nearly thirty miles away. At any rate, the cave derived its name from this legend. But they have commercialized the cave, and a crude tram railway now penetrates its labyrinths. On this tramway thousands of pounds of guano has been brought out of the cave, loaded onto trucks and hauled to the railroad station, most of it going to Marble Falls, some 40 miles away.

And the old ranch that played its prominent role in pioneer history is performing its great service in the industrial affairs of the country. Good homes, nice farms, fine stock, and a bat cave that furnishes annually hundreds of tons of fertilizer for the worn out soils of distant localities.

In the vicinity of the Enchanted Rock, particularly along Crab Apple creek, are some noted old time ranches. It is not known just who first settled in that vicinity. James Riley located on Crab Apple in 1854. Among the other very early settlers were the Mosses, Slators, A. Kneese, Nicholaus Rusche, Jacob Land, Frederick Welgehausen, John Pehl, Adam and Jacob Friess and Mathias Schmidt. The old Moss ranch was really in Llano county, just north of the Enchanted Rock. Every one of these old ranches has its pioneer and Indian time history. The old Riley home, built perhaps in 1855, is still standing, with no evidence of decay or dilapidation. It is a typical old time home, built of logs, with two rooms, a broad hall between, a second story or loft, and has a porch running the entire length of the building. Near it stands the old smokehouse. In its day thousands of tons of buffalo and deer meat, pork and beef has been cured in this old smokehouse, a reminder of the days when people lived at home and drew most of their sustenance from the forest and wild herds. The old Riley ranch house, and the land immediately around it, is now owned by Valentine Beyer, but some two miles west of this old ranch house is the present Riley ranch and two story rock residence. This home was built by Crockett Riley, a son of James Riley. Mrs. Amalie Riley still occupies this fine old home, and she is a most remarkable woman. Now more than seventy years old, educated and refined, active mentally and physically, and a noted hostess and entertainer. She has lived, witnessed and helped make pioneer history. She was born in Fredericksburg, her father being Captain E. Krauskopf, so she is the daughter, the widow and the mother of pioneers, for her own sons were raised on that old ranch. George Riley, another son of James Riley, was for several terms sheriff of Gillespie county. James Riley, originally from Indiana, was a relative of James Whitcomb Riley. Crockett Riley and Tom Shelley were among the very first men to drive herds of cattle from this part of Texas to California. These herds were driven up the Concho river by way of Fort Concho, then across the wild divide to the Pecos, then up the Pecos, far into New Mexico, and then across the deserts of New Mexico and Arizona. Sometime these drives would go for days with but little water for men and horses and with none for the cattle, the men and horses getting only sparingly of the water hauled in the chuck wagon. They had plenty of exciting thrills, and in some instances, disastrous experiences with Indians.

Every one of these old ranches has its real pioneer history. Pack Saddle Mountain was made famous by reason of an Indian fight. The ranching section was most subjected to Indian raids, because there were plenty of horses on all of these ranches, and it was the horses that most attracted the Indians.

In the vicinity of the Enchanted Rock are several noted old ranger camps, perhaps the most noted being the Highsmith camp, only a short distance from the old Riley ranch. But notwithstanding the watchfulness of the frontier forces the Indians would make their frequent and generally disastrous raids just the same, and many are the exciting experiences related by the old timers of narrow escapes during Indian raids.

But nature and conditions have changed in that section. Crab Apple and Sandy creeks used to be running, living streams, with deep pools stocked with fish and beavers. There are still signs of the old beaver dams. But there are no deep pools and no running water any more. Just an occasional spring gives feeble evidence of its present existence. This applies to dozens of other streams, not only in Gillespie county, but throughout this part of the state. Doubtless this is attributable to two main causes. Putting the land in cultivation caused the streams to fill with washed earth; and second, the drilling of numerous wells throughout the country has tapped the sources of the springs that formerly supplied the living water for the streams.

But the most remarkable feature about these noted old ranches is the fact that with the exception of the Pehl and Priess ranches every one of them is today owned by the descendants of the pioneers who established them. Nearly every one of the children and grandchildren of these old pioneers are today prominent citizens of Gillespie county. Some of them are dead, and some have moved away, but those who have moved away are still identified with the old home county and the old home place by the ties of endearment. It is doubtful if there is another old ranching section in the United States with a history equal to this. It is an unusual thing, even in isolated cases, that children, grand-children, and even great grandchildren, can point to an old ranch house or cattle range and say: "That's our's. Grandpa settled there seventy years ago."

There were many other noted ranches in Gillespie county, their complete history deserving more space than is possible in this work.

Among these noted ranches was the Morris ranch. This was never a cattle ranch. Many years ago the property was acquired by Francis Morris, and later by his son, John A. Morris, founder of the Louisiana Lottery. In comparatively recent years it became one of the most noted race horse breeding properties in the United States. There was more fad and fancy than profit about this business and when the heirs came into possession of it they quit the race horse breeding business. Much of the land is now in cultivation, worked by tenants. The property is still owned by the Morris estate.

There were quite a number of ranches in the Harper section. The old Inskip ranch above Harper, was cut into small tracts many years ago, and is now owned by farmers and small stockmen. The Frank Vander Stucken ranch, east of Harper, later became the Hopf ranch, and is still owned by members of the Hopf family, though subdivided into several tracts. North of Harper was the Sultemeier ranch, now owned by Emil Wahrmund. The old Tremlett ranch, on the headwaters of the Pedernales, was another pioneer property. It is now owned by Albert Friederich and August Mosel. Another noted old ranch was the Roundtree ranch at Beaver lake, near Harper. It was cut up and sold off in small tracts many years ago.

Among the noted ranches in the early days were the Marschall, Welge, Rode and Anderegg ranches in the Cherry Spring territory. All of these properties are still owned by the descendants of the original founders.

The Henry Schwethelm and Heinen ranches, on Wolf creek, are noted ranch properties that have changed hands. Most of the Schwethelm ranch is now owned by Otto Henke and his sons, but the old Heinen ranch is owned by different persons.

At one time Charles Schreiner, of Kerrville, owned a large tract of land in Gillespie county, known as the Cottonwood ranch, but it was sold in small tracts many years ago. This ranch was also in the Wolf Creek section. The present George Zenner, John Lott, Emil and Albert Kott, William Henke, Henry and Felix Ahrens, Henry Braeutigam, Bruno Schwethelm, William Roeder, and possible other ranches are out of the old Schreiner ranch lands.

The Hohmann ranch on Crab Apple, owned by Theodore, Emil and William Hohmann, is perhaps the biggest cattle ranch in Gillespie county at present. Much of this ranch property has been acquired in comparatively recent years.

Another old time ranch with a history is the Nott ranch on Klein Branch, now owned by Adolf Dittmar and John Fiedler.

The Peril ranch, on Henderson Branch, is one of the old timers. Most of this old ranch is still owned by Mrs. W. A. Peril and her son, W. R. Peril. W. A. Peril, now dead, located this old ranch many years ago.

The old Hayden ranch, on Spring Creek, is a rather noted property. This property was acquired by Peter Hayden many years ago, and is still owned by the Hayden heirs. Like the Morris ranch, it is now a thriving farming community, managed by E. H. Riley for the Hayden estate.

One of the best known ranches in the county at present

is the Jeff Young ranch, about fourteen miles east of Fredericksburg and near the town of Willow City. This is really an old ranch, with its full share of early day history, but its present day importance is due to the fact that it is one of the greatest breeding and best improved ranches in Texas.

Indian Depredations.

Repeated references have already been made in this work regarding the relations of the early Gillespie county settlers and the Indians. No pioneer county in Texas was subjected to fewer Indian depredations and outrages. Particularly were the German settlers and the Comanche Indians on friendly terms. Practically all of the mischief done in Gillespie county prior to 1860 was the work of the Lipan tribe, or rather, by roving bands of that tribe. As a whole the Comanches lived strictly according to their treaty with Meusebach, but occasionally some mischief was done by depredating bands of Comanches even prior to 1860. Left to their own resources and methods of dealing with the Indians it is doubtful if the German colonists would have ever had serious trouble with the Comanches, and in all probability they would have succeeded in establishing friendly relations with the Lipans and any other tribe in any way identified with this section of country, but when the federal government removed the Indians to reservations, they resented this infringemnt of their rights with all the power and revengeful ferocity of which they were capable. The action of the government, as they saw it, released them from all treaty obligations, and made them the foes, regardless of former friendly relations, of all white people of any community. The hostility and wrath of the Indians would have meant nothing had the government been able to confine them to restricted areas. But the government was unable to do this, and it was a common thing for strong bands of Indians to deliberately abandon the reservation and go on marauding expeditions, stealing and murdering, and returning to the reservation when too hotly pursued. It was the duty of the government agents to see that property stolen by the Indians was returned to the owners when application was made. But in a majority of cases this was not done, the usual excuse being that the stolen property could not be located.

It was during the civil war that the Indians were meanest and the communities most helpless, the majority of men being in the army, and even the federal government and the Confederate government being less able, and perhaps less disposed, to use considerable numbers of men to keep the Indians on reservations or to protect the frontier settlements from Indian depredations.

After the war it didn't take the federal government long to put a stop to Indian troubles.

In the fall of 1846 quite a number of immigrants were killed, presumably by a band of Lipan Indians. This attack was made on an immigrant train encamped on the Guadalupe river.

In 1847 Lieutenant von Wrede and two companions were killed by a considerable band of Indians on the road between Fredericksburg and Austin. This mischief was credited to the Comanches.

In 1855 the Comanches made a raid into the Sisterdale community, killed a young man by the name of Hermann Runge, and drove away a considerable number of stock belonging to the citizens of that community.

One of the most noted outrages was the killing of Henry Arhelger, near Fredericksburg, in 1863. Arhelger and a companion, both in the frontier ranger service, were scouting in the mountains when suddenly attacked by a band of Comanches. Arhelger's companion, riding a swift horse, made his escape, but Arhelger was riding a slow mule, and had to fight it out. It was his heroic fight that gave the affair its prominence. Though poorly armed, he killed one Indian that was left by his companions and perhaps killed others that were carried away. The blood signs were proof that he had wounded several others. The Indians certainly got enough of the fight as they left one dead Indian and did not scalp Arhelger. When found his body was pierced with thirteen arrows, and in his search for water he had wandered considerable distance from the point where the fight took place.

In the early part of 1863 Conrad and Heinrich Meckel were killed by Indians at a point not far from the present town of Loyal Valley.

In 1864 the Comanches captured and carried away Rudolph Fischer, twelve year old son of Gottlieb Fischer. Some eleven years later Rudolph returned to Gillespie county, but he had imbibed too much of tribal life to ever be satisfied with the environments of his childhood. ,The call of the wilds was ever chanting to him, so within a few months he returned to the Indian tribe from whence he came. He was married to an Indian woman and has raised a large family. He received his tribal allotment of land and is said to be at present a substantial citizen of Oklahoma.

On one of their raids the Indians found three women alone in a little log house on the head waters of Spring creek, the men, not aware of the fact that Indians were in the country, having gone away for the day. The women barricaded the house and defended themselves as best they could, and they certainly made a heroic defense. The women had no fire arms but when the Indians smashed the door down, one of the women grabbed a smoothing iron and killed one Indian. The two older women were killed, but the third, a young girl, was carried away. Mr. Ludwig Usener thinks this occurred in 1858 or 1859.

In April, 1862, the Indians killed Heinrich Grobe, who lived on Landrum's creek, known in the early days as a branch of Riley's creek. When killed Grobe was working on a field fence not far from his home, but none of the family knew about the killing until the children went out to assist their father, and found him dead. The mother, assisted by the children, carried the body to the house, and then notified the neighbors of what had happened. The Indians drove off all stock belonging to Mr. Grobe, and thus Mrs. Grobe was left with eight children, the oldest not over fourteen years, to care for as best she could.

On the same day that Mr. Grobe was killed the Indians killed a Mr. Berg some eight miles from Grobe's place. Berg was a brother of the hermit, mentioned elsewhere, and the story is that he was on his way to Fredericksburg, carrying some whisky to town, but after killing him the Indians didn't touch the whiskey, this due, doubtless, to some of their many superstitions, for the Indians were notoriously gluttons for whisky.

One of the worst raids the Indians ever made into this section of the country was perhaps during the first year of the war. On this raid they drove off nearly every horse and mule in the county, the ranches especially suffering. A Mr. Doss had a ranch some miles southeast of Fredericksburg, and quite a number of extra good horses. Some negroes were herding the horses when the Indians attacked them. Some of the negroes were killed and the entire herd of horses driven off. Mathew Zenner, who was riding around looking for some cows, witnessed this exciting episode from the top of a mountain some distance away, unseen by the Indians, but powerless to give any aid. Jost Heinrich Stahl, who lived on Cave creek, had left home early in the morning, afoot and unarmed, to hunt for some cows, and was seen by Mr. Zenner only a few hours before he witnessed the attack of the Indians on the negro horse herders. Mr. Zenner reported the Indian invasion, and neighbors started out to hunt for Mr. Stahl, who had failed to return home. Some days later the searchers found the body some six miles from home, scalped, horribly mutilated and stripped of all clothes except his shoes.

In 1865 a small band of Comanche Indians waylaid and captured Misses Anna and Katherine Metzger as they were returning from Fredericksburg to their home a short distance north of town. Anna, who was about 20 years of age, put up a stubborn fight and finally made an attempt to flee into the timber, whereupon she was killed and horribly mutilated. Katherine, who was only thirteen years old, was carried away. Some months later she made her escape, and reached one of the northern Indian agencies, and was soon thereafter returned to her parents.

In the summer of 1865 Heinrich Kensing and his wife were killed by a band of Comanches between Beaver and Squaw Creeks. They were returning from church when attacked.

It was perhaps in the latter part of 1868 that Hermann Lehmann was captured and carried away by the Comanche Indians, this capture taking place in Mason county, near the present line of Gillespie. He remained with the Indians for many years, during which time he had varied experiences. Some years ago he returned to his own people. He is now well advanced in years, but still gives exhibitions, and is said to be writing a book dealing with his experiences while living with the Indians.

E. Kriewitz was one of the original colonists. He was an educated man, but a typical adventurer and soldier of fortune. He conceived the idea of going with the Indians and living as one of them as a means of keeping the Indians on friendly terms with the colonists. So away he went, and for many months he dressed in breechclout, moccasins, paints and feathers, baring his body to the blizzards of winter and the scorching sun of summer. He lived on Indian fare and learned their language, but what influence, if any, his mission had in protecting the colonists against the Indians is not known. Be that as it may, he evidently got enough of Indian life for he returned to Gillespie county, where he married and raised a family. His was at least a novel idea, an unusual experience and a commendable motive.

In the summer of 1871 A. Keese, who lived on Little Sandy, near the Enchanted Rock, went out to hunt his oxen, in the course of his rounds he stopped at a spring. The nervous actions of his horse caused him to investigate, and the result was that he discovered an Indian creeping along in the brush not far away. Keese promptly killed the Indian, and then raced to his home, closely pursued by other Indians who happened to be not far away when their companion was killed. Some weeks later perhaps the same band of Indians reappeared in the community, and it was evident that they not only came to steal horses, but to kill Keese or some other white person, in retaliation for the death of their tribesman. This was evidenced by the fact that this band worked in daylight, whereas when they came only for the purpose of stealing they usually worked by the light of the moon. Ludwig Spaeth had a little cabin home and a little farm in the Sandy creek community. He was in the field plowing with a yoke of oxen. His son Louis was driving the oxen, and two smaller sons were working in a pea patch near by, no one suspecting that Indians were in the country at that time. Suddenly from a shinoak thicket near by, the Indians fired on Mr. Spaeth, who was then near the middle of the field. He was struck by one bullet and several arrows. Louis, who had an old pistol, and while closely pursued he fired, killing one Indian, and making his escape into a corn field. The Indians did not venture into the high corn, fearing the fate of their companion. Although they could not see the boy, they fired many shots into the corn patch. The other two boys, Frank and Jacob, fled to the house while the Indians were pursuing Louis. After a short time Louis also made his way to the house, and diplomatically reported what had happened. Mrs. Spaeth, a young daughter and an infant, together with Mrs. Keese and August Sagebiel, were at the Spaeth home when the crime was committed. Mr. Spaeth's body was recovered and the community warned of the presence and crime of the Indians. It was Mrs. Spaeth's wish that funeral services be conducted by D. Rode, who lived at Cherry Springs, some eight miles away, and to convey this message to the minister, Louis went alone and afoot, although the Indians were supposed to still be lurking in that vicinity. Mr. Spaeth was buried in the little field, near the spot made sacred by the blood of a good pioneer.

One of the worst characters that ever operated in this part of Texas went by the name of Eastwood. His hiding place was in Kerr county, where he lived in a cave.

This man seems to have been the worst kind of barbarian, his occupation murder, theft and robbery. Some of his crimes were revolting beyond description. When he started on his expeditions he always dressed like an Indian, carrying a bow and arrows, and traveled with the cunning and stealth of an Indian. On some of his expeditions he had companions. Possibly at times these companions were really Indians, but the presumption is that they were generally Americans or Mexicans. Perhaps in 1870, a woman was killed near her home, scalped and multilated. This was a double crime, as the slain woman would soon become a mother. Strong circumstantial evidence indicated that Eastwood was the leader of the gang that did this work, the killing taking place near where Tivydale now stands. Charles Jung, a state policeman, assisted by two other state police, slipped up on Eastland one moonlight night, just awhile before day, and captured him. He was put in jail at Kerrville, but later escaped. But the whole country was aroused, and the officers kept after Eastwood. He was recaptured, but soon after his capture he was taken from the officers, hung and his body riddled with bullets, and that very effectively and economically put an end to the career of one of the worst characters that ever harassed this part of Texas.

And Eastwood was not the only man that went in the garb and with the stealth of an Indian, committing revolting crimes and giving the Indians credit for the deed.

In addition to these enumerated tragedies there were a number of Indian raids during which stock were driven away and different people had narrow escapes. For at least six years, just before, during and just after the war, the citizens of Gillespie county were kept constantly on the look out, and were not infrequently terrorized by marauding bands of Indians, and as the people had practically no arms or means of defense the wonder is that Indian killings were not a hundred times what they were. But all the Indian murders from 1846 to 1870 did not amount to half the number of murders committed by Duff's and Waldrip's gangs.

CHAPTER XII.

CONCLUDING SKETCHES.

The Old Time Freighters Made History.

The old freighter was a big factor in the development of pioneer communities, particularly in Gillespie county. Many of the most prominent citizens of Gillespie county, and this applies to many now living as well as to many who have passed away, were early day freighters. They went through all kinds of weather and over the worst of roads, and they were at all times exposed to the gravest dangers, not only from Indians but from white outlaws, who committed crimes even more heinous and revolting than the Indians did, and then gave the Indians credit for the outrage.

When the season was rainy they dragged through miles of mud, and when it was dry they crept along through clouds of dust. They braved the coldest weather with the fortitude of an Indian. In those days there were no bridges, so the old freighters forded swollen streams, and were often delayed for weeks by high water and impassable roads. Prior to the war most of the freighting for Fredericksburg and Gillespie county was done with ox teams, and while most of the trips were to San Antonio and Austin, each less than a hundred miles from Fredericksburg, in many instances the freighters would make two and three hundred mile journeys, the round trip being four or five hundred miles, and requiring two or three months time. Many loads of freight were hauled from Indianola, Houston, and Galveston to Fredericksburg in the very early history of the town.

Until after the civil war and before the railroad was built, all of the lumber, dry goods, groceries, farm machinery etc., was freighted from Austin and San Antonio, and any old freighter can go along these modern highways and point out to you where he was waterbound, where he got stuck in a mudhole and had to carry his load of freight on his back in order to reduce the tonnage to the point where the team could pull it out, unless some one came along with a good team to hook in with his team and drag the load out. They can show you the places all along the road they tried to reach at night in order to have shelter for themselves and their teams in case of a norther, these camping places usually being on the south side of some bluff or mountain, or in some heavy cluster of timber.

As a big factor in the development of every pioneer community the old freighter has never received his just credit, his true measure of praise. His pay was small, his work was hard, his dangers great, and he was absolutely indispensable to the existence of the community he served.

Some Pinoeer Physicians.

What could be termed regular practitioners and skilled physicians were among the essential but rare persons in the early colony history of Fredericksburg. There were a number of persons among the early colonists who knew how to properly care for the sick, and who were fairly expert in the matter of administering medical treatment, but such persons did not pretend to be doctors, and made no character of charge for such services as they could render.

Dr. A. Keidel, Sr., seems to have been the dean of practicing physicians in Fredericksburg. He was a thoroughly educated and skilled physician, a man who could have built up a large practice and made big money in any prosperous community, but he preferred to live in Fredericksburg, where he did a big practice for very small compensation, for the reason that the people had no money to pay for anything, so it wasn't money but heroic devotion that kept the doctor here. There were other pioneer doctors in Gillespie county, who gave the community many years of their service, and there were others who came, remained awhile and went away, but to the end of his days Dr. Keidel lived in Fredericksburg and made his professional visits to the country for miles around, and when he passed on his son, Dr. A. Keidel, Jr., continued the practice, and his son, Dr. Victor Keidel, a grandson of the original Dr. Keidel, is at present a prominent physician in Fredericksburg.

Among the pioneer physicians, other than Dr. Keidel, were Dr. Schultz, Dr. Schilling and Dr. Althaus. Dr. Schilling was one of the earliest physicians in Fredericksburg and was continuously in the practice up to the time of his death in 1881.

Noted Old Time Communities.

It is practically impossible to get much of the best history of the old communities in Gillespie county. Klein Branch, Harper, Doss, Morris Ranch, Cherry Spring, Crab Apple, Willow City, Luckenbach, Stonewall, Spring Creek, Live Oak, Gold, Eckert, Cave Creek, Meusebach Creek, Bear Creek, Tivydale, Mecklenburg, Albert and Cherry Mountain communities all figure conspicuously in the pioneer day history of the county. The history of every one of these places furnishes history for a deeply interesting book within themselves. Bankersmith, while the name is comparatively new, is one of the old settlements in the county. A switch on the F. & N. Ry., was given this name, but there was an old settlement there long before the railroad was ever built. Cain City, a thriving station on the F. & N. Ry., is one of the beauty spots of Gillespie county. It came into existence with the building of the railroad. With few exceptions the oldtimers in these communities, the only people who could give the early day history, have passed away, and with them went a great deal of the best history ever made by pioneers in the development of a new country, for many of the settlements are much older than the names they now bear. They are all prosperous, peaceful communities, now, with their schools, good homes, good ranches and farms, but the real history of every community in the county is that of hardships, struggles, heroic determination and achievement. They each represent the toil, the sacrifice and devotion to an ideal of some pioneer man and his wife, and the sons and daughters of these old pioneers did their full share of the toiling and suffering, enjoying only the most limited school advantages, and denied even the simplest luxuries enjoyed by the children and younger people of today.

The old settlers in these, then isolated communities, made the kind of history of which any state or any nation can be proud, and they were the kind of people of whom their descendants are justifiably proud.

The Last of the Oldtimers.

In May, 1921, Fredericksburg held the Seventy-fifth Jubilee, celebrating the arrival of the first colonists in 1846. This was the third celebration of the kind held in Gillespie county, the event taking place every twenty-five years. In so far as the records show, only thirty-nine of the old colonists participated in the last celebration. Possibly some other old settlers in Gillespie were living in 1921, but in so far as the records show the following attended the celebration:

John A. Klein, Adam Klein, Christian Strackbein, Mrs. J. W. Anderegg, Christian Feuge, Henry Feuge, Carl Moellering, Chas. Schlaudt, sr., Ludwig Usener, Henry Kordzik, Jacob Schuessler, G. Burrow, M. Pfiester, John Schuessler, Wm. Dannheim, Peter Weber, Peter Meurer, Henry Kammlah, Peter Schandua, Rudolf Eckert, Wm. Kiehne, Henry Moellering, Conrad Hahne, Adolf Quindel, Henry Keller, Wm. Heimann; Mesdames Henry Dietz, M. Pfiester, Wm. Ellebracht, William Feller, G. Burrow, J. W. Braeutigam, Joseph, Jenschke, Conrad Herbort, John Immel, John Schuessler, Aug. Ernst and Julius Klett.

Two other oldtimers present were Daniel and Wm. D. Fritze, of Grandfield, Oklahoma.

The oldest of these persons were very young, most of them mere children, when they first came to Fredericksburg. Not all of them came with the very first colonists, but all of them reached Fredericksburg long before civilization had reached the surrounding country.

Of these thirty-nine persons, so far as known, only nine are now living, these being: John A. Klein, Christian Strackbein, Henry Feuge, Carl Moellering, Ludwig Usener, Mrs. Wm. Feller, Jacob Schuessler, Mason county; Mrs. John Schuessler, Llano; Mrs. M. Klett, Blanco county; Wm. D. Fritze and perhaps Daniel Fritze.

The following old timers have died since the first of January, 1925: Conrad Hahne, Rudolf Eckert, Adolf Quindel, Mrs. J. W. Anderegg, Mrs. Joseph Jenschke.

Gillespie County' War Record.

During the war Gillespie county furnished more than its quota of men and in response to every call subscribed more than its share for liberty bonds and war saving stamps.

The Gillespie county boys stood the highest mental and physical tests, a fine tribute to their inherited qualities and proper training.

It has been impossible to get a complete list of the men who went into the service, as volunteers and as drafted men. The total number to enter the service was 360, but the only way to get the complete list would be from the war department, and that would probably require several months.

The first American officer killed overseas was Lieutenant Louis J. Jordan, of Gillespie county. He belonged to Co. C, 142 Art., and was killed in action near Ludesville, France, by shrapnel, during a heavy artillery bombardment, March 5, 1918. He was 28 years, 1 month and 5 days old.

Private Edmund Brinkrolf, killed in action, both legs shot off and otherwise mutilated. The records as obtainable fail to give place and date.

Private Will Hines, 183rd infantry, 42 division, killed in action during St. Mihiel drive. His body was torn to pieces.

Private Henry Schneider, jr,, and private Alfred Schlaudt were killed in action, but no records as to their company,.nor when and where they were killed.

Private Norman Tobin, 36 Division, killed in action during Meuse-Argonne drive.

Private Alfred Billo, Co. C, 168th infantry, killed in action in Meuse-Argonne; torn to pieces by shrapnel.

The following men died of injuries received or sickness contracted while overseas: Private Walter Eckert, died of spinal meningitis in a hospital in France; Private Emil Beyer died of pneumonia, Oct. 15, 1918, in hospital, Beaume, France; Private Henry Green, died in Kerrville Sanitarium from effects of being gassed while in action; Private Harry Duecker, died March 27, 1922, as result of gas and wounds received in action overseas; Private Dave Farris, died in Kerrville Sanitarium, his death due to complications resulting from being gassed; Private Carlos Alexander, died in Hawaiian Islands, death due to being gassed while in service in France; Private

Willie Enderlin died in New Mexico as result of being gassed. The following died in training camps: Walter Burrow, of influenza, Camp McArthur, Waco, Texas; Felix Grobe, of influenza, at Camp Bowie, Fort Worth, Texas; Hermann Hohmann, died in New York of influenza; Edwin Tatsch, died at Camp Travis, San Antonio, of influenza; Walter Langerhans, died at Camp Sheridan, Ala., of influenza; Henry Koch, died at Camp Mabry, Austin, Texas, of influenza; Eddie Klaerner, died at El Paso, of influenza; Willie Enderlin, died in New Mexico from effects of influenza contracted while in the service.

The oldest man in the casualty list was Lieutenant Jordan, and he was only 28. The average age of all the men in the death list was less than 24 years. Major Alfred P. C. Petsch, present member of the legislature from Gillespie county, was considerably under thirty when he entered the service.

The following received the Croix de Guerre for conspicuous service: Fritz Braeutigam, Corporal Otto Grona and Thomas J. Martin.

Not a single Gillespie county man was disciplined for infraction of military rules. Twenty-two paid the supreme sacrifice, and 338 were honorably discharged.

While these Gillespie county boys were fighting, and while these Gillespie county citizens were contributing their money, and in every way denying themselves common luxuries and complying with food conservation requirements, certain persons, who could not correctly write a sentence in the English language, although they spoke no other language, who didn't know a noun from a verb, a quotation mark from an interrogation point, who couldn't tell the difference between a work on higher mathematics and an unabridged dictionary, were raising a terrible rumpus about teaching only the English language in public schools and using it exclusively in private conversation. This language bugaboo was the crowning farce of humbuggery and pitiable ignorance, plus considerable pure cussedness. Had the German citizens been disposed to engage in hostile plots they would have done so in strict secrecy, and in that event what difference would it have made what language they used. The

German citizens were hounded and harrassed and libeled enough to justify them in hostile actions and resentment, but be it said to their credit they "considered the source," smiled at the nonsense and humbuggery of it, and let it go at that. During the civil war hundreds of them were assassinated by dastardly barbarians, just because some of them were loyal in sentiment to the Union, and courageous enough to die for their convictions, although many of the most distinguished Confederate soldiers were Texas Germans. During the World War they were subjected to the most unjust and cowardly insults, not by real soldiers, real patriots and real men, but by a flock of howling blatherskites, most of whom were fervently shooting hot air, when, for the good of humanity, they should have been in Europe getting shot.

History of the Printing Business.

The first newspaper venture in Gillespie county was a German paper named "Wahrheitsfreund" or "Freiheitsfreund." No records seem to exist, and the memory as to names of people connected with it, seems to be unreliable.

In 1873 the "Wochenblatt" was founded, but soon got in financial straits. E. Wahrmund, Sr., and F. Kneese were at different times during the early existence forced to take over the plant to protect their investment, as the different editors and managers were scholars but no business men. A Mr. Buchen, Harry Schultz and Arved Hillmann edited the paper for them, until James Holten, in 1886, secured the paper by purchase. He continued publication for six years, when he got in financial troubles. Hillmann and Stork, as lessees, then publised the paper for several months, until the plant was tied up by a lawsuit and finally sold by order of court to satisfy claims. Mr. R. Penniger bought the plant in June 1893 and one month later began publication again, which he continued for 23 years. In 1916 Mr. Penniger decided to form a stock company. Shares to the amount of $15,000 were sold and the business incorporated under the name of Fredericksburg Publishing Co. Later in the same year the Publishing Co. acquired the Fredericksburg Standard by purchase from H. W. Kusenberger and the two plants were combined. One of the first gasoline engines in Texas was used in furnishing power to operate the press in Mr. Penniger's time.

During the last 20 years the office had grown so that local business was not enough, and outside business was solicited, resulting in orders from all over the states of Texas, Louisiana, Arkansas and Oklahoma.

At present there are published in this plant, the Fredericksburg Wochenblatt, Fredericksburg Standard, Courier-Record, Missionsfreund, and Kerrville District Bulletin.

Mr. Penniger remained with the Fredericksburg Publishing Company as manager and editor until 1920, when Robert Hanschke died while on a visit in Germany, and Mr. Penniger purchased the "Freie Presse fuer Texas" from his heirs. Mr. Wm. Dietel succeeded him as editor and Mr. Wm. Habenicht as manager. When Mr. Dietel resigned his position as editor, Mr. O. R. Schumacher was appointed in his place, and is at this time editing both, the Wochenblatt and the Standard.

(While this book was being printed, Mr. Schumacher suffered a stroke of appoplexy and died on April 20, 1925, at the age of 60 years.)

After resigning as editor from the Fredericksburg Publishing Company, Mr. Dietel formed a partnership with Mr. A. R. Gold. They founded the "Radio Post," but after a short time Mr. Dietel purchased Mr. Gold's interest and is now sole owner and editor.

Green Harrison founded the Gillespie County News in 1892. Issued same in Willow City for several months and then moved to Fredericksburg, where he continued publication for about 2 years, and then sold to Webster McGinnis, who, about a year later sold to Hy. East. After publishing the paper for several years, he sold to R. T. Gliddon. Mr. Gliddon continued the publication for a number of years and in 1908 sold to Owen Faubion, who changed the name of the publication to Fredericksburg Standard. Under this name the publication was sold by him to H. W. Kusenberger, who continued publication until the Fredericksburg Publishing Company purchased the paper in 1916.

In 1916 the Publishing Company entered into a contract with I. G. Wehmeyer, an all around printer of wide experience gained in the various large offices of the country, for all the mechanical work in its plant. His experience enabled him to put the work on an efficiency basis and the company could contract for a great amount of book work that is ordinarily beyond the sphere of the small town printery. In this way the output was greatly increased.

The officers of the company are, A. P. C. Petsch, president; August Zincke, vice-president; Wm. Habenicht, secretary-treasurer.

Glowing Promises of the German Emigration Campany.

This important and interesting item is stuck in here for the reason that the writer was unable to get a copy of the contract between the colonists and the German Emigration Company, until the preceding pages had been printed. It properly belongs with the history of the formation of the German Emigration Company.

It will be recalled that the first evil spirit to inflict itself on the honest, but impractical, gullible officials of the Adelsverein, was a French land sharper by the name of Burgeois d' Orvanne. He unloaded a worthless grant for a nice cash consideration and then got to be official hot air dispenser for the company. The worst modern hot air artists are pigmies compared to d'Orvanne.

He wrote most of the pamphlets, newspaper bunk, and generally supervised the publicity work for the company. He also manufactured a masterful lot of Utopian dreams and promises. Henry F. Fisher later confirmed this bunk. It served his purpose to do so and what did Fisher and d'Orvanne care about what happened to the German emigrants and the German Emigration Company?

Under d'Orvanne's guiding genius here is what the German Emigration Company contracted to do for the emigrants:

1, To make the rivers navigable. 2, to canalize them, if necessary. 3, to see that steamboat lines were established. 4, to establish and build good roads and bridges. 5, to build churches. 6, to establish savings banks. 7, to establish one or more free schools. 8, to build hospitals, infirmaries, orphan asylums and establish drug stores. 9, to furnish each settlement a grist mill, a sawmill and a cotton gin. 10. to advance the surveying fees on all colonists' lands. 11, to deliver a house to each colonist on his land at a cost of not more than $24.00, which house, as it developed, could not be built for less than $100.00. 12, to transport the colonist from Germany to the colony site, together with unlimited baggage. 13, to keep them in provisions and deliver them goods, implements, farming utensils and material, work animals, horses, oxen, cows and other livestock, all on a credit until the second successive crop had been raised.

D'Orvanne and Fisher knew this was the rankest kind of bunk, at least ninety per cent of it. But it was captivating; it created the craze and that was what Fisher and d'Orvanne were up to, all same modern grafters. Had the company been guided by simple honesty and practical methods, and furnished the emigrants transportation, homes, schools, work stock and reasonable credit until they made a few crops, there would have been no calamity story to tell regarding the German colonists .

But just imagine what a howling success the German Emigration Company, with its pitiable little capital stock of $80,000, would have had building miles of public highways and spanning numerous rivers with expensive bridges; canalizing the Colorado, San Saba, Llano, Pedernales, Gaudalupe and other rivers, and putting steamboats to navigating them. Dallas hasn't been able to get the Trinity river navigated yet. But the oldtimers fell for this rank bunk just as we present day folks fall for similar nonsense.

In Conclusion.

There has never been and there will never be a complete history of Gillespie county. No history of the county will ever be so complete that some important and interesting matters will not be omitted, or, at most, but briefly mentioned. There is little of the county's history of record, and those who know it from personal experience are passing away. In fact, most of them have gone. But in the preceding pages the reader has at least obtained an excellent idea and practical knowledge of the experiences of these old pioneers. They started in poverty, isolation and distress. Notwithstanding this fact they and their descendants have accomplished wonders. In no community in the United States has more been accomplished.

Gillespie county is today one of the wealthiest stock raising and agricultural counties in the United States. This wealth is remarkably well distributed. There are no millionaires and no paupers in the county. They started without land and without money. It can be truthfully said that they dressed in rags, had but little to eat, and at first lived in log huts. They worked hard, endured tortures and privations, acquired land and made it productive, built good homes and made permanent improvements. Nowhere will you find better country homes, better improved and properly cared for farms and stock. And near most of these good country homes you will find some evidence of the first humble home built by some old pioneer seventy or seventy-five years ago. And in a great majority of cases the children or grandchildren of the original founder of that home still own and occupy it. This fact within itself makes wonderful history. Ninety per cent of the present citizenship of Gillespie county are descendants of the first settlers.

According to the records there are approximately 2000 farms in Gillsepie county, and only 50 tenants.

The conservative market value of the farm and ranch lands in the county is $20,000,000. Against this land there are mortgages of less than $450,000, and most of these mortgages are with federal farm loan banks.

The only bonded indebtedness of the county is for public roads and it is very small. No county in the state has better public schools and school buildings, and yet the indebtedness of the districts is very small, many of them owing nothing at all.

Fredericksburg is perhaps the largest unincorporated town in the United States, and yet it is one of the most orderly, beautiful and cleanest towns in the country. They have no city tax at all, and perhaps the lowest tax rate of any county in Texas.

They started with nothing, have managed well and accomplished wonders. Silently, without bluster or pretence they have given a model for home life, civic pride, and industrial achievement that deserves to go as a message and a precept to every community in the world. They have not been perfect, nor have they achieved the perfect, but their work stands as indisputable evidence of the wonderful things they have done, and the exceptionally high record of their character is evidenced by the small per cent of crime in the history of the county. Their criminal dockets are filled mostly by the names of drifting, lawless Americans, and by cases transferred here from other counties. They are the greatest people in the world to attend to their own business. Only great people could have endured what these people have endured, and have done what they have done, and great people do not waste their time attending to the business of others, or fretting, fuming and fussing about insignificant matters.

Only by knowing these people, only by seeing the work they have done can they be properly understood and appreciated.

They have used common sense and common honesty in their public as in their private affairs. They have not been foolishly extravagant nor have they been penurious.

A number of the principal business concerns of Fred·ericksburg were established before the civil war, and are still conducted by some member of the family that established them. There have been fewer business failures in Fredericksburg than in any town of the same size in the United States.

The citizens of Gillespie county have at all times nobly done their part in peace and in war.

APPENDIX

CHURCH HISTORY OF GILLESPIE COUNTY.

The Methodist Episcopal Church South.

(By Rev. R. Gammenthaler.)

In giving a brief history of the Methodist churches of Gillespie county I shall start with the church at Fredericksburg. The first Methodist church in Fredericksburg was organized in the pioneer days—away back in 1850. At that time there were only a few families of Methodists living in the community. The church was erected on the present site in 1855, under the pastorate of Rev. C. A. Grote. The building, which has the same dimensions today as it then had, 40x60 feet, was built of rocks quarried in the hills of the county. The lumber and shingles were hauled with ox teams from a saw mill then in operation in Bastrop county. The rafters measure 8x8 inches, joined at the top by a wooden pin. The cross beams are 3x6 inches. The wooden pins are still intact, and in as good condition today as when first put in.

Prominent among the charter members were Ludwig Kneese, father of Louis, Otto, Henry, John, Ernst and William Kneese; the father of L. F. and Charles Kneese; Mr. Ellebracht, father of Louis and Henry Ellebracht; H. Hoerster, Theo. Buchholz, the Dursts and others. That was at a time when the Indians were roaming about, and as a matter of precaution and safety, heavy iron rings were fastened in the rocks of the building to which worshippers hitched their horses on Sundays. The building was erected at a cost of $1,100. It was remodeled in 1923 at a cost of $2500, but the iron rings were left where they are as a matter of historic interest. After the war betwen the states a sad incident occurred—the division of the church into what is known as the Methodist Episcopal and the Methodist Episcopal South. The congregation has grown to no mean proportions, notwithstanding the fact that many moved away to other quarters of the country. The present membership totals 184.

There are two other Southern Methodist churches in the

county, one at Willow City and the other at Harper. The
present pastors of these three churches are: Rev. R. Gammenthaler, Fredericksburg; Rev. T. H. Davis, Willow City,
and Rev. J. H. E. Willmann, Harper.

The majority of the ministers who served in Fredericksburg have passed away. The old records show the names of
the following ministers:

C. A. Grote, J. W. Devilbis, P. E. H. Bauer, F. Vorden-
baumen, H. P. Young, presiding elder; J. W. Whipple, presiding elder; P. E. C. Pluennecke, John C. Kopp, I. H. Cox,
presiding elder; J. J. Brunow, F. Mumme, J. Kern, J. A.
Schaper, G. Buchschacher, Wm. Knolle, Daniel Schrimpf,
August Scheurich, Ernst Frezel, H. Jordan, Jacob Bader, A.
E. Rector, R. A. Lemberg, Robert Moerner, J. C. Winkel,
O. W. Benold, W. D. Wiemers, A. R. Vetter and the present
incumbent. Of the foregoing list only ten are still living.

The church at Willow City was organized in 1885 and
in 1900 the church building was erected under the pastorate
of Rev. J. T. Lassater. The present total membership of
the Willow City church is 80.

The Harper congregation was organized October 30,
1904, by Rev. J. T. King. The church was built in 1908,
during the pastorate of Rev. R. A. Waltrip, assisted by Rev.
Theophelus Lee, presiding elder. The pastors before the
church was built were: J. T. King, Rev. Barton, and W. E.
Garrison. Since the church was built the pastors have been:
R. A. Waltrip, J. T. Osborn, T. J. Thomason, J. L. Burns, R.
H. Obarr, R. Gammenthaler, O. W. Benold, E. W. Bode, and
J. H. E. Willmann. The present membership of the Harper
church is 42.

METHODIST EPISCOPAL CHURCH.

(By Rev. G. H. Houy.)

The Methodist Episcopal church in Fredericksburg was
organized May 5, 1871, by Conrad Pleunnecke, in the home of
Fritz Kneese, father of L. F. and Charles Kneese, who are
today members of this church. The charter members of the
church were Henry Bratherich, Fritz Kneese, Dorothea
Kneese, L. F. Kneese, Johnna Kneese, Sophie Kneese, Henry

Stiehl, Daniel Stiehl, Mary Stiehl, Hermann Fisher, Elizabeth Fisher, Catherine Feuge, Jacob Treibs, Sr., Catherine Treibs, Jacob Treibs, Jr., Mary Treibs, Fritz Winkle, Anna Winkle, Edward Winkle, Minna Schuessler and Gregina Bratherich. The first stewards were Fritz Kneese, Hermann Fisher and Jacob Treibs, Sr.

The first church was built in 1872, and occupied the site of the present church. The first church was a stone structure, 28x40 feet, and was constructed under the supervision of Carl Jung. The first quarterly conference was held in this church September 23, 1872. This conference was presided over by Rev. Carl Urbantke, the first presiding elder of this district.

The church has enjoyed a steady and satisfactory growth, its present membership being 209, as compared with an original membership of 21. Six boys raised in this church have taken up ministerial work, these being: Daniel Stiehl, Gustav Schulze, A. D. Moehle, G. H. Houy, E. E. Schmidt and Henry Roos. Daniel Stiehl died some two years ago; Gustav Schulze is on the superannuated list and resides at Grit, in Mason County; G. H. Houy, present pastor at Fredericksburg; A. D. Moehle, in active work in the Brenham district; E. E. Schmidt, now in charge of a pastorate in the Meyers settlement near Riesel, Texas. Henry Roos was in charge of a church in Missouri, until he underwent an operation and died March 12, 1925, and was buried at Brenham, the former home of his wife.

The present large, substantial and beautiful church was dedicated February 24, 1924, and was erected at a total cost of approximately $22,000, this cost not including value of the half block of land occupied by the church. The present church has a seating capacity of four hundred. One of the big features of the present church is the basement. This basement is provided with a kitchen and dining hall, the dining hall furnishing accommodations for social gatherings and as a dining room at all times for persons coming to church from their country homes, some of the active members living more than twenty miles from town. In the basement there are also five Sunday school class rooms, a ladies' dressing room, and an extra heating room, equipped with a hot air heater. The church has handsome and substantial furnishings, but nothing gaudy or elaborate, the pews costing around $1700. The church ventilation is excellent and the acostics perfect. Situated in the northwest part of town, it has a beautiful location, commanding a fine view of the picturesque range of hills to the southwest, west and northwest of Fredericksburg.

The parsonage occupies a lot just across the street from the church. It is a two-story building, with eight rooms and a sleeping porch. The original parsonage was built many years ago, but it was remodeled and added to some fifteen years ago.

The church has three choirs. First, the male choir, of which the leader is Henry Fisher, son of Hermann Fisher, one of the churche's charter members; second, mixed choir, of which Henry Fisher is also leader; and the Junior choir, of which Jacob Treibs is leader. Mr. Treibs is a grandson of Jacob Treibs, Sr., and a son of Jacob Treibs, Jr., both charter members of this church, which shows how the descendants of the pioneer founders of this church have stuck together, grown up and worked together in this church.

The present officers are: H. E. Fisher, local preacher; Edward Durst, exhorter; H. E. Fisher, L. F. Kneese, Louis Woerner, Emil Treibs, John Durst, Hermann Schmidt, Ludwig Schmidt, Carl Koenig and Ben Kneese, stewards.

Trustees: Carl Woerner, president; Ed. Durst, secretary; Henry Koenig, treasurer; L. F. Kneese, Charley Kneese, Charley Feuge, Ed. Roos, Louis Ahrens and Arthur Houy.

The following persons served during the construction of the present church, acting in the capacity of building committee: Rev. G. H. Houy, H. E. Fisher, L. F. Kneese, Louis Woerner, Hermann Schmidt and Arnold Houy. Ben Kneese was treasurer of the building fund, assisted by Arnold Houy.

Carl Feuge supervised the masonry work, and Alfred Burrer supervised the carpenter work.

The following pastors have served this church: Gustav Ely, one year; Anton Ulrich, three years; Jacob Ott, three years; George Koch, three years; Otto Reibe, three years; Emil Draeger, three years; J. W. Pfaeffle, four years; Hermann Homburg, one year; Gustav Schulze, four years; G. W. F. Schreiber, four years; Albert Hild, one year; John Hierholzer, three years; G. H. Houy, six years, when on account of poor health he retired for five years; J. A. Traeger, three years; John Kleinknecht, two years; G. H. Houy, now serving fourth year of second pastorate.

The following charter members of the church are now living: L. F. Kneese, Hermann Fisher, Jacob Treibs and Edward Winkle, all of Fredericksburg; Sophie Kneese, now the wife of Rev. Julius Urbantke, living at The Grove, in Coryell county, and Mrs. August Wahl, formerly Mary Treibs, lives eight miles north of Fredericksburg.

EVANGELICAL - PROTESTANT CHURCH
(By Rev. A. Koerner.)

The Evangelical-Protestant Congregation of the Holy Ghost is the oldest in Gillespie County, the pioneer church. Its history begins with the first prayer offered to Divine Providence by the sturdy settlers of 1846 before they went to sleep for the first time on the soil of their new found "Heimat." The majority of the first settlers were of protestant faith. During 1846 and the greater part of 47 the services were held under a large liveoak tree that stood south from the present court-house. Rev. S. W. Basse served as first minister. He preached the first sermon in the old communion church, or "Vereins-Kirche." The cornerstone of this old church, remarkable on account of its architecture (an octagon, each side 18 ft. long and high, covered by an octagonal 10 ft. high slanting roof, that carried an octagonal copula, each side of which was 10 ft. high and of the same width, covered again by an octagonal roof 7 ft. high; total height 45 feet; built entirely by hand from the best trees and stone around the present town), was laid in the spring of 1847, and the building dedicated late the same year. This old landmark of the early German-Texan pioneer days was torn down shortly after 1896. The cornerstone became lost (for that reason even the year of the erection of the old church has been wrongly stated to be 1846) and forgotten, until the present pastor with the help of Mr. Henry Basse and Mr. Klett searched for it and found it on the premises of the late Mrs. J. Klett, where it had served for years a drinking trough for chickens. Today this relic of by gone days has a resting place in the Holy Ghost Church together with the first bell of little more than 80 pounds, that called the first settlers to devotion and prayer.

The old Vereins-Kirche served also as a town-house, meeting place and certainly was intended to be a last place of refuge in the event of a possible Indian attack, for which the strange but most practical octagonal architecture testifies.

The pastors B. Dangers, Hermann and Christian Koch filled the pulpit of the old church up to 1886. The first and last died here. Under Hermann's pastorate the congregation added "Holy Ghost" to its name.

As early as 1849 a number of settlers seceded from the first church and founded the Methodist church. In 1850 an orthodox Lutheran Church was organized, and in the same year the settlers of the Roman Catholic faith, who worshiped up to this year with the Protestants in the old church (but without an ordained priest) ceded their prorata interest in the ownership of the church building to the Protestants for a nominal remuneration and in the year 1887 the present "Evangelical congregation" left the Holy Ghost congregation, led by a dissatisfied pastor.

The cornerstone of the present large church with its beautiful 125 ft. steeple was laid on June 6th. 1888, the church was dedicated on March 31st., 1893. Rev. DeGeller served during those years as pastor.

Under the present pastor, A. Koerner, who accepted the pastorate on Sept. 7, 1919, as the first minister that belongs to a synod (the German Evangelical Synod of North America) since the split in 1887 the congregation enjoys a healthy development. From 1920—22 the interior of the monumental edifice was renovated and beautified; 1922 the 75th. anniversary was celebrated and the present parsonage erected as a memorial of this anniversary.

An item of interest is the fact that the parsonage together with the improvements of the church interior cost approximately the same amount that was paid by the congregation for the whole church building except the helmet of the steeple, namely $12,000. During the years of 1888—1893 only skilled workers received a little more than one dollar a day and hundreds of wagonloads of the big stones used in building the church were broken and hauled to the place for almost nothing or not more than 75c a day.

The helmet of the steeple was constructed in 1907. It is 35 feet high, only first class materials were used and according to the contract with a local firm H. V. Kuenemann, its cost amounted to $605. Today it would not be possible to build it for less than $4000 and the church building as it stands today could not be duplicated for less than $50,000.

Today the church membership includes more than 400 families with more than 2400 souls, almost all living within Gillespie County, or about 25 per cent of the total population.

With its Lord Jesus and its pastor the congregation believes in the ultimate "Union of all faithful Christians on earth. Its old pioneer character has been preserved, and it is now a living and growing church, together with about 50 churches of the same faith in Texas, the largest of which are: The Evangelical Protestant churches at New Braunfels, San Antonio, Houston, Waco, Fort Worth, Seguin, Lockhart, Weimar, Schulenburg, Cibolo, Geronimo, Coupland, Richland. and other towns in Texas.

HISTORIC SKETCH OF ST. MARY'S PARISH.

(By Rev. H. Gerlach.)

The first settlers arrived May 9, 1846. Lay services were held by the Catholics in the house of a school teacher, John Leyendecker, in 1847. These services consisted mainly of prayers and gospel reading. In the fall 1847 the congregation was visited by two missionaries, one a French priest, Father Dubuis, the other one a Spaniard, Father Salarza. They administered the Holy Sacrament of baptism and said mass in one of the verein's buildings, located opposite the present Nimitz Hotel. Father Dubuis spoke German, and he and his companion remained for two weeks. They then visited the surrounding country, going as far as Fort Concho and Fort Mason.

About that time the building grounds for a church and priest's house were bought. It may be interesting to note that the lot on which the first church was built was purchased at a cost of $18.00. The structure was partly of rocks and partly of lumber. The masons were Jacob Metzger and Peter Schmitz; the carpenters, Peter Schandua and Brinkhof.

In the summer of 1848, Rev. Mentzel came to Fredericksburg. The church not being yet completed, he said mass in the priest's house which had been erected shortly before. After a stay of a few weeks this missionary left for Europe. Rev. Hugg, who came after Father Mentzel, stayed three weeks. He then returned to Galveston where he died, a victim to yellow fever.

Father Dubuis paid several missionary visits to Fredericksburg, but never made a permanent stay. The first priest to remain here for a long period was Rev. Mueller, who arrived in 1852 and remained until August, 1855. The Sacrament of Confirmation was administred for the first time in October, 1854, by the first bishop of Texas, Right Reverend Bishop Odin, whose seat was then at Galveston.

Rev. P. Tarrillion came on Dec. 1, 1855, and on December 26 of the same year returned to Galveston. He was followed by Father Zoeller. In 1859 a great orator and missionary of the Society of Jesus, Father Weninger, held a mission. One of the main points he brought to the attention of the faithful was the fact their church had become too small, and, since it was no more adequate to their needs, it was their duty to build a larger and worthier one.

In the course of time the people followed the advice of the famous missionary, and erected a new church under the administration of Father Peter Baunach, O. S. B. A subscription list was started Nov. 10, 1860, and on June 9, 1861, the corner stone of the new building was laid and blessed in presence of Father Peter and all the people. In the stone were enclosed the names of the Pope Pius IX, of the Bishop of the diocese, Bishop Odin, of the Pastor, Father Peter Baunach; the list of contributors, two German newspapers, the "Katholische Zeitung," New York, and the "Wahrheits Freund," Cincinnati; one English paper, "The Catholic Herald," Philadelphia; corn and wheat, a few silver coins and a bottle of wine. The number of subscribers was 136 and among these was a large number of non-Catholics. The work on the Church was a free contribution of the people, and hence the exact cost cannot be given. The amount paid for material was $7687.53.

On November 17, 1861, Father Dubuis, who had visited Fredericksburg several times as a missionary, paid another visit to the congregation. This time however he came on a special mission; he was now Bishop Dubuis. He blessed the new bell on Nov. 21; on the 22, took place the dedication of the new church. The records show that Bishop Dubuis celebrated Solemn High Mass with the assistance of three priests; furthermore, that the ceremony lasted from 8:30 a. m. till 1:00 p. m., and that the people of the whole town, irrespective of creed, were present at the celebration. At the conclusion all united in the singing of Te Deum, while an Indian was ringing the bell.

It is well to recall the times at which this church was erected. Many had gone to war, and those who remained offered their services free of charge. It is but doing those pioneers justice, and honoring their memory, to mention here their names.

The masons who did work from beginning to end: Anton Kraus, John Metzger and Jacob Metzger; this last workman died before the completion of the building. Assistance was given by Christian Kraus, Peter Schmitz, Joseph Jenschke, John Walch and Peter Petsch. The stone cutters were Peter Schmitz, Moritz Hartmann, Mathias Zenner, the carpenters: Frederick Gentemann, John Kunz, Schmidtzinsky and Heep; Zimmermann, Heinrich Cordes, a non-Catholic, Frederick Jordan and Henry Kruse. Those who worked on the roof: Henry Cordes, Frederick Gentemann and John Kunz. Tinner: John Fritz. Special zeal was shown by Wendelin Kohler, Franz Mittel and Franz Stehling.

The baptismal font was cut by Moritz Hartmann and put up Sept. 28, 1864. It is now used regularly since the last two years at the solemnity of the first Communion, when the first communicants renew their baptismal vows over the same font which witnessed the baptism of their parents and grand parents.

Father Peter was called back to his Monastery, Dec. 13, 1866. Rev. Theo. Grundener, O. S. B. succeeded him, and arrived Jan. 7, 1867. He stayed till March, 1868, when Father Peter Tarrillion came as resident pastor. Father Tarrillion remained till Jan., 1900, when he died in San Antonio, of heart failure. Under his administration three new bells were bought for the church.

Father Roch was his successor, but he was not to stay long, for he died, June 14, 1904, a victim to typhoid fever. Father Neisens, who succeeded him, was pastor for nine years, until 1913, during which time the present new church was built.

Then came our present pastor, Rev. H. Gerlach, in Aug., 1913. The growth of the parish soon made it necessary to have an assistant priest, and Father Wolf was the first one to come in that capacity in the fall of 1913. He remained but a short time, and in July, 1914, left for Europe. He was prevented from reaching his intended destination by the declaration of war. Father F. Drees was the next assistant, and he was followed by Rev. R. A. Heinzmann, during which time a separate congregation was organized at Harper, Texas, which was supplied by Father Heinzmann. Father Leo Goertz was his successor. He remained until the fall of 1923, when he left for Divine, Texas, where he now has his own congregation. Since Father Gerlach's arrival, three beautiful stained windows have been purchased for the church.

ST. MARY'S PAROCHIAL SCHOOL.

The first man to make an attempt at teaching a Catholic school in Fredericksburg was John Leyendecker, in 1846, but he received no salary and soon had to give it up. In 1856 Franz Stein taught school, beginning with a class of seven children. Under Father Peter, W. Kelley was teacher; then Christian Kraus. It was in 1870 that the Sisters of Divine Providence came here for the first time and taught school in the old Straube house. The residence formerly used by the

Sisters was bought by Father Tarrillion. It served for a time as a school house, but soon proved too small. Then the old church was remodeled and fitted for a school building.

The Catholic High School.

In 1922 the number of school children had increased to more than 200 and the old church proved inadequate to accommodate this number, and as the expense of properly changing and remodeling it was almost prohibitive, a meeting was held September 1, 1922, to devise means for taking care of the situation. At this meeting it was agreed that a modern new building, to cost approximately $45,000 should be built. A committee composed of Rev. H. Gerlach, advisor; Robert Blum, president; I. G. Wehmeyer, secretary; Felix Stehling, treasurer; Max Blum, Joseph Molberg, Joseph Moritz, Edward Knopp, Matthew Pyka, Willie Pape, Emil Schandua and Adolf Fries were elected to take charge of the matter.

The 27 persons present at the first meeting subscribed $5,000, one individual giving $600. By January members of St. Mary's Parish had pledged about $30,000, while fifty four non-Catholics had subscribed $2305. Architect Leo Dielmann, at the request of the committee, drew up plans for a high class modern building, in all respects meeting the requirements of the state school laws in the matter of lighting, hygiene, fire escapes, etc. He estimated that the building with a basement would cost $40,000. But to bring the cost of the building within these figures it would be necessary for the parishoners to do all excavating for basement and foundation, hauling sand, gravel and crushing the rock, free of cost. Bids were called for, but it then developed that the building could not be completed for $45,000. Another meeting was then held and additional funds to the amount of $10,000 was voted. The contract was awarded April 22, 1923, and the building was completed in January, 1924. It is one of the best school buildings in Texas. It will easily accommodate 400 children, has living quarters for the teachers, a basement equipped for manual training, and answering as a playground in bad weather.

The building was consecrated by Bishop Drossaerts, January 29, 1924.

The motto of the school is "Patriotism, Religion, Science."

In 1922 a Ladies' Auxiliary of St. Mary's School was organized. This organization has done wonderful work. Among other things it was through their efforts that a nutrition teacher was secured, this teacher giving lectures in hygiene to both pupils and parents. The ladies raised $3,736 during three years, donating $1500 to the building fund, and expending the balance for school playground equipment. They also furnished the laboratory and contributed largely to the school library.

It is the aim of St. Mary's High School to secure grade A affiliation with the State University in the fall of 1925.

St. Anthony's Business College.

The St. Anthony's Business College was founded in 1909. The course of study of that institution was intended to give a substantial foundation in commercial training, and make the students up-to-date and efficient business men. It was very successful in this respect, as all its graduates are holding responsible positions here and elsewhere and are well spoken of by their employers. Almost since its beginning, Professor J. M. Dubray was principal of the St. Anthony's College. In 1923 Professor Dubray accepted a position as instructor in the St. Edward's College at Austin. After his departure Professor Huslage taught a term in the college. When the new school building was finished, a commercial course was added to the Course of Study of the St. Mary's School, thus making a special business college unnecessary, and the St. Anthony's College was abandoned.

Societies.

St. Joseph's Society for men. Meets on first Sunday in each month.

St. Ann's Christian Mothers' Society for married Ladies: Meets on second Sunday of each month.

St. Aloysius Society for young men: Meets on fourth Sunday of each month.

St. Rosa's Society for young ladies: Meets on third Sunday of each month.

Sacred Heart Society: Meets on first Sunday of each month.

Holy Child's Society for children: Meets every fifth Sunday.

Catholic Knights of America, Branch 1065, founded in 1915 by Wm. Harwerth, with 30 charter members: Holds regular monthly meetings.

All of the above named societies meet in the St. Joseph's Hall, a fine rock building erected in 1900. This hall is located next to the new school building, and is used for the meeting of all church societies, social gatherings, bazaars, plays and entertainments, given for church, school or other good purposes.

The number of families in the parish is approximately 300. There is also a mission at Harper, with a present membership of about 35 German Catholic families.

LUTHERISM IN GILLESPIE COUNTY.

(By Rev. F. A. Bracher.)

Its Early Beginnings.

When the colony of Fredericksburg was founded in 1846, not a single lutheran pastor lived in the entire state of Texas. Most of the settlers were either free Protestants or Roman Catholics. Among the founders of the new colony, however, there was a small number of loyal Lutherans. They worshipped with the other settlers at the community church (vereinskirche.) But the Lutherans could not subscribe to the doctrines as preached, and naturally longed for their mother church. A devoted Layman from the Wupperthal of Germany, Friederich W. Schumacher, was instructed to look for a pastor. He invited a man by the name of Schneider, then stationed at Victoria, Texas. It later developed that Schneider was not a Lutheran, but a Methodist. There were no Methodists in Fredericksburg at that time, but Schneider remained and induced a number of Lutherans and others to establish a Methodist congregation. This was in 1849. Thereafter the Lutherans met privately to instruct their children in the faith of their fathers.

But before long brighter days dawned. In 1850 the first Lutheran Missionaries came to Texas. Others followed in the succeeding year. They came from Pittsburg, Pa., and from the Pilger Mission of St. Chrischona at Bale, Switzerland. In December, 1851, the first Lutheran Synod of Texas was organized at Houston, Texas. To this synod the little band of Lutherans in the colony appealed for spiritual ministration. Their appeal was not in vain. The Texas Synod at that time had a missionary at San Antonio. The door there was shut. Six families of the colony issued a call to him to come to Fredericksburg. He came in August, 1852. It was the Rev. Ph. Fr. Zizelmann, the first Lutheran missionary of Fredericksburg and Gillespie county. The first few services were held at the community church. Then, when the further use of this building was denied to the little band of loyal Lutherans, a vacant log and clay cabin was rented as a place of worship. Here they met from Sunday to Sunday to rejoice in the everlasting Gospel of God's Word and Luther's doctrine pure; here plans were adopted and preparations made to plant the church of the Reformation. Thus were the early beginnings of Lutheranism in Fredericksburg and Gillespie county.

Its Development.

Zion's Church, Fredericksburg, is the mother church of Lutherism in Gillespie county.

When the first Lutheran Missionary arrived in Fredericksburg in August, 1852, only six families gathered about him. But in the following months family after family was added to this small number. On Jan. 13, 1853, fifteen families under the leadership of the Rev. Ph. F. Zizelmann organized Zion's Church, the first Lutheran congregation of Gillespie county. The following were entered as charter members: F. W. Schumacher, E. C. Shaper, J. F. Shaper, H. Strackbein, J. Aurand, D. Rode, F. W. Rode, W. Reider, G. Roehrig, F. W. Rode, Sr., J. W. Wartenbach, P. Hundhausen, H. Goebel and E. Weber. A sound Lutheran constitution was adopted. G. Roehrig, W. Reider, D. Rode and F. W. Schumacher were elected as the first elders of the congregation. Steps were taken at once to secure a church building. Three prospective sites were selected. A lot was cast to decide where the church should be built. It fell upon Lot

No. 151 on San Saba Street, later commonly known as Main
Street. This site was bought from Jacob Harth for the sum
of $45.00. It was a splendid location. The same year the
building, a massive stone structure 50x36x18, was completed
and consecrated to the services of the Triune God. The ap-
proximate cost of the church was $1200.00. A widow donated
$50.00 for the pulpit. Before the completion of the church
the congregation numbered 28 families. The building of a
church of that size and cost was quite a task in those days.
Money was scarce and means to acquire it very limited.
About the only marketable products were corn and sweet
potatoes. The only markets for these, however, were the
distant forts and the cities on the sea coast 300 miles away.
The hauling of freight to these markets was one of the rare
opportunities to make a little cash. All of the rough work
in the construction of the church was gratuitously done by
the members of the congregation. We will quote just a few
items from the old records. W. R., for instance, donated the
hauling of 136 loads of sand and water and the labors of 124
days. Ph. K. and son contributed each 138 days of carpenter
work and the hauling of about 100 loads of lumber and rocks.
Others labored for days and nights and weeks at the lime
kiln. Even the pastor worked as fireman at the kiln for
many a night. No wonder, that there was rejoicing in the
Lutheran camp after the work was crowned with success.
One of the first ministrations performed in the new church
was Pastor Zizelmann's own wedding on Jan. 1st, 1855. The
wedding services were conducted by the Rev. J. C. Roehm,
who was then stationed at Castell on the Llano. The pastor
of Zion's Church had carried on mission work here since 1852
and established a growing mission.

Three parsonages were built by Zion's church in the
course of its history. The first one, a primitive log cabin of
two rooms, was replaced in 1878 by a stone structure 16x44
feet. This building was extensively and elaborately rebuilt
and remodeled and changed into a massive two story concrete and stone structure with every modern convenience in
1922 during the pastorate of the Rev. F. A. Bracher. Zion
Church has now one of the finest parsonages in the Lutheran
church of Texas. The church building was rebuilt and re-

modeled twice, in 1884 and in 1908. In 1921 the galleries in the church were enlarged and a pipe organ installed at the cost of $3000.00. The four foot stonewall, which encloses the church property, is an unique landmark of the past. It was erected in 1874 by the members of the church.

The following pastors have ministered to the congregation since 1852: Zizelmann, Bohnenberger, Schumacher, Holzinger, Goszweiler, Merz, Weiss, Fiedler, Glatzle and Bracher. To Zizelmann, the founder, goes the credit of establishing the congregation on a sound and firm foundation. Schumacher was pastor during the dark years of the civil war. Holzinger steered the congregation out of the turbulent waters of an unsound emotionalism and radical revivalism back to its sane and sound scriptural and Lutheran moorings. Weiss launched out into the deep and transformed the North and East branch of old Zion into filial congregations. To Glatzle goes the distinction of a long, faithful service of 27 years. During his pastorate the congregation on Jan. 11th, 1903, celebrated its 50th Anniversary, the Ladies Aid, the Luther League and the male and the mixed choirs were organized. In 1917 Rev. Glatzle retired from the ministry and the present pastor, Rev. F. A. Bracher of Wichita Falls, was called to succeed him.

Zion's Church has enjoyed a slow, but continuous growth and progress. From 6 in 1852, it has grown to 160 families. Its membership consists of 172 voting members, 498 communicants and 751 souls. Its contributions for various church purposes outside of the congregation have increased from less than $100.00 to more than $2000.00 per annum. Zion's Church of Fredericksburg has been connected with the First Lutheran Synod of Texas from its organization up to the present time and has become one of its leading congregations.

Evangelical Lutheran St. Paul's Church, North Grape Creek.

The second Lutheran church in Gillespie Co. was organized about twelve miles east of Fredericksburg at North Grape Creek. Previous to this organization the Lutherans of this settlement formed a branch of Zion's church at Fredericksburg. The pastors of this church held occasional services in this settlement at the homes of the people. During a pastoral vacancy, after the resignation of Rev. Weiss from Zion's church, who had accepted a call from Victoria, Texas, about 18 families of this settlement peaceably withdrew from their mother congregation in the city and on Nov. the 9th organized a separate congregation, adopting the name of St. Paul. Gottf. Ottmers, Adolf Quindel, John B. Olfers and Aug. Klett were the first elders of this congregation. In the following year, 1884, Rev. M. Haag, the first pastor, was called. Under his leadership the small congregation at once undertook the building of a church. Four acres of land, situated in a gap between two mountains, was donated to the congregation by Mr. Conrad Herbort. This site was later enlarged to seven acres. The church, which was erected here, was a frame building 25x30x14, with a forty foot spire. At the dedication the choir of Zion's church sang: "The Little Brown Church in the Vale." In 1890 the little church in the vale was renovated and enlarged. The parsonage was built in 1885 and rebuilt in 1895. The congregation has its own cemetery not far from the church. Due to the location it was quite a task to get a well. A number of drillings were unsuccessful.

The fact, that a number of young men entered the ministry from this congregation speaks well for St. Paul's. Among these are the Rode Brothers, Erwin and Arthur, located at present at Lodi, Cal. and at Hallettsville. Tex., respectively; the young Rev. Helmuth Gold, of Syracuse, Neb., and two sons of pastors of the congregation the Rev. Im. Haag of Colecamp, Mo., and the Rev. Wm. Flachmeier, Jr., of Columbus, Tex. The following pastors have served the congregation faithfully: Haag, 1884-1902, Ermisch 1902-1907, Billnitzer 1907-1911, Hannemann 1911-1920. The present pastor is the Rev. Wm. Flachmeier, Sr.

Evangelical Lutheran St. John's Church, Crab Apple.

St. John's church in the beautiful valley of the Crab Apple, about 14 miles North of Fredericksburg, is the third Lutheran church of Gillespie Co. Its history is closely interwoven with the history of St. Paul's church at North Grape Creek. It was served by the same pastors. Its first members also originally constituted a branch of Zion's church.

Around 1880 strenuous efforts were made by a denomination of the Reformed church to enstrange the Lutherans of this settlement from their mother church. To counteract these movements a Lutheran mission was established in the valley of the Crab Apple. From year to year Lutheran services were held, first by Rev. Weiss, of Fredericksburg and then by Rev. Haag, of North Grape Creek, at the Crab Apple school house.

Formal organization took place under Rev. Haag, when eleven families adopted a Lutheran constitution and elected the following elders: Nikolaus Rusche, Aug. Sagebiel, Karl Sagebiel and Julius Rusche. Two acres of land, on the banks of the Crab Apple and adjoining the school house, were donated to the little congregation by Aug. Bruns in 1897. In the same year a beautiful roch church, 45x25, with a graceful steeple, was erected on this site. The cost of this massive and stately little church was only about $600.00. How was this possible? The rocks were quarried and hauled, the lime was prepared at a kiln constructed at the Crab Apple and practically all of the work was gratuitously executed by the members of the church under the leadership of Julius Rusche. On Nov. 21st the church was dedicated to the services of the Triune God by Rev. Haag.—The Enchanted rock, one of the grandest freaks and sights of nature in Texas, which only a few decades earlier was idolized and worshipped by the superstitious Indians, is located about three miles from the church. A special service of Thanksgiving was held on this Rock the day following the dedication.

St. John's Church now numbers some forty families. The latest available statistics present the following figures of the numerical strength of St. Paul's and St. John's church together: families 102, communicants 310, souls 402. The Rev. E. A. Sagebiel of Yorktown, Texas, comes from this congregation.

The Evangelical Church, Fredericksburg.

One of the landmarks of old Fredericksburg was the socalled "Community Church" (Vereins-Kirche) erected in the midst of the town by the Mainzer Adelsverein, and Emigration Association of Germany, which was instrumental in the establishment of the colony. The settlers, who worshiped here, adopted for their congregation the name "Evangelical-Catholic Church." This name was later changed to: "Evangelical Protestant Church of the Holy Ghost."

Quite a number of the members of this congregation were by birth and education formerly Lutherans. After the death of the Rev. C. Koch in 1886 a new pastor was called. It was the Rev. J. Heinzelmann. This pastor, in his convictions, as well as in his practice, was a Lutheran. His loyal stand for Lutheranism caused dissatisfaction, friction and opposition in the congregation. The Lutherans of the congregation, who constituted a small majority, rallied around the pastor. Finally a separation took place. The courts awarded the old Community Church to the Evang. Protestant Congregation and the Church Records to the dissenting Lutherans.

Under the leadership of the Rev. J. Heinzelmann a second Lutheran congregation was organized in the city of Fredericksburg, on March, the 27th, 1887. The first church council was composed of the following members: Rev. J. Heinzelmann, Pres., Jacob Schmidt, Karl Naemky, H. Dietz Sr., Chr. Crenwelge, W. Jordan, W. Kammlah, H. Borchers, P. Schuch, K. Itz, W. Wahrmund, G. Peter and D. Ludwig. Until a church building could be secured the services were held at the Southern Methodist church. In 1889 two lots were purchased in the block adjoining the market square on Austin Street in the so called "Unterstadt" (down town section.) On this site a stone Church, 36x64, with a 75 foot steeple, was erected and shortly thereafter also a parsonage, which was a frame building. The Rev. E. Metzenthin of Austin, the Rev. M. Haag of North Grape Creek and Prof. H. Ernst, of St. Paul Minnesota, participated at the dedicatory services on September, 15th, 1889. The cost of lots, church and parsonage, excluding much labor, gratuitously rendered by members of the church, amounted to about $4000.00. The sum of $5750.00 was expended within the last ten years (1914-1924) for the renovation of the church, the rebuilding of the parsonage and other improvements.

At the time of the organization in 1887 the congregation numbered 80 voting members. It now has a membership of 189 voting members, 555 communicants and 765 souls. A mission society, a Ladies Aid, a mixed choir, a male choir, a Luther League and a church orchestra constitute the various organizations within the church. The Sunday School has an enrollment of 135 children. The following ministrations are recorded in the annuals of the church since 1887: Baptisms 1090, confirmations 1034, weddings 303, funerals 357. The present elders of the congregation are: K. Konzack, pastor; Max Schoenewolf, pres.; Felix marschall, vice-pres.; Alb. E. Klett, sec.; R. H. Eckhardt, treas.; K. Itz, E. A. Grobe, Alf. Gold, O. B. Petsch, Emil Dietrich, R. Olfers, Chr. Ressmann, Ad. Stahl and W. J. Schroeder. The congregation has been successful and fortunate in securing able and faithful pastors.

The following 8 pastors have ministered unto the church since its organization:

J. Heinzelmann, 1887-1891; Dr. W. Steinmann, 1891-1897; J. S. Roehm, 1897-1901; J. C. Kuemmel, 1901-1904; S. C. Zettner, 1904-1905; G. J. Ide, 1906-1911; H. Schliesser, 1911-1914; K. Konzack, 1914 to the present time.

Evangelical Lutheran St. Peter's Church, Doss.

One of the noted, picturesque and historic spots of Gillespie county is Lange's mill in the beautiful Doss Valley about 25 miles northwest of Fredericksburg. At this rustic old water mill another Lutheran congregation had its beginning. It was here on the 13th of September, 1896, under an arbor where six Lutheran families gathered around a Lutheran missionary by the name of Rev. H. Krienke to On the 4th of Nov., 1905, St. Peter's church together with in Doss Valley were F. Hahn, Jr., L. Hahn, Christ. Strackbein, Wm. Geistweidt, Jr., Chas. Geistweidt, and Lorenz Wendel.

In 1898 an appropriate location was bought in the hamlet of Doss and a little frame church was built. This edifice is still used as a church school and on the Sabbaths as a messhall. For a number of years the Rev. C. Ziehe, of Mason, took care of the spiritual needs of this little mission. On the 4th of Nov., 1905, St. Peters church together with Christ church of Cherry Spring called its first pastor. It was the Rev. Muerdter. He was succeeded by Rev. Schubert.

The pastorate of these first two missionaries was of short duration.

A new chapter was opened for this mission in 1910. In this year the Rev. H. Meyer took charge of the work. His labors were crowned with marked success.

The members still remember the unique vehicle, introduced by Pastor Meyer to carry him from home to home and from place to place. It was a Sears Roebuck automobile buggy, the first of its kind to make its appearance in this Hill country. Quite often it refused to respond to the pastor's biddings and to do its duty, especially on an upgrade over the steep hills. In such critical situations the pastor good-naturedly abandoned his innovation and took recourse to the old time, trusty, real horse power machine. The days of the reliable Fords had not yet dawned.

Under the pastorate of Rev. Meyer a large and fine stone church was built. It is perhaps the most beautiful of all the country churches in the Texas Synod, an impressive token of faith and a splendid ornament of the beautiful valley of Doss. From 1917 to 1920 the Rev. Alf. Kluge was pastor of the congregation. Internal dissensions troubled and disturbed the congregational life during these years.

The Rev. H. A. Heinecke was the next pastor. His faithful ministry was chiefly a period of reconstruction. The congregation developed nicely along material and spiritual lines.

Rev. L. Hoefer became his successor in 1923. During his pastorate the drilling of a well at the parsonage, 768 feet deep, was completed. This well cost over $2500.00. At the same time a fine new parsonage, a two-story frame structure, was built at the cost of about $3000.00. It was dedicated in 1924 on the second day of Pentecost. The congregation is now in possession of a splendid church property. The membership consists of 56 families.

Evangelical Lutheran Christ Church, Cherry Spring.

In the northern part of Gillespie Co., about 15 miles from Fredericksburg, a spring, surrounded by wild cherry trees, bubbled from the rocks at the foot of the "Lochberg" in the days of the pioneers. From this fountain the region derived its name: "Cherry Spring." Here Christ Church had its origin.

The beginning of this church dates back to the years of the civil war. In those years a few members withdrew from Zion's church of Fredericksburg and gathered for divine services at the home of Mr. Dietrich Rode, a prominent rancher and farmer of the Cherry Spring region. The military government granted to Mr. Rode a license to preach and he became the spiritual leader of the settlers of his neighborhood. From Sunday to Sunday and from year to year his loyal followers with their families came together at his stately home, a large two-story stone structure, which had a spacious hall for such meetings, to enjoy his renowned hospitality and to attend his divine services. On these Sabbaths Mr. Rode, gratuitously ministered to the bodily and spiritual needs of the people that gathered about him. Far into the years of his old age he baptized, instructed and confirmed their children, lead them in prayer and preaching, pronounced the benediction at their wedding festivals and performed the last rites at their graves. The old Rode home is still a landmark of Cherry Spring.

After the death of Mr. Rode a Lutheran congregation was formally organized and the name "Christ Church" was adopted. In 1902 a nice stone church was erected not far from the old Rode home. After this the Rev. C. Ziehe of Mason ministered unto the people for a number of years.

In 1905 it called a pastor of its own together with St. Peter's church at Doss and has since then been served by the same pastors. Christ church numbers 26 families. The members of this church gave financial aid to their sister congregation at Doss in the drilling of her deep well and in the building of her new parsonage.

Evangelical-Lutheran Trinity Church, Albert.

A broad and productive valley, enclosed by ranges of high, rugged hills on the north and on the south, stretches through Gillespie county from the west to the east. The beautiful Pedernales, a clear and rippling mountain stream, winds through this valley and carries its waters over a rocky bed to the far away Colorado.

In this valley, about 20 miles east of Fredericksburg, between the hamlets of Stonewall and Albert, a new Lutheran mission was established in 1902. A Lutheran missionary by the name of Rev. K. Ermisch located at Kerrville, held the first services here in an old rent house near Albert, owned by Mr. Christian Lindig. The name "Trinity Church" was adopted and the following settlers became charter members of the mission: Andreas Nielsen, Hr. Behrens, Christian Lindig, Chas. Lindig, Ferd. Mayer, Mr. G. Manius, Prof. J. Merz, Wm. Peese and perhaps a few others.

The second missionary, Rev. Kupfernagel, lived in the Community in an old lopsided house at Stonewall. In 1905 a little church was built between Stonewall and Hye at the junction of the Fredericksburg, Austin and Blanco City road on the banks of the Pedernales. Before two years had passed the little chapel proved to be too small for the needs of the growing mission. A larger frame church was erected at the same place in 1904. The little chapel became the nucleus of the first parsonage.

The same year the Rev. M. Heinrich took charge of the work. The congregation's part of the salary at that time amounted to $200.00. The balance was contributed by the Mission Board of the First Lutheran Synod of Texas. Rev. M. Heinrich labored in this field as a faithful servant of his Lord and Master and as a devoted pastor of his flock until 1913. His labors in the Lord's vineyard were blessed with marked success. The mission increased from 23 to 95 families and soon became self-supporting. The parsonage was rebuilt and enlarged.

The next pastor was the Rev. O. Lindenberg, who served the congregation faithfully from 1913 to 1920. A new altar and pulpit and a pipe organ were installed during his pastorate. After the World War Rev. Lindenberg resigned to make a trip abroad.

The Rev. Ph. Peter was his successor and served the congregation from June, 1920, to February, 1923.

A new period of good will, harmony and spiritual and material progress was ushered in under the present pastor, the Rev. P. Leonard. The congregation now numbers 120 families and about 500 souls. A new church, to accommodate the growing congregation, will probably be built in the near future.

Two young men have entered the ministry from this congregation: the Rev. E. Meier, under the pastorate of Rev. Heinrich, and the Rev. E. Arhelger, under the pastorate of Rev. Lindenberg.

A Ladies Aid, a Luther League, a male choir, a mixed choir and a church orchestra belong to the organization of the congregation.

Evangelical Lutheran St. James' Church, Harper.

Harper, a thriving little town on the western border of the county, not far from the head of the Pedernales, about 25 miles from Fredericksburg, ranks first in size, population and business activity among the villages of old Gillespie. It has five churches, a high school, a post office, a bank, a drugstore, a hotel, a light plant, cotton gins, blacksmith shops, garages, business houses of various kinds and about 100 dwellings on an areea of over a square mile. All of the business establishments are located on main street, which has a length of about one mile. The first settlers were almost exclusively Anglo-Americans. But within the last two decades quite a number of German-Americans have established homes, farms and ranches in and around Harper.

For years the Lutherans of this community held membership in Zion's church or in the Evangelical church of Fredericksburg. In 1908 the Rev. C. Stadler was placed in this field as the first Lutheran missionary by the First Lutheran Synod of Texas. He worked here for about two years. The Presbyterians and later the Methodists offered the use of their churches to the Lutherans in a kind and friendly spirit.

The Rev C. P. Leonhard, who had just arrived from abroad, entered the field as its second missionary. A brighter day seemed to dawn for the little mission. But the promising pastorate of Rev. Leonhard was limited to the short duration of about a half a dozen months. He responded to a call of a Lutheran congregation in Alsace, Germany, and returned to the old country. During the many and long vacancies the mission was served by pastors of Fredericksburg and Doss.

The year 1914 stands out as a bright milestone of progress in the history of this mission. The Rev. B. Schleifer, an energetic and active missionary, located at Kerrville, had taken charge of the work in the previous year. The congregation was formally organized with 10 families and preparations were made to secure a church home. Mrs. Sophie Klein offered a site at the head of Main Street to the little mission upon which a church could be erected. It was a splendid location. This donation created a spirit of enthusiasm and activity among the Lutherans. Subscriptions were solicited, first from the members of the mission and their friends at Harper and then from the fellow-Lutherans of the other churches in the county and a nice frame church was erected.

The day of its dedication, July 26, 1914, was a festival occasion of gladness and rejoicing. The Rev. B. Schleifer consecrated the church to the service of the Triune God. The chief sermon was preached by Rev. Th. Bogisch, secretary of the Mission Board. A booklet, written and issued by Rev. Schleifer to commemorate the occasion under the title: "The Building of the Church at Harper (Der Kirchbau zu Harper)," gives a vivid description of the undertaking, crowned with marked success. The membership of the congregation now increased to 26 families, numbering 94 souls.

Various incidents during the World War disturbed the harmony and peace of the congregation and checked its progress. The Rev. B. Schleifer resigned and was succeeded by the present pastor, the Rev. L. Nikolai, who had charge of the work from 1919 to the end of 1924. During the faithful ministry of this servant of the Master the congregation was blessed with a new period of external and spiritual progress. The congregation increased to 37 families of 160 souls. An edifice adjoining the church property was bought and changed into a neat parsonage.

St. James Church of Harper at the present time (1925) forms a mission parish together with Zion's Church of Kerrville, Immanuel's Church of Comfort and St. John's Church of Roosevelt. The Mission Board of the Texas Synod in conjunction with the churches of the parish calls the missionary pastor, renders financial aid in his support and supervises the work.

Services, Church Customs and Special Historical Events of the Lutheran Churches of Gillespie County.

The services are still held in the German Language. At some of the Luther League meetings and on special occasions, however, the English language is also used. The services in most of the churches are usually all day services. In the city of Fredericksburg quite a number of members from the country districts occupy their Sunday houses at the week-end and over the Sabbath. Scores of members from the country own such Sunday houses at various locations of the city, equipped for temporary use and for light housekeeping. At the country churches the people spend the noon repass under arbors and tabernacles. The problem of the requirements of sociability of the church people on the Sabbath day is successfully solved by these unique customs. Usually a number of families of the same relationship will occupy a Sunday house or a Sunday arbor together.

The chief service of worship is held in the forenoon. The Sunday School work, the meeting of the Luther League, choir practice, singing and other religious features are connected with the afternoon services, which are of a more informal nature.

The Church Year is observed by all of the churches. Services are still held on Second Christmas day, Second Easter day and on the Second Day of Pentecost. The Second day services are quite often held out of doors in the forests under the trees. The season of Lent is observed as a special period of spiritual awakening. On the Harvest Home festival most of the congregations decorate their altars and churches with gifts of the harvest. Palm Sunday has become the festival of confirmation. On this day the young catechumens are publicly examined in the fundamentals of Christian faith and life, reconsecrated to the Lord and admitted to Holy Communion.

Aware of the fact that religious education means more than Sunday School special courses of religious instruction are provided for the young in the summer parochial school and in a course of week days instruction for the catechumens, preparatory to confirmation, from September to Easter.

The institution of sponsorship is still held in high honor by the Lutherans of Gillespie county. Not only at the festival of confirmation, but also on the glad wedding day and at other special occasions the sponsors are usually the guests of honor of their godchildren.

The First Lutheran synod of Texas held 6 of its annual conventions at Fredericksburg: in 1855, 1879, 1896, and in 1911 at Zion's Church and in 1922 at the Evangelical Church. In 1896 the Texas Synod passed a resolution to affiliate with the Iowa Synod. At the convention in 1911 the resolution was passed to establish the Lutheran College at Seguin.

On the 31st of October, 1917, the Lutheran churches of Gillespie and the surrounding counties celebrated the Quadricentennial of the Reformation.

This celebration was attended by more than 5000. The following adresses were delivered:
Luther and the 31st of Oct., 1517, _____ Rev. K. Konzack.
Luther at Worms, _____ Rev. C. Lindenberg.
The Blessings of the Reformation, Rev. E. A. F. Hannenmann.
Luther and the Bible, _____ Rev. A. Kluge.
Luther and the Gospel, _____ Rev. B. Schleifer.
Luther and the School, _____ Rev. Ph. Peter.
The Hero of the Reformation, _____ Rev. F. A. Bracher.

The same churches held another joint celebration at the 400th Anniversary of Luther's Stand at Worms, in which the following churches participated: Zion's Church and the Evangelical Church, of Fredericksburg; St. James' Church, of Harper; St. Paul's Church, Mason; St. Paul's Church, North Grape Creek; St. John's Church, Crab Apple; Trinity Church, Albert; Zion's Church, Kerrville; St. Peter's Church, Doss; Christ Church, Cherry Spring; St. James' Church, Llano; Evangelical Lutheran Church, Leiningen.

On May 8, 1921, the Lutheran Churches of Fredericksburg and Gillespie county celebrated the 75th anniversary of the founding of Fredericksburg. On this occasion appropriate and impressive ceremonies were observed at the various churches; and at Zion's Church a pipe organ was dedicated to the services of God.

Another special event of much significance was the convention of the State Luther League at Zion's Church on

the 20th, 21st and 22nd of July, 1923. This was an outsanding
event in the history, and to the honor, of the town and
county. It was an event receiving extensive notice throughout
the country, especially in the columns of the Luther Link.
Zion's Luther League, Alfred Neffendorf, chairman, achieved
great success in the matter of seeing that all visitors were
heartily welcomed and royally entertained. The program
opened with an address of welcome by Rev. F. A. Bracher of
the local Zion's Church; response by the state chairman,
Paul Stricker, of Pflugerville, and closed with an address by
the newly elected president, Walter Bohn, of Austin, and a
farewell address by Rev. Bracher, of Zion's Church.

In conclusion it can be said that the present status of the
Lutheran Church in Gillespie county is most gratifying.
From an insignificant beginning in 1852, it has developed
into the largest and strongest church of Gillespie county. It
now has six pastors, eight congregations and a membership
of 640 families, 1838 communicants and 2926 souls.

Illustrated Section

Prince Solms Braunfels, first Commissioner General German Emigration Company.

John O. Meusebach, second Commissioner General German Emigration Company.

Two Demolished but Famous Landmarks.

Above; ''Sophienberg,'' New Braunfels; first structure erected by German Emigration Co. Below: The Vereins-Kirche, ''the Old Coffee Mill,'' Fredericksburg.

Where the Ancient and the Present Blend.
The Nimitz Hotel, built in 1847, and the first cotton to leave
Fredericksburg by railroad, in 1912.

Nueces River Tragedy.
Top: Where the Germans were camped when attacked by Duff. (See page 58) Bottom: Monument at Comfort. (See page 60.)

Home of the Hermit

Top: Rear of the second story, showing the hermit and the pipe organ.

Bottom: Front view, showing first and second stories. (See page 86.)

Two Old Street Scenes in Fredericksburg.
Top: Street Scene during second Jubilee in 1886. Picture shows where the "Old Coffee Mill" stood in Main Street.
Bottom: Picture taken in 1882, looking northwest from court house.

Guenther's Mill on Liveoak.
Top: (in oval) C. H. Guenther, the builder; the old mill.
Bottom: Pioneer Mills, San Antonio, the husky child of the old
Liveoak Mill.

An Old Mill With a Great History.
Top: Lange's Mill on Threadgill Creek. (See page 127.)
Bottom: Evangelical Lutheran Church at Doss, organized in the old Lange Mill. (See page 206)

Lutheran Churches.
Top: Zion's Church and Parsonage, Fredericksburg. (See page 199)

Bottom: "The Evangelical Church" and Parsonage, Fredericksburg. (See page 204)

Evangelical Lutheran Churches.
Top: St. Paul's Church, North Grape Creek. (See page 202)
Bottom: St. John's Church, Crab Apple. (See page 203)

Evangelical Lutheran Churches.
Top: St. James' Church, Harper. (See page 210)
Bottom: Christ Church, Cherry Spring. (See page 207)

Methodist Churches.

Top: Methodist Episcopal Church, Fredericksburg. (See page 188)

Bottom: Methodist Episcopal Church South, Fredericksburg. (See page 187)

Evangelical Protestant Church, Fredericksburg.
(See page 191)

St. Mary's Catholic Church, Fredericksburg. (See page 196)

St. Mary's Catholic School, Fredericksburg. (See page 197)

Public School Building, Fredericksburg.

See article, ''Progress of Education in Gillespie County,'' Page 148.

ERRATA

No attempt was made to verify every date published in the original edition of 1925. There are a few obvious discrepancies, however, which are noted below.

Page 37. The reference to Meusebach's visit to the Indians for the purpose of negotiating a treaty is noted on this page as being "In July 1847," however it is correctly given on page 42 where it states that he left Fredericksburg for Indian territory late in January 1847.

Page 46. O. C. (Otto) Meusebach was born January 6, 1855. Elizabeth Meusebach Zesch was born January 21, 1862. (These are the dates given in John O. Meusebach's biography published in Vol. I of *Pioneers in God's Hills* in 1960.)

Page 96. The John Peter Tatsch home referred to in the second paragraph was built in 1856, but it was not the *first* stone building in Fredericksburg.

Page 112. "The Mount of the Holy Cross" the writer mentions is and has always been known as "Cross Mountain" (Kreuzberg).

Page 133. The man's name is correctly spelled Diedrich Rode, not "Dietrich Rode."

Page 158. Nimitz did not build the first section of his hotel in 1846. A hotel at this site was begun in 1847 and Nimitz acquired ownership of it in 1855 and expanded it over the years.

Page 159. At the top of the page reference is made to "Judge O. A. Cooley." His name was A. O. Cooley. He was a young lawyer from New York.

Page 191. The pastor's full name is Rev. Henry S. W. Basse.

Page 217. The railroad into and out of Fredericksburg began operations in 1913— not 1912.

Page 220. The reference to the top picture, "Street Scene during second Jubilee in 1886," is erroneous. This picture was taken during Fredericksburg's "Golden Jubilee" in 1896, the fiftieth anniversary of its founding in 1846.

★ ★ ★ ★ ★

It should also be pointed out that the author occasionally made certain philosophical statements or expressed ideas which are obviously personal observations, and may not be based on fact or those which actually prevailed at the time.